THE MEANING OF
RELIGIOUS FREEDOM

ॐ

SUNY Series in Religious Studies
Harold Coward, Editor

THE MEANING OF
RELIGIOUS FREEDOM

ॐ

MODERN POLITICS
AND THE DEMOCRATIC RESOLUTION

FRANKLIN I. GAMWELL

STATE UNIVERSITY OF NEW YORK PRESS

Published by
State University of New York Press, Albany

For information, address State University of New York Press,
State University Plaza, Albany, N.Y. 12246

Production by M.R. Mulholland
Marketing by Bernadette La Manna

Library of Congress Cataloging-in-Publication Data

Gamwell, Franklin I.
  The meaning of religious freedom: modern politics and the
democratic resolution / Franklin I. Gamwell.
    p. cm. — (SUNY series in religious studies)
  Includes bibliographical references and index.
  ISBN 0-7914-2389-1 (alk. paper). — ISBN 0-7914-2390-5 (pbk. :
alk. paper)
  1. Freedom of religion. I. Title. II. Series.
BV741.G36 1995
323.44'2—dc20   94-15524
                                                            CIP

10 9 8 7 6 5 4 3 2 1

For
Donald L. Benedict

CONTENTS

Part 4. The Democratic Resolution

PREFACE

This work asks whether the political principle of religious freedom makes sense. Religious plurality in the modern period has occasioned a distinctive political problematic, of which religious freedom is meant to be the resolution. Given that religions represent comprehensive convictions about human life, however, there is reason to doubt whether conflict among them can be in principle civilized and, therefore, whether politics can coherently legitimate a plurality of religions. This doubt is the more appropriate because, as I will seek to show, widely-held interpretations of religious freedom are compromised by philosophical confusion. But purchase on that confusion, I will argue, leads to a clarification of religious freedom as the constitutive principle of modern democracy.

This problem has occupied my attention for several years. As a consequence, any success I have had in addressing it is accountable to a large company of people who have assisted me. I regret that I can identify and acknowledge only the more proximate debts. Students at The Divinity School of The University of Chicago pursued the problem with me in several courses, and their own work on the problem has refined my formulations. Through many conversations, Martin E. Marty and David Tracy have educated me in matters pertinent to this work, and I am the beneficiary of patient and pointed criticism from Paul Griffiths. Philip E. Devenish and Schubert M. Ogden read the entire manuscript, and their critical comments and suggestions have saved me from many mistakes. In addition, several anonymous readers for SUNY Press have significantly influenced the outcome. Some of this company may judge that I have not fully appreciated the force of their proposals for revision, but I am immensely grateful for their attempts to help me.

With gratitude and admiration, I take the liberty of dedicating the book to the Reverend Donald L. Benedict, whose prophetic Christian witness first provoked my interest in the proper relation between politics and religion.

I express my appreciation for permission to include here material that I have also included in the following publications:

"Review of Kent Greenawalt, *Religious Convictions and Political Choice*" (*The Journal of Law and Religion* 8 [1990]); "Moral Realism and Religion" (*The Journal of Religion* 73 [1993]); "Democratic Discourse: Modern Politics and Religious Freedom" (*The Annual of the Society of Christian Ethics*, 1994); "A Foreword to Comparative Philosophy of Religion" (*Religion and Practical Reason*, ed. Frank E. Reynolds and David Tracy [Albany, N.Y.: State University of New York Press, 1994]). I also thank Joseph Pettit, who thoughtfully edited the entire manuscript, and Charles Mathewes, who thoughtfully prepared the index.

PART 1
THE MODERN POLITICAL PROBLEMATIC

1

INTRODUCTION

Among the political changes that occurred in the West in the eighteenth century, no other was more profound than the revolution summarized in the terse formulation: "Congress shall make no law respecting an establishment of religion, or prohibiting the free exercise thereof." The radical character of these clauses is measured by the fact that no other political prescription is more widely accepted as an expression of distinctively modern politics. There has been enduring and sometimes confusing disagreement about the identity of the modern age. But there is virtual unanimity that a credible reading of modernity must make sense of the new relation between politics and religion that is given classic statement in the First Amendment to the United States Constitution.

It is not surprising, then, that the meaning of these clauses and the character of this new relation have themselves been the subject of continual disagreement. This debate has been especially prominent in the twentieth century, due to the increasing complexity of our common life in the United States and the increasing plurality of religious convictions, and this special importance is reflected in the increasing attention given to the religion clauses by the United States Supreme Court. It follows that the Republic has never been more uncertain about the relation between politics and religion to which it is committed. Roughly speaking, there is a persistent division between contemporary separationists and contemporary religionists. For the former, the constitutional disestablishment of religion means that religious convictions are properly separated from the activities of the state; for the latter, the constitutional protection of religious exercise means that religious conviction is essential to civic virtue and the well-being of the civil order. Both positions endorse the First Amendment, but neither has been able to persuade the other that it does so consistently. Religionists claim that separationists not only disestablish religion but also deny its free exercise; on this critique, the "wall of separation" creates a secularistic civil order. Separationists claim that religionists not only affirm the free exercise of religion but also establish religious conviction; on this critique, religion cannot be essential to the civil order unless some particular religion is a necessary condition of civic virtue.

The present work seeks to answer the question: What, if anything, is the proper relation between modern politics and religion? So formulated, of course, the question makes no explicit reference to the United States or to the religion clauses of its constitution, and this is because I do not intend directly to enter current contention regarding the First Amendment. On the contrary, this work withdraws the spotlight from the peculiarities of the United States in order to give sustained attention to more general or philosophical aspects of the problem, that is, the conditions common to the relation between politics and religion in any modern community. I choose this course because I believe that an appropriate interpretation of the Republic's religion clauses depends on philosophical clarity, and I am further persuaded that the current impasse between separationists and religionists is largely controlled by philosophical confusion.

On my reading, the current contention is largely futile because those who disagree commonly assume an understanding of religion that prevents a consistent understanding of modern politics. I have in mind the pervasive assumption that religious beliefs cannot be the subject of public debate; they are solely matters of faith or confession in the sense that the differences among alternative religious convictions cannot be publicly assessed. I will call this "the theory of religion as nonrational," because it holds that distinctively religious convictions are not expressions of reason; their claims to validity do not belong to a rational order of reflection, and, in that sense, they cannot be rationally validated or assessed. As we shall see, differing adherents of this theory sometimes mean differing things by "nonrational"; in particular, we may contrast those who hold that religious convictions are "subrational" and those who insist that affirmations of faith are "superrational." In either case, however, it remains that religious claims cannot be rationally assessed or publicly debated, and, on this theory, I will argue, the distinctively modern relation between politics and religion cannot be coherently formulated. At least in this respect, then, an appropriate reading of the United States Constitution waits on philosophical clarity regarding the relation of politics to religious convictions.

This is not to say that the meaning of the First Amendment is settled by asking and answering the philosophical question. Whatever the answer to that question, it is a further matter to determine what the religion clauses prescribe. In addition to philosophical clarity, a constitutional interpretation requires some explicit or implicit theory of constitutional hermeneutics—that is, a method with which we may understand for ourselves in our situation the meaning of the religion clauses as written and ratified in the eighteenth century. Perhaps these clauses do not in fact stipulate a coherent constitutional principle. But even if this is the conclusion that we are bound to accept, we cannot reach it unless we first clarify the conditions, if any, given which modern politics and religion can be coherently related. In other words, the question about the First Amendment includes but is not exhausted by the philosophical question to which this work is addressed, and no attempt to complete the hermeneutical task can be successful if it is informed or controlled by philosophical confusion.

On the other hand, the relation between the hermeneutical and philosophical questions means that significant proposals regarding the philosophical problem have been advanced by those who also endorse the First Amendment. Thinkers who commend one or another understanding of the religion clauses have generally maintained that these interpretations are coherent. Moreover, thinkers who have sought a coherent understanding of modern politics have generally argued that the theory defended is also a proper interpretation of the First Amendment. Because it will be important to consider the relevant claims of some of these thinkers, reference to the United States will be frequent in the course of this work—and, indeed, I will offer some comments about the import of my philosophical conclusions for interpretation of the United States Constitution. But this does not gainsay that the two questions are distinct and that the focus of the discussion here abstracts from the hermeneutical problem.

Alternatively stated, then, the present work is addressed to what I will call the "modern political problematic," and this problematic may be expressed in the question: What, if anything, is the proper relation between politics and religion, given that the political community includes an indeterminate plurality of legitimate religions? With this formulation, I assume that an indeterminate plurality of legitimate religions is a distinctively modern characteristic of the political community. The human adventure has, of course, always been characterized by religious diversity, and only within the last century have we come to appreciate how profound the differences among religions can be. Summarily speaking, however, premodern religious diversity more or less exclusively coincided with differences between societies or political communities, so that a plurality of religions internal to a single political community is, on the whole, a modern development.[1] Also speaking summarily, then, we may say that medieval Western communities in which the modern age first emerged were characterized by an overwhelming Catholic religious uniformity, and this uniformity was sustained by the authority of the Catholic church. Thus, the emergence of an appreciable plurality of religions internal to these communities is coincident with the erosion of this authority and is a part of their transition to modernity.

My formulation of the modern political problematic stipulates that modern politics properly legitimates the plurality of religions. One might object that this stipulation begs the question against those who claim that modern politics can substitute force for the authority of the Catholic church and its tradition, such that all religions or all religions save one are coercively proscribed. The totalitarian experiments in the modern West are terrifying confirmations that this claim has been politically influential. But the important question is whether there are any other grounds for a political community inclusive of religious plurality, and, therefore, I stipulate that diverse religions are legitimate.

In calling this plurality of legitimate religions indeterminate, I mean that no limitation is politically prescribed, that is, any religion accepted by members of the political community is legitimate, and some may object more insistently to this aspect of the modern political problematic. Formally, at least, indeterminate religious plurality is not the only alternative to overwhelming religious uniformity. A modern political community might be characterized by a limited or determinate plurality, for instance, diverse religions all of which claim to be Christian. It may seem all the more important to credit this third alternative because many modern political com-

---

1. I do not mean to assert that religious diversity was or is entirely absent from premodern political communities; indeed, the Roman Empire, especially prior to Constantine, included an extensive plurality of religions. I here intend simply a summary comparison of the modern and premodern situations.

munities seem to be or to have been illustrations of it. Numerically minor exceptions aside, for instance, the religions in the English colonies in America at the time of their union were, some might say, all expressions of Christianity. But I seek to clarify the general problem of modern politics, and, so understood, the problem is not usefully formulated in terms of a limited plurality of religions. At least some modern societies have so developed as to include religious diversity more extensive than Christianity, or Christianity and Judaism, or even Western religions. Given that such a course is at least a possibility, the modern political problematic generally or in principle should be formulated in relation to the more extensive case. In other words, a resolution that is pertinent to the situation of greater religious plurality will also be pertinent to the situation in which that plurality is more limited, but the converse, at least if the limitation is essential to the resolution, will be false.

In principle, moreover, only coercion could limit the religious diversity that a modern Western society might include; that is, an indeterminate plurality of religions is, as a matter of principle, the only alternative to the religious uniformity that was effected by authority. Whatever its specific conditions, including the advances in transportation and communication that introduced people in the medieval West to other beliefs and practices, doubt about the Catholic church and its traditions was, at least implicitly, doubt about religious authority as such. A question about the authority of a given religion cannot be answered by appeal to the authority of another religion, because that response leaves one with the question of which authority to accept. Thus, the erosion of Catholic authority was in principle the increasing freedom explicitly to choose one's religion and, therefore, to affirm any religion with which one might become familiar—and this freedom can, as a matter of principle, be limited only by force. Peter Berger expresses this logic of the matter by saying that modern life faces "the heretical imperative"—where "heretical" is used with a meaning derived from the Greek verb *hairein*, to choose, and the imperative, therefore, is the requirement that one explicitly choose one's religious conviction (see Berger 1979: 23f.). In what follows, then, I will take for granted that the plurality of religions properly constituting the modern political problematic is indeterminate, so that the term "plurality of legitimate religions" implies this further qualifier.

Of course, it might be asked why a plurality of legitimate religions should be thought to constitute a significant political problem. A summary answer is possible given only the widely shared understanding that religious convictions include adherence to fundamental or comprehensive beliefs regarding reality and human purpose. Since differing religions at least may differ with respect to these beliefs, it follows that adherents of two or more legitimate religions may find themselves in political conflict—as, for instance, religious adherents in the United States disagreed for religious reasons about slavery in the nineteenth century and about possible entry into the European war in the nineteen thirties. The significant problem, then, is this: How in principle can such political conflict be ordered or governed? Since the grounds in conflict are fundamental or comprehensive, there seems to be no common principle that could override the conflict and, thereby, civilize or unite the political community. To be sure, the state might seek coercively to impose an order, but, at least to first appearances, this course can only deny the legitimacy of at least one of the religions involved.

In sum, a legitimate plurality of religions seems to be in principle a prescription for political instability or civil war, and the modern political problematic may be reformulated: How, if at all, is politics consistent in principle with a plurality of legitimate religions? So to formulate the question is to focus on the political problem. But this focus may be changed in order to make clear that the issue is also a religious one. If legitimate religious diversity precludes an overriding political principle, then no religious adherent has grounds in principle to be a citizen. Thus, one may also ask: How, if at all, may adherents of a plurality of legitimate religions consistently be citizens of the political community? Since the political problem occurs by virtue of possible political conflicts among adherents of differing religions, the two formulations refer to the same problem. We may say, then, that the modern political problematic is a question in both political philosophy and philosophy of religion.[2]

---

2. Moreover, if one means by "theology" critical reflection on the convictions and practices of a given religious community or tradition, such that the term should always be qualified by the name of some or other particular religion, then the modern political problematic is also a theological problem. In Christian theology, for instance, the question may be formulated: How, if at all, may Christians consistently be citizens in a political community in which a plurality of other religions is also legitimate? *Mutatis mutandis*, any other specific kind of theology permits of a statement of the modern political problematic.

Still, some may assert that a resolution to this problematic is obvious. It is often said that a political community inclusive of diverse religions is possible if adherents of each religion are tolerant of those who adhere to others. Indeed, no exhortation has more widely expressed the modern political attempt to affirm religious plurality than the call for religious tolerance. In itself, however, this exhortation only restates the problem, which may now be formulated: What does tolerance mean, such that adherents of a plurality of religions might all agree to tolerate each other? The answer to this question is not obvious, precisely because a religious conviction identifies the comprehensive terms in which to assess all political convictions—including, one might think, the affirmation of tolerance. If we are told that tolerance means the affirmation of civil peace as an overriding value, we may ask how an indeterminate plurality of religions might all include this affirmation. Civil peace is inescapably the peace of some or other political order, and conflict will be about the character or content of this ordering. Whether the disagreement is more important to the parties than civil peace would seem to depend on the religious convictions in question, precisely because they are comprehensive. On what grounds, then, can one believe that civil peace will be in principle overriding?

Without some further explanation, in other words, the call for toleration is simply the exhortation that the modern political problematic should be solved. Indeed, the first use of the term during the sixteenth and seventeenth centuries in Europe, when the Reformation had led to enduring religious conflict, was simply imperative, so that the call for toleration begged for theoretical backing. On a widely accepted reading, in other words, the long years of religious wars in Europe first impressed on modern political thought what I have called its distinctive problematic (see, e.g., Stout: 3, 235; Toulmin: 16-17; Rawls 1993: xxii–xxv), and political theory sought to answer the question: In accord with what understanding of the political community, if any, may the hope for toleration be given reasonable grounds?

As this formulation of the question suggests, one might well use the term "toleration" as the name of that political principle for which modern political thought requires a coherent statement. By virtue of its history, however, this term is also associated with the attempt to maintain an established or politically favored religion even while "dissenting" or nonestablished religions are permitted in the political community. I seek to avoid this association because, as I will argue, toleration in this sense is not a coherent solution of the modern political problematic. Alternatively, then, one might use "disestablishment" to name the solution to the modern political problematic. But this term is also troubled by associations that I seek to avoid. Some hold, for instance, that disestablishment is consistent with a secularistic state, and, in order to proscribe that possibility, some religious adherents insist, the First Amendment also includes the free exercise clause.

In contrast to both alternatives, then, I will use "religious freedom" to identify the political principle, if there is such a principle, in accord with which a plurality of legitimate religions internal to a political community is consistent with its unity. That it is *religious* freedom makes the legitimacy of religions explicit, and that it is religious *freedom* insists on their plurality. I emphasize, however, that the term is introduced here simply in order to name that principle rather than to assert its character. Here at the outset, in other words, religious freedom merely identifies the question to be pursued—namely, what, if anything, does religious freedom properly mean? On the assumption that such a meaning can be clarified, of course, one may also assert that it is the proper philosophical meaning of disestablishment and toleration, and I endorse that assertion. Still, I judge that clarity will be best served if the discussion is principally cast in pursuit of a coherent formulation of religious freedom.

My thesis is that religious freedom coherently means nothing other than a free political discourse that is also a full political discourse because it includes adherents of a plurality of religions, that is, a political discussion and debate in which differing religious convictions are or can be publicly advocated and assessed. I will call this "the democratic resolution" and will seek to show that only this resolution can be redeemed as an answer to the political and religious formulations of the modern political problematic. On this reading, religious freedom means that democratic discourse is the principle of political unity, and democratic civility is the constitutive political virtue consistent with all religious adherence.

It is apparent that this thesis takes exception to the theory of religion as nonrational. If I am correct that this theory is pervasively assumed, then it follows that the meaning of religious freedom I seek to defend contrasts with several other proposed understandings. In the second part of this work, I will seek to defend the critical claim that no proposal consistent with the theory of religion as nonrational is a coherent resolution to the modern political problematic. The third and fourth parts of the work, then, pursue a constructive effort to clarify and defend the claim that religious freedom can mean full and free political discourse. But I will be in a position more fully to formulate this thesis and outline the book only subsequent to an attempt to clarify "religion" and "politics" as the central terms of the modern political problematic. Accordingly, the following chapter seeks to formulate and defend the meanings of these terms that will inform the subsequent inquiry, and, at the conclusion of the chapter, I will offer more precise statements of the thesis and of the character of the remaining discussion.

2

THE TERMS OF THE PROBLEMATIC

To ask about the relation between religion and politics is to imply that the two are distinct. An address to this question, then, requires a clarification of this distinction or, what comes to the same thing, related definitions of the two terms. In other words, our first task is to understand as precisely as we can the question by which the modern political problematic has been identified: How, if at all, is *politics* consistent in principle with a plurality of legitimate *religions*? In order to clarify this question, moreover, its central terms must be defined in a manner that does not answer the question persuasively, that is, does not arbitrarily beg the question against any candidate answer. On the one hand, the definition of religion cannot be dependent on the particular convictions of a historically given religion or set of religions, because the modern political problematic involves an indeterminate plurality of religions. On the other hand, the definition of politics cannot be dependent on some historically given political community or political system, for instance, that of the United States or Great Britain, because this would arbitrarily assume that religious freedom is a coherent political principle only if it is coherent within the constitution of that political community. We can make the point, then, by saying that we require formal definitions of religion and politics as such.

It is not immediately clear that this requirement can be met, because the attempt formally to define either religion or politics as such is widely thought to be futile. Formal definitions of religion as such are, perhaps, especially suspect. Many scholars in religious studies find that the phenomena properly or plausibly called religious are so varied and complex as to preclude the possibility of any fully general definition. Accordingly, these scholars choose to study one or some but not all such phenomena and insist that any explicit or implicit definition of religion is selective, so that it can be justified only with respect to some particular purpose in religious studies.

John Hick, for instance, asserts that "religion" is a "family-resemblance concept," in the sense that each of its referents "is similar in important respects to some others in the family, though not in all respects to any or in any respect to all" (Hick: 3, 4). Similarly, some scholars hold that the proper or plausible uses of "politics" are so varied that any definition offered is historically specific, in the sense that its exemplifications constitute a historically emergent class of communities.

The attempt to clarify the distinction between "religion" and "politics" is further complicated because, to first appearances, the two terms do not refer to differing instances of the same thing. "Religion" is frequently used, at least in the first instance, to identify a specific form of culture. In a widely influential discussion, for example, Clifford Geertz says that a religion is a system of "sacred symbols" and, therefore, a pattern of culture (Geertz: 90f.) "Politics," on the other hand, is frequently used, at least in the first instance, to identify a specific form of human association. John Dewey, for example, says that politics occurs when the public "is organized and made effective by means of representatives who...care for its especial interests by methods intended to regulate the conjoint actions of individuals and groups" (Dewey: 35). Since a distinction is also a comparison, the definitions we require for the present inquiry must somehow compare a form of culture with a form of association.

Still, if religion is a form of culture and politics is a form of human association, they have in common the fact that both are somehow related to human activity. As a consequence, we speak not only of religion but also of religious activity and not only of politics but also of political activity—and, as a further consequence, we also speak of religious association and political culture. This common relation to human activity suggests that our attempt to distinguish religion and politics might focus on definitions of religious and political activity. In order to assure that these definitions are formal in the sense we require, we might first seek formally to identify human activity as such and then ask whether this understanding is itself sufficient to distinguish between the two specific forms of activity central to the modern political problematic. In pursuing this approach, we should note, we are not necessarily bound to agree with all of the varied and complex ways in which "religious activity" and "political activity" are in fact used. One of the matters to be assessed is whether common usage should, in the interests of general understanding, be reformed.

The question, of course, is not whether "religious activity" or "political activity" is another term for human activity as such. I assume as noncontroversial that some human activity is not religious and some is not political, so that these terms identify specific forms of activity. The question to be pursued, then, is whether a formal understanding of human activity as such itself implies certain distinctions among its specific forms or aspects. We may ask, in other words, whether the formal character of human activity as such is self-differentiating, and, if so, whether two of its specific forms or aspects can be appropriately called religious and political respectively.

As mentioned, this approach requires that one first develop a formal understanding of human activity as such. The first section of this chapter seeks summarily to clarify and defend such an understanding.[1] In the second section of the chapter, I will seek to show how this understanding does indeed provide the basis for the formal definitions of religion and politics we require. Religion, I will propose, is the primary form of culture in terms of which humans explicitly ask and answer what I will call the comprehensive question. Politics, I will propose, is the primary form of association in which humans explicitly ask and answer the question of the state. In the final section of the chapter, I will outline with greater precision the attempt to solve the modern political problematic that will occupy the remainder of this work.

Human Activity

It is widely agreed that humans may be distinguished from other things because we understand ourselves. Human individuals, it has often been said, not only are but also understand that they are. Strictly speaking, of course, we are not always aware of ourselves. We are sometimes in a state of dreamless sleep, and we can become unconscious in a way that excludes all understanding. It is more accurate to say, then, that human individuals are distinguished by the

---

1. In the Appendix to this work, I seek to develop more extensively the formal understanding of human activity as such that, in this chapter, I present summarily. See the section entitled "Human Activity and the Comprehensive Question." This entire chapter is immensely indebted to the work of Schubert M. Ogden, and my definition and discussion of religion is nothing other than an attempt to appropriate his formulations for the purposes of the present inquiry. See especially Ogden 1992: chapter 1.

capacity for self-understanding, and we exist in our distinctively human state at those times in our lives when this capacity is exercised. I will use the term "human activity" to mean this distinctively human state of human individuals, so that human activity always includes or is constituted by a self-understanding. On this account, the life of a human individual is an identifiable series or career of activities, some of which are distinctively human activities because they are constituted by self-understanding.

"The primitive stage of discrimination," writes Alfred North Whitehead, "is the vague sense of reality, dissecting it into a three-fold scheme, namely, The Whole, That Other, and This-Myself" (Whitehead 1938: 150). When we understand ourselves, we simultaneously understand at least some other things in at least some measure. This is because understanding necessarily discriminates or distinguishes, so that we could not be aware of ourselves without a simultaneous awareness of things that are not ourselves. Indeed, an awareness of oneself includes one's understanding of other things, in the sense that one's understanding of those other things also constitutes the self. Moreover, self-awareness also includes an understanding, at least in some measure, of some "whole" or larger reality of which self and others are parts. Only with respect to this larger reality can one distinguish between self and others. This is because a distinction identifies not only difference but also similarity, and to understand the similarity between self and others is to identify, in one respect, some larger reality to which both belong.[2] Summarily, then, in each of our distinctive activities we understand ourselves and, therefore, some larger reality of which we and others are parts.

Because or insofar as humans live with self-awareness, they also lead their lives. In other words, an activity that understands itself thereby chooses in some measure what it is or will be. To be sure, some theories of human existence deny human freedom. Self-awareness is said to be "epiphenomenal," in the sense that no reference to it is required in order to identify or account for any given

---

2. In order to avoid misunderstanding, I should perhaps underscore that I mean by the "larger reality" nothing other than whatever is implied by the fact of similarity between things that are understood. One might hold, for instance, that the similarity implies nothing more than a mere collection of self and others; in that event, it remains that this collection is the larger reality with respect to which one understands its members.

human activity, and, on this view, human science is defined as a search for causal relationships similar to those pursued by the sciences of nonhuman existence. But to treat self-understanding in this way is in truth to deny that it occurs. Granting that a human activity is in some measure the effect of causes other than itself, these others cannot effect an understanding of the self, because they would thereby effect an understanding of their effects. The self that is understood already includes whatever determination the environment has contributed; thus, a self-understanding transcends other-determination. Let the effects of others be as extensive as you please, the completion of a human activity still waits on how it chooses to understand itself.

To be distinctively human is, in other words, to exercise our distinctive freedom, and this may be more apparent if we say that self-understanding is the choice of one's purpose. Humans not only live but also lead their lives because they complete their activities by choosing with understanding what they will pursue. In its awareness of other things, an activity understands causes of which it is an effect; in its awareness of itself, an activity understands effects of which it will be the cause. Each human activity "arises as an effect facing its past and ends as a cause facing its future" (Whitehead 1961: 194). Self-understanding, we may also say, is the way in which humans choose to add themselves or make a difference to the larger reality of which they are parts.

Still, if all distinctively human activities choose their own purposes with understanding, this does not mean that our self-understanding is always *explicit*. "Explicit understanding," as I use the term, refers to our conscious thoughts, and it is obvious that our conscious thoughts are always fragmentary, in the sense that no human activity is conscious of all things completely. As a consequence, every human activity also includes or is constituted by understandings that are *implicit*, by which I mean understandings that are excluded from conscious attention but without which our explicit awareness could not be what it is. Thus, for instance, one's conscious thoughts may focus on things other than oneself, perhaps on the activities of another human individual or something she or he says, with the purpose, say, of subsequently offering advice to her or him or otherwise making a contribution to the conversation. Since one's explicit understanding of the other individual depends on this purpose, the conscious thought could not be what it is without the implied self-understanding. Alternatively, one's conscious thoughts may attend to one's purpose, and some of one's understandings of other things remain implicit. This distinction between explicit and implicit understanding is important to the present work because, as I will try to show later in this chapter, religious and political activity as such may be formally distinguished in terms of their differing explicit understandings.

But, now, if an activity is distinctively human when it includes an explicit or implicit self-understanding, then all human activities include, at least implicitly, an understanding of human activity generally or as such. This is simply an application of the logical dictum that the particular implies the general. To understand that something is red is, at least implicitly, to understand that it is colored; to understand that Abraham Lincoln was President during the Civil War is to understand, at least implicitly, that he was a nineteenth-century United States citizen. Similarly, any particular self-understanding implies an answer to the general question: What are the characteristics common to the diverse self-understandings of all human activities, actual or possible? Or, again: What are the conditions of possibility of human activity as such, of which this particular self-understanding and any particular self-understanding are exemplifications? To be sure, one may ask whether there are characteristics common to all particular self-understandings—or, if there are, whether it is possible to identify them. But these questions answer themselves, since self-understanding and, therefore, understanding in some measure of others and some larger reality, are precisely such characteristics.

We may also say that every human activity chooses, at least implicitly, an understanding of human purpose as such, the common character or characteristics of all human purposes. This follows because self-understanding is a choice of some particular purpose, a decision about how one will make a difference to the larger reality of which self and others are parts. In all of our distinctively human activity, then, we lead our lives by choosing, at least implicitly, an understanding of human life as such, the purpose by which it is identified, and I will call this an activity's "comprehensive self-understanding." Our particular purpose, whether explicitly or implicitly understood, is always an expression of what we take to be the purpose of the human adventure. John Dewey, to choose one example, claimed that pursuit of the "all around growth" of all human individuals, which he also called the democratic ideal, is the purpose of human life as such (see Dewey 1957: 186).

Clearly, he could not mean by this that all human activity does, without compromise or corruption, pursue the democratic ideal. It is apparent, in other words, that we may be mistaken in what we take to be the comprehensive purpose. Our particular choices may express a misunderstanding of the characteristics exemplified in or implied by all human activity. If, for instance, the purpose of the human adventure is as Dewey believed, a given individual might so understand herself or himself as to pursue her or his own wealth or pleasure at the expense of the growth of all humans and thereby imply that the comprehensive purpose is not identified by the democratic ideal.

But comprehensive self-understandings that are mistaken cannot be merely misunderstandings or mere ignorance. Because the character of human activity as such is implied by any given activity, any understanding of oneself includes, at least implicitly, the valid comprehensive self-understanding. In this sense, we can never fail to understand correctly the purpose of all human activity. Thus, when we choose a particular purpose that exemplifies a mistaken understanding of the human adventure, we both affirm and deny, at least implicitly, the comprehensive purpose. In other words, any choice that implies a comprehensive misunderstanding can only be, at least implicitly, a duplicitous choice. When we so choose, we correctly understand the comprehensive purpose and could have chosen to exemplify that purpose without compromise or corruption.

For this reason, the valid comprehensive self-understanding is moral in character; it is a norm or ideal that every human activity ought to exemplify or express without duplicity. Conversely, an invalid understanding of the comprehensive purpose is immoral precisely because it is duplicitous. Given that ought implies can, human activity as such could not be morally bound to understand itself in accord with the comprehensive purpose were this not always a possible choice. But it is always a possible choice because all self-understandings and, therefore, every choice with understanding of a particular purpose, include, at least implicitly, a valid understanding of human purpose as such.

We may also say that the comprehensive purpose is the comprehensive condition of all valid moral claims. Moral claims purport to identify purposes that are prescribed or proscribed, and these claims may be more or less specific. Most purport to be valid only for individuals within certain circumstances. To prescribe, for instance, that eligible United States citizens ought to exercise their right to the franchise is to identify a particular purpose that is, if the prescription is valid, required only of certain people at certain times in their lives. But any specific moral claim that is valid can only be a specification of the comprehensive purpose to certain circumstances. The comprehensive moral norm or ideal, in other words, must be implied without inconsistency by all other valid moral claims, and, in this sense, the former is a necessary condition of the latter. But, then, this purpose is also the sufficient moral condition of all valid moral claims. In addition to the comprehensive purpose, there are no other conditions of valid moral understandings except the certain circumstances to which this purpose is specified, for instance, the circumstances in which United States citizens find themselves at certain times in their lives. The comprehensive purpose, we may summarize, is the necessary and sufficient moral condition of the validity of all moral claims, and this is what I mean in calling it their comprehensive condition.

Religion and Politics

On the account presented in the previous section, our distinctively human activity is constituted by an explicit or implicit self-understanding, so that we choose with understanding how we make a difference to the larger reality of which we are a part. Thereby, we also choose, at least implicitly, an understanding of human activity as such or the purpose that is the comprehensive condition of the moral enterprise. Given this formal characterization of human activity as such, we are now in a position to pursue the formal definitions of religion and politics we require in order to formulate the modern political problematic, that is, to clarify the question: How, if at all, is politics consistent in principle with a plurality of legitimate religions, or, what is the meaning of religious freedom? Adequate definitions of religion and politics will be achieved, I have suggested, if we can show (1) that the formal character of human activity as such is self-differentiating, in the sense that it implies certain distinctions among specific forms or aspects of itself, and (2) that two of these forms or aspects of human activity can be appropriately called religious and political respectively.

The idea that human activity as such is self-differentiating may be illustrated by noting that the previous section mentioned a distinction between two aspects of the understanding with which we lead our lives. Because our conscious thoughts are always fragmentary, I have said, every human activity includes or is constituted by both explicit and implicit understandings. Still, this distinction is solely analytic, in the sense that there is no human activity in which one or the other is absent. In other words, this distinction refers solely to aspects of any given activity and never to a difference between some human activities and others—as, for instance, a coin always has two sides. In contrast, religious and political activity seem to be differing kinds of activity in a sense that is nonanalytic. In other words, religious activity is not necessarily also political, and political activity is not necessarily also religious—as, for instance, a silver coin is not necessarily also copper or vice-versa (although a coin may be both silver and copper if, say, it is silver-plated). We may formulate this point by saying that "religious" and "political" seem to identify specific *forms* of human activity, that is, kinds of human activity that may be exemplified in some particular activities and not in others.

But, now, precisely the analytic distinction between explicit and implicit understandings may be used to explain how specific forms of human activity might be differentiated. Because our conscious thoughts are always fragmentary, differing kinds of activity may be distinguished in terms of differing kinds of explicit understandings. Since understandings may be represented as answers to questions, differing forms of human activity may also be identified in terms of differing questions that are explicitly asked and answered or addressed. On this account, then, religious and political activity might be defined in terms of the differing questions to which each is an explicit address.

In itself, however, this possibility does not confirm that these specific forms of activity may be clarified in the formal manner that we require. It seems apparent, for instance, that "Christian religious activity" and "British political activity" might be defined in terms of the questions that each explicitly addresses—for instance, "what is the Christian conviction about human life?" and "what should the government of Great Britain do?" Were the definition of "religion" dependent on the Christian religion, however, the question of religious freedom could not be properly formulated, since, on this definition, we would ask only about consistency between politics and diverse exemplifications of Christianity. Again, were the definition of "politics" dependent on British political activity, the question of religious freedom could not be properly formulated, since, on this definition, we would ask only about consistency between British politics and a legitimate plurality of religions. Neither definition can serve our purposes, because both are dependent on given historical conditions and, therefore, neither is implied by the formal character of human activity as such. But I believe that we can achieve understandings of "religious activity" and "political activity" that are not similarly bound to particular historical events or conditions—as I will now seek to show, attending first to the meaning of religion.

As I noted earlier, "religion" is frequently used, at least in the first instance, to identify a form of culture. Hence religious activity cannot be identified without first clarifying the relation between human activity and culture. Considerable discussion in recent philosophy has focused on the relation between understanding and culture, especially in the respect that understanding involves language. If our distinctive activity is constituted by understanding, many have argued, then activity cannot be human without the use of or participation in language, because conscious thought is linguistically constituted. Even without seeking precision regarding this claim, we may affirm one of the principal conclusions to which, for many, it leads: Because language is a particular cultural creation, our distinctively human activities are mediated by some or other particular culture. On this account, conscious thought is always a fragmentary interpretation in terms of cultural concepts and symbols and, thereby, expresses an individual's participation in a cultural lifeworld. Accordingly, I will identify the relation between activity and culture in the following formal way: Culture consists in the concepts and symbols in terms of which human activities explicitly understand themselves and other things and the larger world to which they make a difference.

Because religion is a specific form of culture, it now follows that a particular religion is a set or system of shared concepts and symbols in terms of which humans ask and answer some specific question, and a formal definition of religion requires an identification of this question. In the previous chapter, I mentioned the widely-shared understanding that religious convictions include adherence to fundamental or comprehensive beliefs regarding reality and human purpose. Beginning with this approximation, we may recognize that the question by which religion and religious activity might be formally identified has already been discussed. For we have seen that the choice of a particular self-understanding always includes, at least implicitly, the choice of a comprehensive self-understanding. Thus, we may say that every human activity asks and answers, at least implicitly, the comprehensive question, namely, what is the valid comprehensive self-understanding? Since the choice of a self-understanding is nothing other than the choice of a purpose, the comprehensive question may also be formulated: What is the comprehensive human purpose?[3]

Just because every human activity asks and answers this question, at least implicitly, an address to it cannot itself identify specifically religious activity. But we have already said that religion is a form of culture and, therefore, a religion is a set or system of concepts and symbols in terms of which humans *explicitly* understand themselves. Accordingly, I will mean by religion the primary form of culture in terms of which the comprehensive question is explicitly asked and answered.[4] It then follows that all human activity is not religious. On the contrary, our activity is religious only when or insofar as we explicitly understand ourselves and the larger reality in terms of some or other particular religion.[5]

Moreover, it is just because we ask and answer the comprehensive question, at least implicitly, in all of our activity that religion is important in human life. As we have seen, the comprehensive self-understanding that is expressed in the way we lead our lives may be invalid. We may choose our particular purposes with a duplicitous conviction about the comprehensive purpose. For this reason, humans raise explicitly the comprehensive question, and the specific

---

3. It is worth nothing that this question asks about the *material* character of human activity as such. If, as the earlier discussion asserted, the *formal* character of human activity as such consists in the choice of some or other particular and, therefore, some or other comprehensive self-understanding, then the material character of human activity as such is the valid comprehensive self-understanding.

4. Because culture consists in concepts and symbols in terms of which humans explicitly understand themselves, to say that religion is a form of culture in terms of which the comprehensive question is explicitly asked and answered is redundant. But it is a useful redundancy, underscoring, as the text proceeds to make clear, that religious activity is a specific form of human activity because it asks and answers the comprehensive question explicitly.

5. Similarly, this understanding of religion does not imply that all human individuals or societies are religious—however pervasive religion may be in human history. On the contrary, the character of human activity as such implies the *possibility* of religion, in the sense that it implies the comprehensive question and, therefore, the possibility that this question is asked and answered explicitly.

function of religion is so to represent in concepts and symbols the valid answer to this question that religious adherents believe it. In other words, the specific function of religious activity is so to address the comprehensive question explicitly as to cultivate in the lives of religious adherents comprehensive self-understandings that are not duplicitous or, as I will say, are authentic. Accordingly, the comprehensive question may be reformulated: What is the authentic comprehensive understanding, or what is human authenticity as such—or, again, what makes human activity as such authentic?

In so formulating the question that is addressed in religious activity, I do not mean to deny that this same question may be properly identified in terms other than those I have used. Paul Tillich, for instance, defines religion in terms of the question of ultimate concern, where this asks about "the meaning of Being for us" (Tillich: 22), and Reinhold Niebuhr says that religion relates human action "to the totality of things conceived as a realm of meaning" (Niebuhr 1942: 44). More generally, it has often been asserted that religious activity is concerned with the ultimate meaning of human life. But these formulations may be so understood that their difference from the question of human authenticity as such is solely verbal. To understand what makes human activity as such authentic *is* to identify the source and character of our ultimate meaning. I have chosen to speak of authentic human activity only because the contrast between authenticity and inauthenticity, perhaps more readily than that between meaning and its absence, is appropriate to the moral character of religious convictions—and, as we shall see, the moral aspect of religion is especially pertinent to the relation between politics and religion.

Still, the formulation "what makes human activity as such authentic?" offers terms in which to make clear that an answer to the comprehensive question includes, as Tillich's reference to "Being" and Niebuhr's to "totality" suggest, a metaphysical as well as a moral aspect. We have seen that an understanding of oneself or one's purpose includes an understanding in some measure of some larger reality or whole in which self and others are distinguished and to which one's choice will make a difference. It follows that a comprehensive self-understanding includes an understanding of the larger reality or whole in which self and *all conceivable others*, all other things that might be understood, are distinguished. An answer to the comprehensive question, in other words, includes an understanding of reality as such and, in this sense, a metaphysical aspect. Every religion, then, includes a metaphysical claim about the character of reality and, further, the claim that reality so understood makes human activity as such authentic, at least in the sense that reality as such permits human authenticity.

On the other hand, every religion includes the claim that human activity makes itself authentic and, in this sense, a moral aspect. Because self-understandings are self-determined or chosen, and because this choice may express duplicity, the valid comprehensive self-understanding identifies how human activity as such ought to make a difference to the larger reality of which it is a part. In representing an answer to the comprehensive question, then, every religion claims to represent the comprehensive moral norm or ideal and, therefore, the comprehensive condition of all valid moral claims. Moreover, it is proper to say that the moral aspect of religion is its inclusive aspect. Although a religion is always something more than its metaphysical claim, because it is concerned with the valid comprehensive self-understanding as well as the comprehensive character of reality, a religion is finally nothing other than its comprehensive moral claim. This is because the character of human authenticity as such includes or implies its relation to the character of reality as such, and the converse is not the case.[6]

It should be clear the the definition of religion I have proposed depends on nothing other than the formal character of human activity as such and, therefore, is itself formal in the sense that a statement of the modern political problematic requires. This is because the comprehensive question and the possibility of addressing this question explicitly are both implied by the choice of a self-understanding. Of course, one might ask why the form of culture that has been identified is appropriately called religion. But if we refuse to use "religion" in this way, we will be bound to find some other term to identify the primary form of culture in terms of which the comprehensive question is explicitly asked and answered. Given that all human activity must ask and answer the question about human authenticity as such and may do so inauthentically, the

---

6. In saying that an answer to the comprehensive question is a comprehensive moral claim, I do not mean to deny that there is another use of "moral claim" in which it is limited to claims about more or less particular purposes or actions that express the valid understanding of human authenticity as such. Because they are constituted by particular purposes, all human activities ask and answer not only the comprehensive moral question but also another moral question to which the more limited use of the term "moral" refers.

explicit address to this question is a distinct and important function of culture. One might, then, ask any who doubt this definition of "religion" to suggest a more appropriate name for cultural systems or formations that serve this function.

A more direct response to the doubt, however, is the recognition that each of the so-called axial or post-axial religions more or less obviously illustrates the understanding I have proposed. I have in mind especially Buddhism, Christianity, Confucianism, Hinduism, Islam, and Judaism. To be sure, each of these traditions is internally complex, and it is an open question in each case whether we should speak of one religion or more than one that claim the same name. If the latter, however, I expect that the inner complexity of any such tradition results in two or more cultural systems each of which consists in concepts and symbols in terms of which the comprehensive question is explicitly asked and answered.

Moreover, I judge that the comprehensive question allows one to distinguish the specifically religious character of these traditions or their differing expressions from cultural systems or formations generally considered nonreligious, for instance, political formations. This is not to deny that one or more of the traditions in question may include terms in which questions other than the comprehensive one are explicitly asked and answered.[7] In other words, religions and the activities and associations constituted thereby in a given society may be more or less culturally and socially differentiated. As a matter of fact, religions are rather highly differentiated in most modern societies and have been more or less diffuse in some premodern societies. In the latter, then, cultural formations and activity properly called religious are also properly called, say, political— although they are religious and political in differing aspects.[8]

---

7. On the account I gave above, the distinction between specific forms of human activity, for instance, religious and political activity, is nonanalytic in the sense that it *may* distinguish between particular activities. But this means that a given activity also may be an instance of more than one specific form, for instance, may be both religious and political. In contrast, a distinction between aspects of human activity, for instance, between explicit and implicit understanding, is analytic, meaning that all human activity exemplifies both aspects.

8. The appeal to so-called axial or post-axial religions as apparent illustrations may elicit the objection that this understanding of religion excludes so-called pre-axial or archaic religions. I am not competent to

But if religious activity may be defined in terms of an explicit address to the comprehensive question, attention to the axial or post-axial religions also suggests that explicit address to this question is not always religious. As those examples illustrate, it is characteristic of religions that their modes of expression, including their practices, are highly symbolic or figurative, in contrast to the language used in, say, philosophical discussions of metaphysics and morality. To note this fact is to underscore that the distinguishing function of religious activity is to cultivate in the lives of religious adherents authentic comprehensive self-understandings. Precisely because religious activity has this function, in other words, religion as a form of culture refers to some or other system or formation of concepts and symbols that is distinguished by the answer it represents to the comprehensive question.[9] But if a religion represents some or other such answer, then it is always possible to ask whether that answer is valid. Accordingly, one may distinguish from religious activity another specific form or activity in which the comprehensive question is

---

discuss this objection in an informed way, but I suspect that it is not finally as telling as it may initially seem to be. If the point is that a pre-axial religion is particularistic, in the sense that its understanding of human authenticity is limited to a particular collectivity, then it might be argued that such particularism includes a belief about other collectivities—either that authenticity is not possible in other collectivities or that authenticity in other collectivities is of an entirely different order. Beliefs such as these are, perhaps, among those that adherents of axial religions are especially concerned to criticize, and this suggests that pre-axial religions in their own way ask and answer the comprehensive question. Whether or not it is exemplified by archaic religions, however, a form of culture implied by the character of human activity in general and of which the axial religions are more or less obvious exemplifications commends itself as an appropriate formal characterization of the term "religion."

9. Another way to make this point is to say that the figurative modes of expression characteristic of a religion have the meanings that they have only with reference to the answer to the comprehensive question that they help to represent. As a symbol that constitutes Christian activity, for instance, "Jesus" is a part of the cultural system in which Jesus is said to be the Christ, or, alternatively stated, if "Jesus" has some other meaning, it is a different symbol. In contrast, philosophy as a form of culture refers to some or other set of concepts and symbols in terms of which philosophical activity may attend to diverse answers to the questions of philosophy. Accordingly, it is characteristic of philosophical modes of expression that they seek, at least insofar as possible, to be literal in distinction from figurative.

explicitly addressed, namely, a form in which humans critically reflect on one or more claims about human authenticity as such, that is, seek to assess the validity of that claim or those claims.

The general point here is that we may ask and answer questions in two basic ways. On the one hand, a question may be so addressed as to make a claim to validity, either explicitly or implicitly; on the other hand, the same question may be so addressed as critically to assess or validate claims that purport to be the valid answer to it. We might also make the point by saying that questions may be asked and answered decisively, on the one hand, and critically, on the other. The latter activity is a secondary form of reflection, in the sense that it presupposes the former as the object of explicit attention. Because humans choose their purposes with understanding, in other words, the primary form of human reflection is decisive in character, that is, consists in the making of claims with which or by which we lead our lives. Accordingly, critical reflection is secondary in the sense that its function is to assess the claims with which we do or might lead our lives when, for whatever reasons, we question their validity.

Given this difference, we may say that religious activity, which seeks to cultivate in the lives of religious adherents the understanding represented in some or other particular religion, asks and answers the comprehensive question explicitly and decisively. For this reason, religion is a primary form of culture. In distinction from religious activity, then, we may refer to specific forms of activity in which the comprehensive question is asked and answered critically, and these include the secondary forms of theology, philosophy of religion, and philosophical theology.

To assert this distinction is not, however, to separate religious activity from critical reflection on religious claims or convictions. The fact that generally acknowledged religious communities or traditions typically include or are closely related to individuals and associations whose principal vocation is theological or philosophical reflection confirms that religious activity itself implies the importance of this vocation, at least in certain circumstances. Precisely because the validity of a given religion can be called into question, the critical assessment of its claims is especially important to those who have adhered to it when, for whatever reasons, they have reason to doubt its representation of human authenticity. Accordingly, a religious association may include theological and philosophical activity, because these are necessary to the religious activities of its members. For the same reason, the results of theological and philosophical reflection sometimes subsequently function religiously, that is, become concepts and symbols in terms of which activity seeks to cultivate authentic self-understandings.

This is not to say that critical reflection on some comprehensive claim or claims can be practiced only within religious associations, since it may well be pursued by individuals who are not themselves religious adherents, for instance, by individuals seeking to decide whether to become religious adherents. But when members of a religious association pursue this activity because it is required by their religious adherence, we may say that theology and philosophy are religious activity that has become self-critical. The distinction between religious activity and critical reflection on its distinctive claims is important to the thesis of this work. If, as I will argue, religious freedom is a coherent political principle only on the affirmation that religious convictions can be publicly debated or assessed, then the modern political problematic can be resolved only if all religious activity can become self-critical.

It is important to note that the definition of religion proposed here is more inclusive than use of the term sometimes intends. At least in some circumstances, for example, nationalism and humanism might be understood as cultural systems in terms of which individuals seek to cultivate a conviction about human authenticity as such and, therefore, are, on my definition, religions. Both in academic discussion and in that of the wider public, however, "religion" is often reserved to mean cultural formations from which nationalism and humanism are distinguished as secularistic convictions. On this common usage, in other words, religion is defined in terms of a certain kind of answer to the comprehensive question, such that secularistic answers are another kind.[10] This more narrow definition of religion has been especially important to the discussion of religion and modern politics. Some hold, for instance, that the modern separation of religions from the state constitutes a secularistic state, and this claim would not make sense if secularism is itself a religion. Again, the more narrow definition is at least implied by the very different claim that the First Amendment to the United

---

10. Alternatively stated, my account may be called a functional definition; that is, religion is identified as a philosophically differentiated function of culture. In contrast, common usage implies a substantive definition; that is, religion is identified as a specific kind of performance of the function in question (cf. Berger 1967: 175–77).

States Constitution prescribes state neutrality only with respect to the differences among religions and, therefore, not with respect to the difference between religion and secularism.

In the course of this work, I will seek to show that the modern political problematic can be solved only if religion is defined in the broad sense I have proposed. Religious freedom, in other words, can only mean the freedom of all activities or associations identified by explicit adherence to some or other comprehensive conviction. On this account, the proper relation between the state and religion, in the narrow sense, is in principle identical to the proper relation between the state and secularism. Still, it will be useful, in order to engage the current discussion of politics and religion, to have some understanding of the more narrow sense of religion, in accord with which religion and secularism are said to be alternative kinds of answers to the comprehensive question.

At least for present purposes, I judge, the following characterization will suffice: Narrowly defined, religion is the primary form of culture in terms of which the comprehensive question is explicitly asked and answered and, further, so answered that human authenticity is derived from the character of reality as such. In saying this, I mean that the distinction between authentic and inauthentic human activity is identified by the relation of human activity to reality as such or ultimate reality. Whether that ultimate reality is understood as Yahweh, Allah, "emptiness," or in some other way, it is understood to be the ground of human authenticity. The point may also be expressed by saying that religion, narrowly understood, so addresses the comprehensive question that ultimate reality is said to authorize human authenticity.

It may be wondered how or in what respect this definition is indeed more narrow than the one I have previously sought to clarify. Since I have said that every answer to the comprehensive question includes a metaphysical aspect, it may seem that all religions in the broad sense ground human authenticity in ultimate reality. In fact, however, the metaphysical aspect of a given religion may or may not determine that religion's distinction between authentic and inauthentic human activity. Individuals may explicitly believe, for instance, that authentic human activity is identified by, say, the pursuit of maximal human flourishing and further believe that reality as such is either indifferent or hostile to human flourishing. On this conviction, it remains that reality as such makes human activity authentic, in the sense that the larger reality is indispensable to and permissive of human flourishing. But humanism, so construed, denies that ultimate reality *authorizes* human authenticity, and a cultural formation identified by this conviction is, therefore, a secularistic religion.

For want of an alternative, I will use the term "theistic religion" and cognate expressions to speak about religion in the narrow sense. But I wish to underscore that, in doing so, I use "theistic" in a strictly formal sense. If this term commonly identifies the affirmation of a God in the sense of a supreme being or an individual transcendent to the world, I here intend solely the belief that human authenticity is authorized by ultimate reality, however that reality may be understood. In contrast to "theistic religion," then, I will use "religion" and cognate expressions without a qualifier when I intend the broad sense of the term or when the distinction between narrow and broad senses is not essential to the point at issue.

Assuming that what has been said serves to define religion as a central term in the modern political problematic, the formal distinction between religion and politics we are seeking now waits on a definition of politics. As we turn our attention to political activity, we may begin by recurring to the general proposition that specific forms of human activity can be identified because the explicit understandings constituting distinctively human life are always fragmentary. If religious and political activity are different, they can be distinguished in terms of differing kinds of explicit understandings and, therefore, the differing questions that are explicitly asked and answered. Assuming that politics is also a specific form of human activity, its identifying question must differ from the comprehensive question. In other words, political activity must be clarified by a question about some *non*comprehensive aspect of our lives and the larger reality to which they belong.

But just as religious activity has not been defined directly because "religion" is frequently used, at least in the first instance, to mean a specific form of culture, so political activity should be defined in relation to the body politic, because, in the first instance, "politics" is frequently used to mean a specific form of association. We may use "human association" in general to mean the relation or relations between or among the distinctively human activities of contemporary individuals. On its most inclusive meaning, in other words, human association occurs whenever one individual understands the understandings of a contemporary, or whenever there is communication between individuals. What we commonly refer to as associations are, then, constituted by complex patterns of communicative action and interaction among individuals—frequently among large numbers of individuals, as, for instance, in economic or cultural or political or religious organizations.

In order to distinguish a particular association, it is typically sufficient if one refers to its location, including the time and place in which its communication began, and the purpose that orders the communication among its member individuals, the purpose that they explicitly and commonly pursue. For instance, a particular university may be distinguished by reference to its origin and its pursuit of higher education. Accordingly, a specific form of association, which abstracts from any particular instances, might be identified by the distinctive purpose that all particular instances, each given its own location, exemplify. But, then, this purpose may be formulated in terms of the distinctive question that orders communication in that kind of association, the question that is addressed explicitly and in common. Given the definition of religion that has been proposed, for instance, religious association is the specific form of association that asks and answers the comprehensive question in terms of some or other particular religion, that is, has as its purpose the cultivation of that answer in the lives of its adherents.

I now propose that politics is the primary form of association in which the question of the state is explicitly asked and answered. On this understanding, the state is the set of governing activities through which all activities and associations within a given society or community are explicitly unified or ordered and, therefore, is always some or other particular state. The question of the state may be formulated: What should the activities of the state be, or what should the state do? Since the primary purpose of asking and answering this question in association with others is to determine what the state's activities will be, a political association in the sense defined includes its own state. At the same time, the definition intends to make clear that a body politic is not necessarily identical to its state, since the former includes all relations among the governed through which the state's activities are explicitly determined. As a specific form of activity, then, political activity may be identified as participation in politics or in the body politic.

This understanding of politics does not mean that all human societies include a more or less differentiated political association. Historically, it has often been the case that governing activities have been more or less coincident with leadership of the religious community. But politics as a specific form of association means only that it *may* be differentiated, as typically has been the case in modern societies. Moreover, the proposed understanding does not even require that politics itself is universal to human societies. Some communities may be or have been ordered by custom in a measure that could lead us to doubt whether they are characterized by governance at all. As a self-differentiation of human activity as such, however, the definition of politics asserts only the possibility of an association that is distinguished in terms of asking and answering explicitly the question of the state.[11]

Clarity may be served by noting that "politics" is often used with a broader meaning than the one I have proposed. On this broader meaning, political activity occurs whenever individuals participate explicitly in determining the larger institutional and cultural structures of their society, including, say, the structure of the economic order or the system of education or the language by which a society is characterized. In contrast, I choose to identify politics by reference to one kind of larger structure, namely, that effected by the state, because the principle of religious freedom is generally understood to be a political principle in this specific sense, that is, it proscribes certain state activities.[12] Accordingly, I will use the term "political process" to mean the larger set of political activities through which the activities of the state are determined and the term "body politic" to mean the political association, that is, individuals

---

11. Since the concept "human association" is implied by the formal understanding of human activity as such, so too is the possibility of an association whose purpose is to effect unity among associations. I recognize that the reference to governance requires further precision or qualification in order fully to identify politics. Not all governance is political; for instance, an economic institution or a university includes an association that explicitly effects the institution's unity, but we call such governance political only on an extended meaning of the latter term. In the first instance, then, political governance generally means the explicit ordering of a group of individuals large enough to constitute what we call a society. Of course, precision now requires that one define a society, but this requirement does not need to be met for purposes of the present work.

12. I expect but will not seek to argue that the conclusions I reach can be appropriated without considerable difficulty to identify the proper relation between politics, on the broader meaning of the term, and a plurality of legitimate religions.

governed by the state insofar as they may legitimately participate in the political process and, in that sense, are citizens.[13]

As the definition I have offered insists, politics should be understood as a form of association in which the question of its own state is addressed not only explicitly but also decisively. This is simply to repeat that there is no body politic unless there is a state in which governance is effected. The purpose of the political association is to determine what the activities of the state are or will be. Of course, the question of the state may also be asked and answered critically; that is, claims about what the state should do may be explicitly assessed—and political activity may also take this form. As I have emphasized, the body politic is not necessarily exhausted by the activities of its own state but, rather, includes all those activities through which its members explicitly and commonly determine what the state does. Accordingly, debate or argument about actual or proposed activities of the state, that is, communication in which the political question is asked and answered critically, may itself be a form of participation in the political association.[14] This circumstance will be important to the argument of this work. I will seek to show that religious freedom as a political principle has no coherent meaning unless a political association can

---

13. Strictly speaking, I distinguish between the body politic or political association and the political community, because I use the latter to mean all of the activities and associations governed by the state. Hence, the political community at least may include individuals who are not members of the body politic. In other words, the terms "political community" and "society" are coextensive, but the former refers to the relevant activities and associations as prescribed, proscribed, or permitted by the state. But this distinction between the political association and the political community is not important to the present inquiry.

14. The fact that political argument as well as political decision can be political activity is, I judge, one reason why politics is properly defined as a specific form of association, and political activity is defined as participation in this kind of association. For the same reason, the use of the term "primary" in the definition of politics (the primary form of association in which the question of the state is explicitly addressed) is not equivalent to its use in the definition of religion (the primary form of culture in terms of which the comprehensive question is explicitly addressed). Since culture consists in the concepts and symbols in terms of which humans explicitly ask and answer questions, a primary form of culture is one in terms of which humans address some question decisively. In other words, a primary form of culture consists in the concepts and symbols for some primary form of

be constituted by a free discussion and debate that includes differing religious convictions.

The Present Purpose

It may be useful summarily to state the conclusions of the preceding section. I have defined religion as a form of culture implied by human activity as such, specifically, the primary form of culture in terms of which the comprehensive question is explicitly asked and answered, so that a religious conviction claims to represent the comprehensive condition of all valid moral understandings. Accordingly, religious activity is the form of activity in which we understand ourselves in terms of some or other particular religion. The function of religious activity is so to represent an answer to the comprehensive question as to cultivate comprehensive self-

---

reflection, in distinction from the secondary form of critical reflection. As the primary form of association in which the question of the state is addressed, politics determines the activities of the state. Precisely because it is an association that does so, however, participation in the political process may include secondary or critical as well as primary or decisive forms of reflection. Thus, political philosophy, which is a secondary form of reflection, at least may be political activity, although theology, philosophy of religion, and philosophical theology are not religious activities.

It also follows that primary forms of human activity are not necessarily defined by primary forms of reflection, that is, by asking and answering some questions decisively. This is because primary forms of human activity are distinguished in relation to different functions that are fundamentally important to living with understanding. Since humans always live with a comprehensive self-understanding, one fundamentally important function of human activity is to cultivate authentic comprehensive self-understandings, so that religious activity as a primary form of human activity is defined in relation to a primary form of culture. Since humans always live together, a second fundamentally important function of activity is to effect authentic governance, so that political activity as a primary form of activity is defined in relation to a primary form of association.

We may also speak of a secondary form of association identified in terms of the question of the state. Political parties and special interest groups, for instance, are political associations that presuppose the body politic in which they participate. Still, it would not be proper to say that activity within such associations exemplifies a secondary form of activity. Such associations participate in the political process, so that the activity within them is political activity.

understandings that are authentic. The importance of critical reflection on the claims of a religion is implied by adherence to it, because the religion in question claims to be valid, and when members of a religious association pursue such reflection because it is required by their religious adherence, we may say that religious activity has become self-critical.

Politics has been defined as a form of association implied by human activity as such, specifically, the primary form of association in which the question of the state is explicitly asked and answered. Political activity, then, is participation in the political process. The state is the association within the body politic that effects governance of the political community, such that the political association includes but is not necessarily exhausted by the state. Although the purpose of politics is to determine the activities of the state, it is also the case that critical reflection on the question of the state may itself be political activity, namely, when participation in the political process takes the form of argument or debate.

These definitions now permit a formal statement of the distinction between religious and political activity. The two kinds of activity differ because the former attends explicitly to human activity as such and the latter attends explicitly to only some human activities, namely, those of a particular state. Alternatively, we may say that religious activity addresses explicitly the question of the comprehensive human purpose, whereas politics addresses explicitly the question of a noncomprehensive purpose, namely, that of ordering or governing the activities and associations within a given society. This distinction between the two also implies a formal relation between them. Precisely because the activities of the state are human activities, the claims of a given religion mean that governmental activities should be decided or determined in accord with that religion's understanding of the comprehensive moral ideal or comprehensive human purpose. In other words, a religious conviction claims to represent the comprehensive condition of politics. The point is all the more apparent if the question of the state is reformulated: What activities of the state are authentic? This question, as all questions about human authenticity, is properly answered only if these activities or their purposes are understood as particular exemplifications of human authenticity as such.

It is also apparent, then, that the relation between politics and religion has become distinctively problematic in modern political communities because these communities include a plurality of legitimate religions. Given that a plurality of religions may include a substantive plurality of claims about human authenticity as such, religious freedom appears to preclude a common principle in terms of which the authenticity of the state's activities may be determined. Modern communities appear to preclude a principle of political unity or, alternatively formulated, a political principle that can be consistently affirmed by adherents of all religions.

It will be important to the subsequent discussion to clarify here that the modern political problematic is a *constitutional* issue. I use the term "political constitution" to mean the explicit principles, written or unwritten, in accord with which the state as such, and therefore, politics as such are defined in a given political community. In other words, the constitution defines the body politic as such and identifies in general the process through which the state's activities are to be determined. Accordingly, constitutional principles are those on which all individuals who are political participants should explicitly agree.

In saying that the modern political problematic is a constitutional issue, I mean that it cannot be credibly solved as a particular political problem, in the sense that the political constitution is silent with respect to the relation between politics and religion and the character of that relation is left to the political process or statutory law. The incoherence of this resolution follows from the character of religious convictions. Since a religious conviction claims to be the comprehensive ideal in accord with which *all* political activity is to be evaluated, the relation of politics to religion is properly an aspect of the political association as such and, therefore, a constitutional issue. Were the constitution silent on this relation, this silence would imply that the comprehensive condition of all authentic politics may differ from time to time in the life of the body politic, and that implication is inconsistent with the comprehensive character of the moral ideal. If religious freedom has a coherent meaning, it is a constitutional principle.[15]

Unless otherwise noted, I will in what follows speak of the constitution's meaning in order to refer to its *explicit* meaning. A constitutional principle, as any claim or understanding, may be said

---

15. The United States Constitution could have denied the *constitutional* establishment of religion simply by remaining silent on the relation of politics to religion. It is noteworthy that the First Amendment proscribes to Congress *any law* "respecting an establishment of religion."

to have *implicit* as well as explicit meanings; that is, its full meaning includes whatever understandings are implied but not explicitly stated. It might be argued, for instance, that a constitutional principle explicitly proscribing war implies that human activity is necessarily inauthentic if, under any circumstances, it purposefully causes the death of any human individual, so that this latter understanding is an implicit meaning of the constitution. Just because the more general claim about human authenticity is not explicitly stated, however, those who agree regarding the explicit meaning of the principle may disagree as to whether the more general claim is a part of the full meaning of the constitution, that is, whether the more general claim is in truth implied. It is, then, the explicit meaning of the constitution that should be explicitly affirmed by all members of the body politic. Alternatively stated, the explicit meaning of the political constitution is an affirmation or set of affirmations that all political participants should be taught, so that the state has a duty to insure that this teaching occurs. When I speak of the meaning of religious freedom, then, I intend that meaning whose teaching is a concern of the state.

The thesis I will seek to defend may now be restated as follows: Religious freedom means nothing other than a political expression of the comprehensive question. Because the modern political problematic cannot be resolved by an answer to this question, I will argue, a modern political community must be constituted by the question itself. A political community constituted by an answer to the comprehensive question includes what has generally been called an established religion, that is, a religious conviction that the political constitution identifies as official. Because a constitution identifies the principles of politics as such, religious establishment means that explicit agreement on a particular answer to the comprehensive question identifies the body politic, so that the state has a duty to insure the teaching of this claim. Accordingly, religious establishment is patently inconsistent with a plurality of legitimate religions. Since a nonestablished religion at least may differ substantively with the religion that is established, the meaning of religious establishment is that any nonestablished religion at least may be illegitimate.

To be sure, it is always an open question whether two different religions do differ substantively. Cultural formations or systems are particular human creations, so that religions may differ with respect to the concepts and symbols in terms of which the comprehensive question is asked and answered even while the meaning of their answers is identical. Still, a plurality of legitimate religions may include substantively different convictions, so that a solution to the modern political problematic must be consistent with this possibility—and it is this possibility with which religious establishment is inconsistent.[16] Because it is this possibility that religious freedom affirms, I will henceforth speak of different religious convictions in the sense that includes substantively different understandings of the comprehensive ideal or human authenticity as such.

It is because religious establishment is inconsistent with a plurality of legitimate religions that "toleration," in the sense that includes an established religion even while it permits dissenting religions, is not a coherent resolution of the modern political problematic. Nor does the fact that political communities constituted by this principle (for instance, Great Britain) have maintained their stability over long periods of time count against this conclusion. It is not a necessity of human activity that the principles explicitly affirmed by individuals, associations, or political communities are coherent. On the contrary, incoherent understandings may be explicitly endorsed notwithstanding that individuals and communities cannot act in accord with them. Thus, an incoherent principle relating politics and religion may command the explicit assent of citizens over long periods of time although, in fact, at least

---

16. Generally speaking, the establishment of a given conviction regarding human authenticity as such has also meant the establishment of a given religion. In other words, certain concepts and symbols in terms of which the comprehensive question is explicitly and decisively asked and answered are also constitutionally affirmed, so that the state supports certain forms of ritual activity or worship. It is an interesting question whether the establishment of a given comprehensive conviction requires the establishment of a religion. On one reading, at least, John Dewey's *A Common Faith* proposes an understanding of politics that includes the establishment of a given understanding of "God," even though it also allows that this conviction might be mediated by differing cultural systems (see Dewey 1934: 82–83). Also, some of the 18th century American colonies and, subsequently, states seem to have practiced "multiple establishment," although the differing religions were differing expressions of Christianity. But I will not pursue this question here. My concern in this work is the political relation between substantively different religious convictions, so that, for present purposes, I will mean by religious establishment the constitutional affirmation of a particular answer to the comprehensive question.

some members of the body politic act in a manner that is inconsistent with the principle. For instance, adherents of a tolerated
religion may also accept the establishment of another religion.
Alternatively, the affirmation of an established religion by all or most
citizens may be merely verbal or "honored in the breach."

If some believe that toleration solves the modern political
problematic, others insist that modern politics must or can be
constitutionally secularistic, so that "disestablishment" or "the
separation of church and state" is or can be an explicitly secularistic
principle. There is no question that secularism has been widely
persuasive in modern life. Indeed, one might say that modern moral
philosophy has been dominated by the belief that differences between
moral and immoral and, therefore, assessments of the state's
activities can be validated independently of claims about reality as
such. It is not my purpose in this work to defend or to contest that
belief.[17] Whether or not that belief is true, I will argue, a secularistic
meaning of religious freedom is also incoherent. Indeed, the attempt
so to understand religious freedom that either secularistic or theistic
religion generally or as such is explicitly affirmed is, I will argue, in
truth the establishment of a particular religion. In other words,
either attempt constitutes the political community by an answer to
the comprehensive question, and this is why the modern political
problematic can be solved only if religion is understood in the broad
sense.

Because religious freedom cannot mean an answer to the
comprehensive question, to repeat the thesis, a modern political
community must be constituted by the question itself. To constitute
a community by a question is, I hold, to constitute a free discussion
and debate regarding proposed answers. On this thesis, then, the
modern political problematic is solved only by the constitution of a
free political discourse that is also a full political discourse because it
seeks to understand the character of human authenticity as such or
the comprehensive purpose in its relevance to the activities of the
state. On a coherent understanding of religious freedom, in other
words, adherents of differing religions may engage in religious
activities that are also political activities, just insofar as the religious
activities address the comprehensive question as a contribution to
the political process. That adherents of *differing* religions may so act
politically implies that the free discussion of human authenticity

---

17. I have contested it in a previous work (see Gamwell).

must also be a free debate, that is, must include not only the making of diverse religious claims but also the critical assessment of them. Thus, the view of religious freedom for which I will argue requires that religious activity as such may, as I have put it, become self-critical, in the sense that religious claims or convictions can be publicly assessed or validated.

As I mentioned in chapter 1, the present thesis about religious freedom takes exception to the theory of religion as nonrational, that is, the theory that religious convictions are not expressions of reason in the sense that their claims to validity do not belong to a public or rational order of reflection and assessment. Accordingly, the conclusion I will seek to commend denies that religious freedom can be coherently understood in a manner consistent with this theory. Part two of this work—or chapters 3, 4, and 5—seeks to sustain this critical claim through attention to three views of religious freedom that constitute alternatives consistent with the theory of religion as nonrational. I will call these, respectively, the "privatist," "partisan," and "pluralist" views of religious freedom. One or more of these names may appear to be polemical, at least to those who advocate one or another of the three views, and it is true that I have so characterized them as to suggest that none of the three is a successful resolution of the modern political problematic. But I intend that this conclusion will be redeemed by argument. In each case, I will seek to assess the relevant view by entertaining the proposal of a representative thinker and so criticizing the coherence of his position that any other formulation of the view in question must display a similar failure.

Taken together, these critical discussions are meant to show that the modern political problematic cannot be solved if one does not contest the theory of religion as nonrational. In other words, the three views of religious freedom in question exhaust the alternatives consistent with that theory. Formally speaking, understandings that deny religious establishment and also deny the public assessment of religions may assert that (1) none of the religious convictions in the community is important to the politics, or (2) some of the religious convictions in the community are important to politics, or (3) all of the religious convictions in the community are important to politics. Since the distinctions among none, some, and all are logically exhaustive, so are the formal alternatives identified by these distinctions.

My intent, then, is that these alternatives, each considered as a view consistent with the theory of religion as nonrational, are the three views of religious freedom I will criticize. The privatist view holds, in a sense to be clarified, that none of the religious convictions in the community is important to politics, and I will examine this view through attention to the political conception of justice advanced by John Rawls. The partisan view holds, in a sense to be clarified, that some of the religious convictions in the community are important to politics, and I will examine this view through attention to the classic proposal advanced by John Courtney Murray. The pluralist view holds, in a sense to be clarified, that all of the religious convictions in the community are important to politics, and I will examine this view through attention to the relation between religious convictions and political choice developed by Kent Greenawalt. In each case, as I have mentioned, the criticism is designed to show that no formulation of the view in question can be coherent.

Summarily, then, parts one and two of this work seek to clarify the modern political problematic and the reasons why public discussion of religious freedom so readily results in confusion. The intent of these first two parts is to gain a hearing for parts three and four, in which I will argue for what I will call "the public view" of religious freedom. On this view, the valid comprehensive conviction is important to politics, and, therefore, modern politics is coherently constituted by a full and free political discourse or by the comprehensive question itself. Part three will present a statement of the public view of religious freedom. In chapter 6, I will approach this statement by reviewing the understanding advanced by Sidney E. Mead, who, in my judgment, has appreciated more fully than any other student of the problem the terms required to make sense of America's "lively experiment." But even Mead's formulation is, as I will try to show, not fully adequate. Because, on the public view, the political community is constituted by the comprehensive question, I will, in chapter 7, examine the rationality of religion and, in that way, reach a restatement and completion of Mead's proposal.

Part four will attempt sufficiently to pursue the public view of religious freedom that at least the most obvious objections to its understanding of politics and religion are seen to be without merit. In chapter 8, I will consider objections focused on the claim that this view identifies a coherent principle of political unity. In chapter 9, I will consider objections focused on the claim that this view identifies a principle all religious adherents can consistently accept. To show that religious freedom on the public view is a coherent political principle adherents of a plurality of legitimate religions can consistently accept is, as I will attempt to clarify, to show that it prescribes democratic discourse and democratic civility and, therefore, may also be called the democratic resolution to the modern political problematic.

PART 2
NONRATIONAL RESOLUTIONS

3

THE PRIVATIST VIEW: JOHN RAWLS

Several students of modern political thought have argued that the ruinous religious wars of the early seventeenth century were the principal political condition of the emergence of religious toleration. As a political principle, in other words, toleration expressed a commitment to political life independent of religious (or at least theistic religious) differences. So Quentin Skinner concludes:

> The acceptance of the modern idea of the State presupposes that political society is held to exist solely for political purposes.... For as soon as the protagonists of rival creeds showed that they were willing to fight each other to the death, it began to seem obvious to a number of *politique* theorists that, if there were to be any prospect of achieving civil peace, the powers of the State would have to be divorced from the duty to uphold any particular faith. (Skinner, 2:352)

Citing Skinner, Jeffrey Stout holds that civil peace required this modern conception of the state because religious convictions appealed to authority, so that conflict among them could not be adjudicated by appeal to reason.

> Any point of view in which religious considerations or conceptions of the good remained dominant was, in the early modern context, incapable of providing a basis for the reasonable and peaceful resolution of social conflict. Incompatible appeals to authority seemed equally reasonable, and therefore equally suspect, as well as thoroughly useless as vehicles of rational persuasion. (Stout: 235)

Whatever the merit of this historical reading, it is clear that modern political thought has frequently endorsed the privatization of religion, precisely in the sense that "political society is held to exist solely for political purposes" and, therefore, is properly "divorced from" religious activities and their claims or convictions. It is also widely believed that this is the meaning of the religion clauses of the First Amendment to the United States Constitution. Indeed, it is appropriate to say that the privatization of religion is, more often than not, the understanding that informs those in contemporary America who insist that religion should be separated from the state and whom, therefore, I earlier called separationists. The two should be separated in the sense that political association should be constitutionally independent of all comprehensive convictions, so that none of the religious convictions in the community is important to politics. I will call this "the privatist view" of religious freedom.[1]

On one account of the privatist view, the political constitution can coherently privatize religion because all comprehensive claims, theistic or secularistic, are, in the nature of the case, subrational. In other words, no religious conviction is either valid or invalid, so that commitment to a comprehensive ideal cannot express an exercise of reason but only a decision. Since this account agrees that every evaluative affirmation implies some or other ultimate ideal, it follows that all value judgments, particular or general, are finally subrational. They imply a judgment that can only be chosen and, therefore, can never express an exercise of reason. Accordingly, the legislative process properly displays a kind of reasoning by convention or is positivistic, that is, can appeal only to prior agreements that were themselves mere decisions of citizens that happened to be common— and, in this sense, "political society is held to exist solely for political purposes." Karl-Otto Apel has called this combination of private or subrational values and public or positivistic facts the "complementarity-system" of modern political thought (Apel 1979a: 37, emphasis deleted). As Apel also notes, this system is articulated especially in

---

1. Some who might own the name "separationist" may do so on the grounds that all *theistic* claims should be privatized; that is, the modern political process should be constitutionally secularistic. The important point at the moment is that the privatization of theistic religion is not, on my usage, an instance of the privatist view. On the contrary, the privatist view holds that the political process is dependent on no comprehensive convictions, so that it is independent of secularism as well as theistic religion. Within the theory of religion as nonrational, the privatization of theistic religion is one expression of what I call the partisan view, and, as such, I will return to it in chapter 4.

the massive achievement of Max Weber, so that, on this account, religious freedom is a part of the "rationalization" of the West, in the sense of this term that Weber introduced (see Apel 1979a).

We may readily see, however, that this account, which we may call the classic account of the privatist view, cannot solve the modern political problematic. Because religious activity asks and answers the question of human authenticity as such, every religious conviction claims to represent a self-understanding that ought to be exemplified without duplicity in all human activity. In other words, a religious conviction necessarily claims to be valid, and an understanding that is neither valid nor invalid because it merely expresses a decision could not be an answer to the comprehensive question. To assert the complementarity system is to deny all religious convictions or to deny that the comprehensive question is a sensible one. Alternatively stated, no religious adherent could consistently accept this account because its meaning of "religious freedom" explicitly denies what every religious conviction affirms: So far from merely positivistic, the activities of the state ought to be authentic, that is, ought to exemplify purposes that imply without contradiction the valid comprehensive self-understanding or the comprehensive purpose. Thus, the constitutional claim that all comprehensive claims are subrational cannot legitimate any religion and is not a coherent understanding of religious freedom.

But if the complementarity system is inadequate to our problem, there is a considerably more subtle account of the privatist view in which the assertion that comprehensive convictions are subrational is explicitly refused. On this second account, it remains that "political society is held to exist solely for political purposes," but the question of whether religious convictions can be valid is simply begged. The comprehensive question, we are told, is not pertinent to politics, such that political thinking may simply refuse the order of reflection that question identifies. As a political principle, then, religious freedom is said to mean just this refusal.

It is not inappropriate to call this second account an expression in political theory of the recently widespread belief that we may "think without foundations" and, therefore, a "nonfoundational" account of the privatist view. Notwithstanding its simple refusal of thought about human authenticity as such, however, this second account is at least consistent with the claim that comprehensive convictions cannot be rationally or publicly assessed. Whether one explicitly asserts that ultimate ideals are subrational or simply refuses to allow in politics the order of reflection that their assessment would require, the common consequence is an understanding of the political process from which the rational or public assessment of religious claims is excluded. It is in this sense, then, that the privatist view, on either account, is one alternative for those who insist on the nonrational character of such claims.

We may consider the privatist view on its nonfoundational account by attending to the proposal advanced by John Rawls in his recent *Political Liberalism*. Although "religious freedom" is not an important term in Rawls's formulations, the attempt properly to relate a conception of justice to a plurality of comprehensive doctrines is central to his thought. Indeed, it is not too much to say, I judge, that religious freedom is, on my meaning of the term, *the* conception that *Political Liberalism* seeks to articulate and defend. In any event, I will attend to his proposal in the measure and respects required to understand his solution to the modern political problematic and, accordingly, will not seek to review his work as a whole, which includes address to many related questions in political thought.

Religious Freedom and the Political Conception of Justice

Rawls is surely best known for his massively influential *A Theory of Justice*. It is also well-known, however, that the theory he there advanced has been revised through a series of subsequent writings that culminated in *Political Liberalism*.[2] On Rawls's own accounting, this development in his thought was required because his earlier work presents its conception of justice as part of a comprehensive doctrine and, to this extent, is "unrealistic" (xvi). Given that modern democratic culture "is always marked by a diversity of opposing and irreconcilable religious, philosophical, and moral doctrines" (3–4) and that this diversity "is a permanent feature of the public culture" (36), the theory of *A Theory of Justice*, precisely because it is another such doctrine, cannot realistically expect the common support or affirmation of democratic citizens. Thus, Rawls's later work, culminating in *Political Liberalism*, has sought so

---

2. The important writings between *A Theory of Justice* and *Political Liberalism* that are most pertinent to the present discussion include Rawls 1980, 1985, 1987, and 1988. All citations from Rawls in this chapter are taken from *Political Liberalism*.

to revise the theory as to articulate systematically the all-important "distinction between a political conception of justice and a comprehensive philosophical doctrine" (xvi). Since this distinction is introduced in order that political theory may be consistent with a diversity of comprehensive doctrines, we may say that Rawls has sought so to revise his earlier work as to solve the modern political problematic.

On Rawls's usage, a comprehensive doctrine is or includes a moral conception that "applies to a wide range of subjects [or aspects of practice], and....includes conceptions of what is of value in human life and ideals of personal character, as well as ideals of friendship and of familial and associational relationships, and much else that is to inform our conduct, and in the limit to our life as a whole" (13). A comprehensive doctrine, Rawls sometimes says, is or includes a comprehensive conception of the good (see 179), and this "determinate scheme of final ends and aims" is, at least sometimes, related to "a view of our relation to the world—religious, philosophical, or moral—by reference to which these ends and attachments are understood" (302). It is apparent, then, that answers to the comprehensive question or religious convictions, as I sought to identify them in the previous chapter, are at least some among the comprehensive doctrines that Rawls has in mind, so that a plurality of the latter includes a plurality of the former. For present purposes, we may use the two terms synonymously.[3]

If a comprehensive doctrine includes a moral conception applied to many subjects, a political conception of justice is a moral conception that is "worked out" for a particular subject, namely, the "basic structure" of society (11), its "main social institutions—the

---

3. Rawls would insist, I expect, that only some comprehensive doctrines are what I have called answers to the comprehensive question. On his intention, in other words, his term is more inclusive, because he distinguishes between a "fully comprehensive" and a "partially comprehensive" doctrine. The former "covers all recognized virtues and values within one rather precisely articulated system," and the latter "comprises a number of, but by no means all, nonpolitical values and virtues and is rather loosely articulated" (13). Rawls would say, I expect, that answers to the comprehensive question, on my usage, are more or less equivalent to what he means by a fully comprehensive conviction. For present purposes, however, we may abstract from this difference. As I will try to show, Rawls's political thought seeks simply to refuse the comprehensive order of reflection, on either meaning, and it is this refusal that I seek to assess.

constitution, the economic regime, the legal order..., and how these institutions cohere into one system" (301). The all-important distinction between a political conception and a wider or comprehensive doctrine means that the former "is neither presented as, nor derived from, such a doctrine applied to the basic structure of society, as if this structure were simply another subject to which that doctrine applied" (12). Rawls also expresses this all-important distinction by saying that a political conception of justice must be "presented as a freestanding view" (12), that is, must be "limited to...'the domain of the political'" (38). "We try, so far as we can, neither to assert nor to deny any particular comprehensive religious, philosophical, or moral view, or its associated theory of truth and the status of values" (150) and, therefore, to work out principles of justice "independently of any wider comprehensive...doctrine" (223). A political conception of justice is also distinguished, then, from a conception of justice; that is, the latter has a broader meaning because it also includes any understanding of justice that is presented as part of or dependent on a comprehensive doctrine.

A freestanding conception of justice is, Rawls maintains, properly called a liberal conception, because liberalism as a political theory is properly traced to the emergence of religious pluralism in "the Reformation and its aftermath," especially in "the long controversies over religious toleration in the sixteenth and seventeenth centuries" (xxiv). But, then, "political liberalism," as Rawls uses the term, must be distinguished from "a comprehensive liberal moral doctrine such as those of Kant or Mill" (145) or of *A Theory of Justice*, because the latter "unrealistically" presents a liberal political theory as part of a comprehensive doctrine. On Rawls's usage, political liberalism seeks realistically to answer the question: "How is it possible for there to exist over time a just and stable society of free and equal citizens, who remain profoundly divided by reasonable religious, philosophical, and moral doctrines" (4)?

Since political liberalism must be independent of wider doctrines, it is worked out in terms of "certain fundamental ideas seen as implicit in the public political culture of a democratic society" (13). A political conception of justice begins with "the most deep-seated convictions" that are shared by democratic citizens because they are implicit in the "traditions of a modern democratic state" (300), that is, in "its system of law and political institutions, and in the main historical traditions of their interpretation" (67). This approach is thoroughly appropriate, Rawls contends, because the plurality of comprehensive doctrines is, at least in part, "the natural outcome of the activities of human reason under enduring free institutions" (xxiv). Since the fact of pluralism is in part the consequence of modern democracy, in other words, there is reason to expect that democratic political culture includes the required resources with which to solve the modern political problematic.

Within the "shared fund" (8) of ideas, some are more general than others. The rejection of slavery, for instance, is a "settled" conviction at a lower level of generality than the basic idea that citizens are free and equal. Starting with more general or fundamental ideas, then, one seeks to formulate a general political conception that is "congenial to our most firmly held convictions.... at all levels of generality" (8), and success in this attempt may require adjustments in either the general conception initially proposed or in our "judgments about particular institutions and actions" (26). "It is a mistake to think of abstract conceptions and general principles as always overriding our more particular judgments. These two sides of our practical thought (not to mention intermediate levels of generality in between) are complementary, and to be adjusted to one another so as to fit into a coherent view" (45). In a now famous expression, Rawls calls this approach to political theory the pursuit of "reflective equilibrium" (8). If one finds a conception of justice in terms of which democratic citizens achieve reflective equilibrium, then one has uncovered "the conditions of the possibility of a reasonable public basis of justification on fundamental political questions" (xix), the plurality of comprehensive doctrines notwithstanding.

The fundamental ideas implicit in democratic culture to which Rawls appeals are ideas of society and the person. He emphasizes persistently that these are political ideas, meaning that they are independent of any wider doctrine because their pertinent meaning is limited to "how citizens are to think of themselves and of one another in their political and social relationships as specified by the basic structure" (300). "The fundamental idea...of society" is that of "a fair system of cooperation over time" (14), that is, cooperation involving "the idea of fair terms of cooperation" or "terms that each participant may reasonably accept, provided that everyone else likewise accepts them" (16). "The fundamental idea of the person" (18) is that of "citizens as free and equal" (19). To say that citizens are free means that they have "two moral powers," namely, a "capacity for a sense of justice," that is, a capacity "to honor fair terms of cooperation" (302), and a "capacity to form, to revise, and rationally to pursue" (19) a conception of the good, one that at least may be comprehensive. Citizens are equal, then, in the sense that they have "these powers to the requisite minimum degree to be fully cooperating members of society" (19).

The two moral powers may also be identified, respectively, as capacities to be reasonable and to be rational (see 305). If the distinction between a political conception and a comprehensive doctrine is all-important in Rawls's proposal, so too is a distinction between the reasonable and the rational. "The reasonable and the rational are taken as two distinct and independent basic ideas," meaning "there is no thought of deriving one from the other" (51). A person is reasonable in the sense that she or he has the capacity "to engage in fair cooperation as such, and to do so on terms that others as equals might reasonably be expected to endorse" (51); that is, the capacity to be reasonable is the capacity for a sense of justice. In distinction, "the rational...applies to a single, unified agent (either an individual or corporate person) with the powers of judgment and deliberation in seeking ends and interests peculiarly its own" (50), that is, the capacity to be rational is the capacity to form and pursue a conception of the good. That these two "basic ideas" are independent means that "merely reasonable agents would have no ends of their own they wanted to advance by fair cooperation; merely rational agents lack a sense of justice and fail to recognize the independent validity of the claims of others" (52).

In sum, reasonable persons can commonly accept terms or principles of justice notwithstanding that they differ regarding their own ends or regarding comprehensive doctrines. Rawls also makes this point by saying that reasonable agents are willing to recognize "the burdens of judgment" (54), especially with respect to comprehensive doctrines. For several reasons, sincere and intelligent people, even after discussion, may not agree (see 54–58) in "many of our most important judgments" (58), and reasonable people accept the consequences of this fact for "the use of public reason in directing the legitimate exercise of political power" (54). Precisely because the reasonable and the rational are independent, then, political liberalism may hope to propose a publicly justified and freestanding conception that neither asserts nor denies any of the comprehensive doctrines. The distinction between the reasonable and the rational is all-important to Rawls because it implies and is implied by his distinction between a political conception and a comprehensive doctrine.

Having articulated these ideas of society and the person, Rawls
proposes that a publicly justified conception of justice may be
achieved by using "the idea of the original position" (22). This idea
is, he says, "a device" that "serves as a means of public reflection and
self-clarification" (26) because it "connects the conception of the
person and its companion conception of social cooperation with
certain specific principles of justice" (304). Given that political
liberalism seeks reasonable terms of cooperation, one may formulate
these terms by asking what principles citizens or their representatives would commonly choose or agree on were they forced to
deliberate under a "veil of ignorance" (27) or certain restrictions on
information. Because the reasonable is independent of the rational,
the veil of ignorance must hide from the parties all knowledge of
their conceptions of the good or those of the citizens they represent.
In other words, Rawls's notion of the original position may be
understood, at least for present purposes, as nothing other than his
insistence that political liberalism must be freestanding or independent of any comprehensive doctrine.[4] It seems appropriate to say,
then, that the device of the original position seeks to identify "the
reasonable point of view" with respect to principles of justice. "We
can, as it were, enter this position at any time simply by reasoning for
principles of justice in accordance with the enumerated restrictions
on information" (27).

It may be wondered how citizens or their representatives so
restricted could agree on any principles of justice. After all, "merely
reasonable agents would have no ends of their own they wanted to
advance by fair cooperation" (52), and the point of justice is fairness
among citizens who pursue diverse ends or conceptions of the good.
Absent all reference to ends, in other words, justice might seem to be
without content. But Rawls insists that this problem is solved by an
"index of primary goods arrived at from within" (40) the freestanding

---

4. Rawls enumerates a number of restrictions on the parties to the original
position—for instance, none of them know what social position they or their
constituents occupy or their special talents or their race or ethnic group, sex
or gender (see 24–25). So far as I can see, however, all of the other restrictions
are implied in Rawls's insistence that parties are ignorant of their or their
constituents' "religious, philosophical, or moral" doctrines (24). To admit
knowledge of the other things he enumerates is to admit the possibility that
these particular conditions are considered good, so that parties to the original
position seek principles of justice biased toward some wider doctrine of the
good.

view. Because citizens as political persons have two moral powers, namely, the capacity for a sense of justice and the capacity to form, revise, and pursue a conception of the good, they also have "two corresponding higher-order interests in developing and exercising these powers" (74). Accordingly, a liberal conception of justice may identify primary goods that are "essential...to realize the higher-order interests" (76). Precisely because these goods are essential to any citizen, irrespective of his or her determinate conception of the good, they are, as the freestanding view generally, "independent of any particular comprehensive doctrine" (180). "However distinct their [conceptions of the good]...and their related religious and philosophical doctrines," all citizens "require for their advancement roughly the same primary goods, that is, the same basic rights, liberties, and opportunities, and the same all-purpose means such as income and wealth, with all of these supported by the same social bases of self-respect" (180). A freestanding conception of justice is not devoid of content, then, because it identifies in principle how these primary goods are fairly distributed and shared.

Notwithstanding the distinction between a political conception and a comprehensive doctrine that *Political Liberalism* seeks systematically to articulate, Rawls continues to hold that any who take what I have called "the reasonable point of view" and, therefore, all parties in the original position will, after due reflection, affirm the two principles of justice, including the lexical priority of the first, for which he argued in *A Theory of Justice*:

a. Each person has an equal right to a fully adequate scheme of equal basic liberties which is compatible with a similar scheme of liberties for all.

b. Social and economic inequalities are to satisfy two conditions. First, they must be attached to offices and positions open to all under conditions of fair equality of opportunity; and second, they must be to the greatest benefit of the least advantaged members of society. (291)[5]

To the specific political conception identified by these two principles Rawls gives the name "justice as fairness."

---

5. There is one change in the formulation of these principles between *A Theory of Justice* and *Political Liberalism*. For Rawls's explanation of the change, see 331f.

Given that the principles of justice are freestanding, political liberalism implies "the priority of the right" (173) or, what is the same thing, implies "that the reasonable is prior to the rational" (25, n. 28). In a liberal democracy, in other words, "the principles of political justice impose limits on permissible ways of life" (174) and, therefore, on "permissible conceptions of the good" (180) or comprehensive doctrines. If a given comprehensive conception or doctrine implies individual or associational pursuits that "transgress those limits," that conception or doctrine has "no weight" (174), and political liberalism implies "an ideal conception of citizenship" (213) that includes adherence to only permissible comprehensive doctrines. Also included in this "ideal conception" is the view that public or political advocacy, at least with respect to the basic structure, should be "conducted in terms of the political conception of justice" (44).

It is normally desirable that the comprehensive philosophical and moral views we are wont to use in debating fundamental political issues should give way in public life. Public reason— citizens' reasoning in the public forum about constitutional essentials and basic questions of justice—is now best guided by a political conception the principles and values of which all citizens can endorse. (10)[6]

It is, then, the freestanding or solely political character of justice as fairness that allows us to call this proposal nonfoundational in character. In seeking "neither to assert nor to deny any particular comprehensive...view, or its associated theory of truth and the status of values" (150) and, therefore to present "a reasonable conception... in terms of certain fundamental ideas viewed as latent in the public political culture of a democratic society" (175), Rawls proposes to justify principles for the basic structure by simply refusing the comprehensive order of reflection. Political liberalism simply avoids, explicitly and implicitly, all wider claims, because "it approaches all questions from within its own limited point of view" (xx). Not only

---

6. Rawls does affirm the assertion of comprehensive doctrines as a part of political debate about decisions other than those of "constitutional essentials and matters of basic justice." But it follows that such assertion is pertinent to politics only insofar as it is consistent with freestanding principles of justice, and it is with respect to the latter than comprehensive convictions are privatized. See Rawls 1993: 230, 235, 246.

does it refuse to say which comprehensive doctrine is true, "it does not,..., use (or deny) the concept of truth; nor does it question that concept, nor could it say that the concept of truth and its idea of the reasonable are the same. Rather, within itself the political conception does without the concept of truth" (94). Individual citizens may go "beyond the reasonable....in line with their own comprehensive views" (153), but the claims of political liberalism are independent of whether any comprehensive doctrine is true (see 126n.34).

Rawls makes the same point, then, when he says that political liberalism is "political and not metaphysical" (10), because "metaphysical" here refers to the order of reflection in which a comprehensive conception of human life and the human good is worked out. He seeks "to develop a political conception of justice without presupposing, or explicitly using, a particular metaphysical doctrine" (29, n. 31). Again, Rawls says that "political liberalism applies the principle of toleration to philosophy itself" (10), because this means that philosophy, in the sense of a comprehensive order of reflection, is irrelevant to the domain of the political.[7] In distinction from philosophy, the order of political reflection is limited to historically specific ideas that are at least implicit or latent within the political culture of a modern democracy, and, therefore, political liberalism says nothing, explicitly or implicitly, about the proper character of moral thought, political or otherwise, in any other historical context.

I will not pursue or seek to assess Rawls's argument for the two principles of justice as fairness, because the more pertinent question

---

7. At one point, however, Rawls does say that political liberals must disagree with a comprehensive doctrine whose adherents contend that their beliefs "are open to and can be fully established by reason" (153), and this disagreement would seem to be philosophical in character. Similarly, Rawls is sensitive to the suggestion that "to develop a political conception of justice without presupposing,..., a particular metaphysical doctrine,..., is already to presuppose a metaphysical thesis: namely, that no metaphysical doctrine is required for this purpose." To this suggestion, he responds: "Following the precept of avoidance, I should not want to deny [this claim]....What should be said is the following: If we look at the presentation of justice as fairness and note how it is set up, and note the ideas and conceptions it uses, no particular metaphysical doctrine about the nature of persons, distinctive and opposed to other metaphysical doctrines, appears among its premises, or seems required by its argument. If metaphysical presuppositions are involved, perhaps they are so general that they would not distinguish between the metaphysical

is whether any freestanding view of justice can solve the modern political problematic. "Justice as fairness" is "but one example of a liberal political conception; its specific content is not definitive of such a view" (226)—or, to say the same, "political liberalism is a kind of view" (226) that allows for variant examples (see 7) that differ in terms of the particular freestanding principles they advance. To be sure, one cannot fully commend political liberalism without showing that some specific example of it can be endorsed by all democratic citizens in reflective equilibrium. But any particular example presupposes that the all-important distinction between a political conception and a comprehensive doctrine, or between the reasonable and the rational, is a coherent basis on which to identify what I call religious freedom. It is this distinction that *Political Liberalism* is principally concerned to defend and, similarly, it is this distinction that I am principally concerned to discuss.

Precisely because any specified principles of justice are worked out as a freestanding view, Rawls continues, there is reason to ask whether the priority of right that they imply and the associated ideal

---

views—Cartesian, Leibnizian, or Kantian; realist, idealist, or materialist—with which philosophy has traditionally been concerned" (29n.31).

But this attempt by Rawls to avoid philosophy appears to involve a philosophical claim. To concede that a reasonable or political conception of justice may presuppose a metaphysical thesis but only one that is general in the sense Rawls suggests is to make or imply a claim that purports to be true, in distinction from reasonable. In other words, the distinction between the reasonable and the true is itself a distinction that must be true. Although Rawls refuses to deny that his proposal presupposes a particular metaphysical doctrine, the point of the criticism is that he cannot consistently refuse to affirm it. Moreover, his account of it is a highly controversial metaphysical claim. The assertion that there may be metaphysical presuppositions so general that they do not distinguish between the metaphysical views with which philosophy has traditionally been concerned is itself a denial of many traditional philosophical views. I refer to those in which metaphysics asks about the a priori or necessary conditions of human activity. Agreeing with these traditional metaphysical views in this respect, I hold that Rawls's assertion implies the denial, in distinction from the mere refusal, of the comprehensive order of reflection as I have defined it. Hence, it is not surprising that political liberalism also denies that any comprehensive doctrine is "open to and can be fully established by reason." I will pursue the nature of comprehensive reflection in chapter 7 and, more fully, in the Appendix to this work.

conception of citizenship, including the commitment to permissible comprehensive doctrines, are in fact acceptable to all democratic citizens. Since a comprehensive religious, philosophical, or moral doctrine is indeed comprehensive, it follows that a citizen can coherently accept a given political conception of justice only if its principles are compatible with her or his comprehensive view. But modern democracy includes a plurality of such doctrines, so that one may doubt whether such coherence will characterize the view of citizens generally. In sum, why should one expect that the plurality of comprehensive doctrines will all be permissible ones?

This question leads Rawls to insist that political liberalism must be "presented in two stages" (140). In the first stage, principles of justice are worked out as a freestanding view, and the second stage considers whether such principles "may establish and preserve... stability given the reasonable pluralism" (133) characteristic of a democratic society. I previously noted Rawls's conclusion that *A Theory of Justice* is "unrealistic" (xvi). Since it presents principles of justice as part of a comprehensive view, it cannot expect common support in a society characterized by a plurality of incompatible comprehensive doctrines. Rawls also makes this point by saying that *A Theory of Justice* failed to solve the problem of stability (see xvii).

A stable democratic society, Rawls explains, requires a "public conception of justice" (66), the necessary conditions of which include, first, that "everyone accepts and knows that everyone else accepts and publicly endorses" that conception (201) and, second, that the "full justification" of that conception is "also...publicly known, or better, at least...publicly available" (67). One among a plurality of comprehensive doctrines cannot meet either condition except "by the oppressive use of state power" (37), that is, nondemocratically. In contrast, the freestanding or political conception of justice advanced in *Political Liberalism* allows a publicly known or publicly available "full justification" for principles of justice, because this justification is not dependent on a comprehensive view but, rather, is developed from the shared fund of ideas implicit in the public culture. Still, it must be shown how, given the plurality of comprehensive doctrines, a political conception can be one "everyone accepts and knows that everyone else accepts" and, thereby, one that solves the problem of democratic stability. "The second stage" in Rawls's presentation pursues this task.

In political liberalism, Rawls maintains, the problem of stability is solved by showing that a given political conception of justice "can gain the support of an overlapping consensus of reasonable religious, philosophical, and moral doctrines in a society regulated by it" (10). Thus, an overlapping consensus with respect to specified principles of justice means that the comprehensive doctrines in question are all permissible ones. It is, then, one of the necessary conditions of "a satisfactory political conception" that it "can be the focus of an overlapping consensus" (141). In other words, a stable democratic society is one whose freestanding principles of justice enjoy not only the common "public basis of justification" in the political culture but also diverse "nonpublic bases of justification belonging to the many comprehensive doctrines and acceptable only to those who affirm them" (xix). The nonpublic bases on which citizens accept the principles of justice "belong to what we may call the 'background culture'" (14) and are variant. "All those who affirm the political conception start from within their own comprehensive view and draw on the religious, philosophical, and moral grounds it provides" (147). Or, again: "The political conception is a module, an essential constituent part, that in different ways fits into and can be supported by various reasonable comprehensive doctrines that endure in the society regulated by it" (144–45).

As a "model case of an overlapping consensus," Rawls asks us to consider three views. One is a religious doctrine that leads to "a principle of toleration" and underwrites "the fundamental liberties of a constitutional regime"; a second is "a comprehensive liberal moral doctrine such as those of Kant or Mill"; a third is "a pluralist view" that includes independent liberal principles of justice and "a large family of nonpolitical values" (145). All three views, Rawls explains, may "lead to roughly the same political judgments and thus overlap on the political conception" (146), so that they form a consensus of reasonable doctrines.

Rawls emphasizes that the question of stability is answered by a consensus among *reasonable* comprehensive doctrines. To first appearances, the idea of a "reasonable comprehensive doctrine" may seem to involve something like a category mistake. As merely reasonable, agents express their capacity to affirm fair terms of social cooperation, that is, terms they can expect all other reasonable citizens with differing comprehensive doctrines to accept. Hence, a reasonable comprehensive doctrine may seem to be, inconsistently, one that we could expect those with incompatible comprehensive doctrines to accept. It is apparent, however, that this is not Rawls's meaning. On the contrary, a comprehensive doctrine is reasonable when or insofar as it "organizes and characterizes recognized values so that they are compatible with one another and express an intelligible view of the world" (59), and its adherents endorse "some form of liberty of conscience and freedom of thought" (61); political liberalism "supposes that a reasonable comprehensive doctrine does not reject the essentials of a democratic regime" (xvi). In other words, adherents of a reasonable comprehensive doctrine affirm "in a more or less consistent and coherent manner" (59) political toleration of a plurality of reasonable doctrines. "Reasonable persons will think it unreasonable to use political power, should they possess it, to repress comprehensive views that are not unreasonable, though different from their own" (60).

It seems appropriate to say, then, that, for Rawls, the necessary and sufficient condition of a reasonable comprehensive doctrine is that its adherents more or less consistently accept the idea of political liberalism.[8] Thus, when Rawls says "that the history of religion and philosophy shows that there are many reasonable ways in which the wider realm of values can be understood so as to be either congruent with, or supportive of, or else not in conflict with, the values appropriate to the special domain of the political" (140), the phrase "reasonable ways" is redundant. So to accord with a political conception of justice *is* to be reasonable. If I understand correctly, in other words, a reasonable comprehensive doctrine is one that allows its adherents more or less consistently to affirm the requisite distinction between the reasonable and the rational. A reasonable comprehensive doctrine is a more or less consistent comprehensive doctrine that is consistent with political liberalism.

Political liberalism "takes for granted not simply pluralism but the fact of reasonable pluralism" (xviii). Rawls's point here is that no

---

8. Since a reasonable comprehensive doctrine is one whose adherents can more or less consistently accept principles of justice that others with differing reasonable doctrines may also more or less consistently accept, to be reasonable is also the willingness to recognize that other comprehensive doctrines may be reasonable, notwithstanding that one does not agree with them or thinks that they are false. That other beliefs with which one differs may be reasonable may also be the case with respect to political judgments. Since political liberalism is a kind of theory, to be reasonable in the sense that one is able to accept freestanding political principles is the willingness to recognize that other freestanding political proposals may be reasonable, notwithstanding that one does not agree with them. See Rawls's discussion of "the idea of public reason" (212–254).

freestanding conception of justice could enjoy an overlapping consensus given "the fact of pluralism as such" (36), because the latter
includes or may include "unreasonable and even irrational (and
sometimes mad) comprehensive doctrines" (126)—for instance, one
that requires adherents "to use the sanctions of state power to
correct, or to punish, those who disagree" (138). Rawls concedes, in
other words, that the modern political problematic cannot be solved
if the comprehensive doctrines that claim the larger number of
adherents are not reasonable and, therefore, political liberalism succeeds only if unreasonable doctrines win sufficiently few adherents
that they "do not undermine the unity and justice of society" (xvii).
Still, what political liberalism takes for granted is, Rawls believes,
plausible. As we noted earlier, the plurality of religious, philosophical, and moral doctrines in modern democratic societies is, at
least in part, "the natural outcome of the activities of human reason
under enduring free institutions" (xxiv)—and at least insofar as this is
the case, one may expect that the plurality is reasonable.

In Western history, for instance, we may suppose that Catholics
and Protestants in the sixteenth and seventeenth centuries initially
accepted experiments with toleration "as a mere modus vivendi,"
that is, an agreement based on a "fortunate convergence of interests"
(147). In such a situation, each party is prepared to pursue its interest
at the expense of others and thus break the agreement should it
become advantageous to do so. But if free institutions endure, then
citizens in a political community so constituted may, over time,
"appreciate the good those principles accomplish both for themselves
and those they care for, as well as for society at large" (160). As a consequence, comprehensive doctrines are so adjusted and revised as to
become reasonable, and those that claim the larger number of
citizens may constitute a reasonable plurality.

Because Rawls takes a reasonable plurality for granted, it may
appear that he has solved the problem of stability by stipulation; if all
comprehensive doctrines are consistent with political liberalism,
then, so it may seem, there is, by definition, an overlapping consensus. To draw this conclusion is, however, to confuse a reasonable
comprehensive doctrine with a permissible one. The latter refers to
the priority of some particular liberal conception of justice; given the
principles of justice it specifies, comprehensive doctrines are
permissible if their adherents can pursue their conceptions of the
good without transgressing the limits set by those principles. All
permissible doctrines are indeed reasonable, but not all reasonable

doctrines are permitted by a specified liberal view. In other words, a doctrine is reasonable if it allows the affirmation of political liberalism as such, recognizing that "liberalism is a kind of view" (226) of which there are many variants. In order for any specified liberal conception of justice to be satisfactory, then, it must "gain the support of citizens who affirm different and opposing though reasonable comprehensive doctrines" (24n.27), and this is just to repeat that the second stage in presenting any specified political conception of justice is to show that it "can be the focus of an overlapping consensus" (141).

I will not review the arguments Rawls makes for why justice as fairness might be successful in this second stage of its presentation, because, as I have said, the important aspect of his proposal for present purposes is the idea of political liberalism as a kind of theory. Assuming that an overlapping consensus can be achieved, this idea seeks to show "how it is possible for there to exist over time a just and stable society of free and equal citizens, who remain profoundly divided by reasonable religious, philosophical, and moral doctrines" (4).

The Privatist View: A Critique

Once the second stage in Rawls's presentation of political liberalism is added to the first, some may question whether in truth his solution to the modern political problematic is, in my sense of the term, privatist. On my account, the privatist view holds that none of the plurality of religions in the community is important to politics, and Rawls insists that a satisfactory liberal conception of justice requires an overlapping consensus of all reasonable comprehensive doctrines or convictions. Precisely because these are reasonable comprehensive doctrines, however, the common ground of this consensus includes the affirmation that a conception of justice is limited to "the domain of the political" (38) and, thereby, separated from all comprehensive convictions, and it is in this sense that Rawls's proposal exemplifies the privatist view.

For Rawls, in other words, none of the religious convictions in the community is important to politics precisely in the sense or respect that the principles of justice are freestanding. They neither assert nor deny and are, therefore, independent of any wider doctrine, so that their "full justification" (67) depends solely on certain fundamental ideas implicit in the political culture. The overlapping consensus, we may say, is or includes an agreement that comprehensive doctrines are privatized. We can also make this point by saying that the differences among differing comprehensive doctrines in the consensus are irrelevant to politics, at least insofar as it determines the basic structure, because political liberalism "approaches all questions from within its own limited point of view" (xx).

Nothing more clearly confirms the separation of principles of justice from all comprehensive views than the fact that political liberalism asserts "the priority of right" (173) and, therefore, sets limits on permissible conceptions of the good. The point is also confirmed, then, when Rawls makes explicit the consequence of this priority—namely, that political discussion and debate, at least insofar as its object is the basic structure, does not properly include comprehensive philosophical and moral views. "Public reason...is now best guided by a political conception the principles and values of which all citizens can endorse" (10). Rawls's proposal is privatist, then, precisely in the sense that it is nonfoundational or justified by appeal to historically specific ideas. Our task now is to assess whether nonfoundational liberalism is a coherent resolution of the modern political problematic and, therefore, a coherent understanding of religious freedom.[9]

---

9. Because political liberalism takes for granted the fact of reasonable pluralism, one might object at the outset that Rawls has not offered a political proposal that legitimates an *indeterminate* plurality of religions. This objection maintains that a condition has been set on the kind of religion that religious freedom legitimates. Rawls's response is that religious freedom cannot legitimate a religion whose adherents cannot accept the principle of religious freedom. Although I take that response to be correct, I am also inclined to think that the objection has merit. Rawls appears to believe that accepting the principle of religious freedom must be "more or less consistent and coherent" (59) with the material content of one's religious conviction and is, therefore, a material condition of religious pluralism. In contrast, I will argue that accepting the principle of religious freedom is a formal condition of religious adherence, that is, adherents should affirm, whatever answer their religion gives to the comprehensive question, that all claims advanced in the political process can be publicly assessed. Because this difference cannot be clarified until the alternative understanding is developed in parts three and four, I will not pursue this criticism here. My argument in this chapter seeks to show that Rawls's solution to the modern political problematic, even granting what political liberalism takes for granted, is incoherent.

Rawls himself notes that "the most obvious" objection to political liberalism as he has worked it out is that an overlapping consensus is itself "a mere modus vivendi" (145). A common or public affirmation of certain freestanding principles of justice that is based on diverse nonpublic reasons or diverse comprehensive convictions is, this objection holds, unstable, because it is "contingent on circumstances remaining such as not to upset the fortunate convergence of interests" (147). But this objection is misguided, Rawls responds, because an overlapping consensus has a "moral object and moral grounds" and "is stable with respect to changes in the distribution of power among views" (148).

The moral object of the consensus is the freestanding conception of justice, developed from common affirmations or fundamental ideas implicit in the public culture. In contrast to a mere "convergence of self- or group interests" (147), moreover, the consensus has moral grounds:

> All those who affirm the political conception start from within their own comprehensive view and draw on the religious, philosophical, and moral grounds it provides. The fact that people affirm the same political conception on those grounds does not make their affirming it any less religious, philosophical, or moral, as the case may be, since the grounds sincerely held determine the nature of their affirmation. (147–48)

Finally, because it is in these respects moral, an overlapping consensus is stable in a sense that a mere modus vivendi is not. The latter depends on "happenstance and a balance of relative forces" (148), such that a redistribution of political power in favor of one party may cause that party to give up the agreement and seek to impose its will on the others by force or the threat of force. In contrast, an overlapping consensus "is stable with respect to changes in the distribution of power among views" (148). So long as the political conception is affirmed on moral grounds, each party will continue to support it.

Still, the critic may doubt that this response is successful. Whatever may be said about its object, the consensus on this object cannot be stable with respect to shifts in the distribution of power without having moral grounds. If "the fact that people affirm the same political conception on...[different comprehensive] grounds does not make their affirming it any less religious, philosophical, or moral" (147–48), then Rawls asserts that a common affirmation has moral grounds if each party participates on grounds she or he *thinks* are moral. Presumably, then, an overlapping consensus is, in Rawls's mind, distinguished from a modus vivendi because the latter is, for the parties involved, required by the distribution of power rather than what they think to be moral. Given that Rawls so defines a modus vivendi, the critic might concede that an overlapping consensus indeed differs from it. But the critic may wonder whether she or he has been answered solely by definition and, therefore, persuasively.

In charging that Rawls's overlapping consensus is itself a modus vivendi, one may mean that it is not based on *valid* moral grounds, that is, a consensus by virtue of a common affirmation of valid moral principles. A modus vivendi, then, is not simply an agreement required by the distribution of power but, rather, an agreement that is accidental, in the sense that it depends on what parties to it merely think morally to be the case, in distinction from what morally is the case. Of course, any explicit consensus depends on what people think to be the case. But a valid moral agreement may be taken to mean a consensus with respect to which all parties have or could have convincing reason for what they think to be the case, precisely because what they think to be the case is valid. Such a consensus is stable in the sense that changes in thought that might threaten it are in that respect invalid, and convincing arguments to this effect can be advanced. Given this wider meaning of "modus vivendi," the objection concludes, Rawls's overlapping consensus is indeed "contingent on circumstances remaining such as not to upset the fortunate convergence of interests" (147). The relevant change in circumstances is not, as Rawls has it, a redistribution of political power but, rather, a change in what people merely think morally to be the case. Because the convergence is not based on valid moral grounds, it is indeed "fortunate," and nothing other than accident prevents changes such that some no longer think there are moral grounds for the political conception of justice.

To the objection so formulated, Rawls will reply that enduring free institutions may themselves condition the comprehensive doctrines that tend to command large numbers of adherents in a democratic society. Given such conditioning, an overlapping consensus may not be significantly threatened by shifts in what parties to it think. But this appeal to the effect of enduring democratic institutions is another way of saying that the consensus has a freestanding moral object as well as diverse moral grounds, that is, the reply reasserts that political principles can be publicly justified by appeal to the historically specific ideas of a modern democratic culture. Clearly, then, Rawls's principal response is that a valid moral consensus, as I have identified it, requires agreement on a comprehensive doctrine, and this begs the question against political liberalism. In other words, the charge that his idea of an overlapping consensus is that of a mere modus vivendi can be sustained only by so defining "modus vivendi" that one rejects solely by definition the idea of a political conception of justice and, therefore, its distinction from a comprehensive view. Accordingly, the objection is also persuasive.

Rawls answers in a similar way if one charges that political liberalism is dualistic because two differing kinds of justification are both necessary conditions of its success. On the one hand, the conception of justice must be freestanding; that is, it requires a public basis of justification in the political culture. On the other hand, the conception of justice must be the focus of an overlapping consensus; that is, it requires diverse, nonpublic bases of justification belonging to the many comprehensive doctrines. This dualistic justification, one might object, is problematic, because it implies that principles of justice both are and are not publicly justified. To this charge, Rawls responds: "The dualism in political liberalism between the point of view of the political conception and the many points of view of comprehensive doctrines is not a dualism originating in philosophy. Rather, it originates in the special nature of democratic political culture as marked by a reasonable pluralism" (xxi).

On this response, if I understand correctly, this second objection also implies that a conception of justice must be a part of some comprehensive doctrine. Only from a point of view that originates in philosophy or is philosophically comprehensive does the dualistic appeal appear to deny as well as to affirm a public basis of justification. But "the dualism in political liberalism....originates in the special nature of democratic political culture." In other words, the dualism in points of view is not itself asserted from the comprehensive point of view but, rather, from within the domain of the political. From this latter point of view, the appeal to an overlapping consensus does not deny the public basis of justification, because the consensus has as its object precisely the freestanding conception of justice. This critic also begs the question against a nonfoundational approach to principles of justice, because she or he stipulates that their justification can only be comprehensive.

If, for Rawls, both objections that we have discussed reject the idea of a political or nonfoundational conception of justice persuasively or by stipulation, the critics may now insist that, in a similar manner, his own proposal merely assumes or stipulates the distinction between freestanding principles of justice and a comprehensive doctrine. In other words, the controversy appears to be a standoff. The contending positions do not in fact argue with each other, because each can only address the issues in terms of its own assumptions. But Rawls holds that his assumptions commend themselves, because a comprehensive point of view cannot solve the modern political problematic. Indeed, this is *the* argument for political liberalism. We should choose a nonfoundational approach to politics, he claims, because "a democratic society is always marked by a diversity of opposing and irreconcilable religious, philosophical, and moral doctrines" (3–4). The idea of a political conception of justice is required if modern democracy is to make sense.

The critics may deny that this consideration resolves the issue. Rawls's claim is conclusive, they may contend, only on the assumption that modern democracy does make sense or that the modern political problematic can be solved, and, they may continue, this assumption, if inconsistent with the comprehensive point of view, should also be rejected. At least in the context of the present inquiry, however, the critics have now become unconvincing. For the question that we seek to answer in this work is whether there is a coherent understanding of religious freedom. If Rawls succeeds in showing that the only successful criticism of a nonfoundational understanding is external, that is, dependent on assumptions he does not make, then he has advanced a coherent solution to the modern political problematic.

So far as the present inquiry is concerned, then, the only pertinent criticism of Rawls is an internal one, and it remains to consider whether the claim that political liberalism solves the modern political problematic is consistent within its own point of view. Although I have been greatly assisted in thinking about this problematic by the proposal Rawls advances, I am convinced and will now try to show that there are good reasons to doubt its internal coherence. The principal problem may be summarily formulated in the following way: Although Rawls holds that apparent objections to his proposal are all external, because they assume that a conception of justice must be part of a comprehensive view, this assumption is in truth internal to his proposal, because he stipulates that at least some democratic citizens affirm it. The citizens I have in mind are those who adhere to religious or comprehensive convictions, in my sense of this term. In other words, Rawls's proposal fails to solve the modern political problematic because, so far as I can see, the meaning of religious freedom that he asserts cannot be consistently accepted by any religious adherent.

To clarify the point, I assume, as I noted earlier, that the plurality of comprehensive doctrines from which a freestanding conception of justice is independent at least includes a plurality of religions, each of which represents an answer to the comprehensive question: What makes human activity as such authentic? But no adherent of a religion in this sense could consistently accept a freestanding conception of justice or, what comes to the same thing, the priority of certain principles of justice that set limits for permissible conceptions of the good. On the contrary, every religious adherent necessarily asserts that the valid comprehensive understanding of human authenticity is prior to, because it identifies or justifies, permissible moral conceptions as such.

To be sure, Rawls may contend that I have missed the point. Acceptance of political liberalism is not inconsistent with religious adherence, given only that the adherent participates in an overlapping consensus. To say that she or he affirms the priority of her or his comprehensive conviction is simply to say that all parties in an overlapping consensus "start from within their own comprehensive view and draw on the religious, philosophical, and moral grounds it provides" (147), so that "the political conception is a module, an essential constituent part, that in different ways fits into and can be supported by various reasonable comprehensive doctrines that endure in the society regulated by it" (144–45). But this idea of an overlapping consensus includes a claim that any religious adherent must reject, namely, the claim that her or his comprehensive conviction is one of various, substantively different comprehensive doctrines that can support a conception of justice or is one of many "nonpublic" bases of justification. To the contrary, a religious adherent necessarily asserts that the valid answer to the comprehensive question is the *only* basis on which a proper conception of justice can be justified —and this is to repeat that a religious adherent is bound to take the comprehensive rather than politically liberal point of view.

We may reformulate the difference if we recall from the discussion in chapter 2 that a religious conviction, because it claims correctly to understand human authenticity as such, purports to

identify the necessary and sufficient moral condition or comprehensive condition of all valid moral claims. On Rawls's political
liberalism, however, no answer to the comprehensive question can be
either necessary or sufficient to the justification of principles of
justice. A given religious conviction cannot identify a necessary
moral condition of justice, because the political conception of justice
requires only an overlapping consensus of the reasonable doctrines in
the society regulated by it; in other words, justification in terms of a
given comprehensive conviction is one of many nonpublic bases of
justification that is required only if there are citizens who adhere to
that conviction. A given religious conviction cannot identify a
sufficient moral condition of justice, because justification requires
the overlapping consensus; in other words, it is a necessary condition
of justification that other reasonable comprehensive convictions
support the principle of justice. But this is just to repeat that the
justification of politically liberal principles is freestanding or
"independent of comprehensive religious, philosophical, and moral
doctrines" (144), and it is precisely this nonfoundational conception
of justification that no religious adherent can consistently accept.

Consider, then, Rawls's "model case of an overlapping consensus," consisting of a "religious doctrine" that affirms toleration
and constitutional liberties, "a comprehensive liberal moral doctrine
such as those of Kant or Mill," and "a pluralist view" that affirms
liberal political principles independently of "a large family of nonpolitical values." All three views, Rawls holds, "lead to roughly the
same political judgments and thus overlap on the political conception" (145–46). In truth, however, there is no consensus among these
views, because the idea of an overlapping consensus includes the
affirmation that this very consensus justifies freestanding principles
of justice, and at least the first two of the three cannot consistently
join a consensus on this affirmation. At best, then, only the third
view accepts political liberalism.

To this formulation of the critique, a defense of Rawls might
reply that the nonfoundational mode of justification is not itself an
object of consensus; on the contrary, common affirmation extends to
only the principles of justice and the fundamental ideas in the
political culture that those principles express, precisely because the
parties to the consensus differ regarding the nonpublic bases of
justification. But this reply contradicts Rawls's insistence that a
politically liberal conception of justice must be public, meaning,
among other things, that its "full justification" is "publicly known,
or better, at least...publicly available" (67). Moreover, this condition,

which makes the conception freestanding, is essential to Rawls's proposal. Absent a public justification, political liberalism is not in truth a proposal in political thought, that is, an alternative in accord with which democratic citizens may commonly understand themselves. Absent a public justification of freestanding principles, in other words, Rawls's proposal reduces to an observation about current democratic politics and the point at which diverse conceptions of justice in fact do or may converge. As a mere observation, political liberalism would not be a conception of justice at all.

So far as I can see, then, Rawls's proposal is internally incoherent precisely because "the distinction between a political conception of justice and a comprehensive religious, philosophical, or moral doctrine" is "basic" or all-important to political liberalism (174). Given this claim, it follows that there must be a justification for *this distinction* that is acceptable to all citizens. But this is a distinction no religious adherent can consistently accept, because the distinction asserts that principles of justice may be justified independently of any comprehensive conviction.

To be sure, it might be said that this internal critique has failed to recognize the difference between reasonable and rational justification. "The reasonable and the rational are...two...independent basic ideas" (51). As all citizens, religious adherents can accept a political conception as one that is reasonable, even if, for them, freestanding principles of justice are not rationally justified. But this response only repeats the problem, because the distinction between the reasonable and the rational is another way of formulating the distinction between a political conception of justice and a comprehensive conviction. The point is, then, that any citizen who is also religious cannot consistently accept Rawls's distinction between the reasonable and the rational. In the sense that a reasonable comprehensive doctrine is more or less consistent with freestanding principles of justice, there is simply no such thing as a reasonable religious conviction or reasonable answer to the comprehensive question.[10]

---

10. This is not to deny that we can distinguish among differing religious adherents those who are reasonable and those who are not. My point is simply that the distinction is not properly the one Rawls takes it to be, namely, a distinction between those who do and those who do not accept the idea of a freestanding conception of justice. What we can properly mean, I hold, is a distinction between religious adherents who do and those who do not recognize that comprehensive convictions can be publicly assessed and, therefore, those who are and those who are not prepared to discuss and

In sum, political liberalism as a mode of political thought is bound to assert that this very mode of political thought, including its distinction between a political conception and a comprehensive view and its distinction between the reasonable and the rational, commends itself to all democratic citizens because it is or can be the object of an overlapping consensus among the diverse religious, philosophical, and moral doctrines that win significant numbers of adherents in an enduring democratic society. Thus, this proposal may be summarized in the claim that all citizens of a democratic society may endorse the proposition: There are principles of justice independent of any particular comprehensive view that all citizens have reason to accept. So far from commanding a consensus, however, this proposition cannot be consistently endorsed by any citizen who is also a religious adherent. For any such citizen is bound to believe that no citizen has reason to accept any principles of human activity independent of the valid answer to the comprehensive question. At best, in other words, the consensus that Rawls's political liberalism requires is joined only by those who deny all comprehensive convictions, citizens who believe that principles of justice are independent of any particular answer to the comprehensive question because no comprehensive conviction is valid.[11]

---

debate political claims about the character of human authenticity as such. In this sense, a reasonable religious adherent is, as I will discuss in part four, democratically civil.

11. Because he refuses to affirm that public reason includes a debate among religious convictions, Rawls's overlapping consensus is, so far as I can see, finally "a mere modus vivendi" (145) and is so in his own sense of this phrase, namely, an agreement dependent on a political "balance of relative forces" (148) or required by the distribution of power. Adherents of a plurality of incompatible comprehensive doctrines may, as a matter of fact, agree to certain principles of justice, each believing that these principles are justified by her or his own comprehensive convictions. But no religious adherent can accept that these principles are freestanding. Hence, any such adherent is bound to believe that invalid comprehensive doctrines do not identify valid grounds on which to accept the principles. Given a suitable shift in political power, the adherents of any given comprehensive conviction are bound to break the agreement and use the coercive power of the state to teach what they take to be the valid answer to the comprehensive question. This is precisely because the validity of the answer cannot be argued or redeemed in public discussion and debate.

To be sure, Rawls will point out that, by stipulation, the comprehensive doctrines in question accept a conception of justice that includes toleration as a political principle, and it follows, he will argue, that no religious

To be sure, this conclusion may leave only doubt that there are political principles all citizens have reason to accept, given a plurality of legitimate religions. But this is just to repeat that a plurality of legitimate religions constitutes the modern political problematic. The only conclusion that the preceding discussion has sought to warrant is that Rawls's proposal does not solve that problematic. Moreover, we are now in a position to conclude that any other proposal that exemplifies the privatist view on its second or nonfoundational account must also be incoherent. Any such proposal must assert that political society exists solely for political purposes, in the sense that political principles are freestanding, and simply refuse the comprehensive order of reflection. Since that proposed meaning of religious freedom is precisely the one that no religious adherent can consistently accept, any such proposal fails to solve the modern political problematic.

In sum, the second or nonfoundational account of the privatist view is in truth no more than verbally different from its first or classic formulation. Since the attempt merely to refuse the comprehensive order of reflection is inconsistent with every answer to the comprehensive question, the second account, as the first, is in truth a denial of all comprehensive convictions.[12] On either account, the meaning of religious freedom is so identified that it explicitly denies

---

adherent could consistently seek to impose through the power of the state any comprehensive doctrine. The point is, then, that on Rawls's proposal adherence to a religion that affirms political toleration of incompatible comprehensive doctrines is inconsistent, because the adherent is bound to believe that this political principle can be justified only in terms of the valid answer to the comprehensive question. A similar inconsistency is involved, so far as I can see, if one says that the basis of religious freedom in America is properly found in the nonrational Christian convictions of the Baptist or Quaker churches of the eighteenth century. On this account, American citizens as such do not have valid grounds on which to affirm the First Amendment to the United States Constitution unless they affirm the comprehensive conviction expressed in these religions. Because the validity of this conviction cannot be publicly defended, it follows, in contradiction to religious freedom, that the state ought to teach or support the teaching of these convictions.

12. I will argue in chapter 7 that the denial of all comprehensive convictions is itself an answer to the comprehensive question and, therefore, is self-contradictory. If that argument is sound, then one may conclude that the turn in Rawls's thought from *A Theory of Justice* to *Political Liberalism* has failed to achieve its principal purpose, namely, to propose a political theory that is not itself part of a comprehensive doctrine.

the comprehensive order of reflection and, therefore, explicitly denies what every religious adherent affirms, namely, that her or his conviction is valid. Because neither account legitimates any religion, the privatist view is not a coherent resolution of the modern political problematic.

4

THE PARTISAN VIEW: JOHN COURTNEY MURRAY

In this second part of the inquiry, we are attending to proposed understandings of religious freedom that might be advanced within what I have called the theory of religion as nonrational, that is, the claim that answers to the comprehensive question cannot be rationally or publicly assessed or validated. Thus, for instance, Rawls's political liberalism seeks simply to refuse the comprehensive order or reflection, and, because that refusal intends to be silent with respect to the truth of comprehensive claims, it is an alternative open to those who hold that religious convictions are nonrational. But Rawls's proposal in particular and the privatist view in general are, I have argued, incoherent. Because, on this view, none of the religious convictions in the community is important to politics, the question with which the previous chapter leaves us is whether the theory of religion as nonrational is consistent with religious freedom if some or all of the religious convictions in the community are important to politics.

The view to which I will now attend holds that the political process is constitutionally dependent on *some* religions, in the sense that a certain class of comprehensive convictions is important to politics. On this reading, religious freedom proscribes to the state any discrimination among the religions within the certain class but not the encouragement or support of this class as such. I will call this "the partisan view." My definition of it is formal, in the sense that one or another expression of this view might endorse constitutional support of any putative class of religions. For instance, the partisan view is exemplified in the claim that government may or should encourage secularistic religion as such, given only that it does not prefer one secularistic conviction to others. Thereby, the partisan view is expressed in the claim that religious freedom means the privatization of theistic religion. On another expression, the partisan view holds that modern politics is dependent on some religions because the government may or should support theistic religion as such and, therefore, the constitutional prescription of state neutrality does not extend to nondiscrimination between theistic religion and secularism. To first appearances, perhaps, this latter expression may seem the more plausible. Given that the term "religion" has traditionally been used to mean theistic religion, religious freedom would seem to include and, perhaps, be identical with theistic religious freedom. In any event, I will focus in the following discussion on the partisan view in favor of theistic religion, although I will seek to show in conclusion that the incoherence of the view in that expression must likewise convict any other exemplification.

The chosen focus is all the more important because the propriety of state preference for theistic religion has recently received widespread endorsement in the academic and larger public discussions. I will call this endorsement "the Religionist position," capitalizing "Religionist" in order to express the preference for theistic religion. Generally, this position is advanced on the grounds that nondiscrimination among theistic religions with preference for theistic religion as such is the express meaning of the religion clauses of the First Amendment to the United States Constitution. If, on the whole, the Supreme Court has, at least since *Everson v. United States* in 1957, so understood disestablishment that it proscribes not only laws that "prefer one religion to another" but also those that "aid all religions [that is, theistic, in distinction from secularistic, religions]," the latter prohibition is, Religionists claim, without constitutional warrant. Gerald V. Bradley, for instance, has argued in detail that the prevailing meaning of religious "establishment" in the United States of the eighteenth century was governmental recognition of and support for a particular and thereby official theistic religion—and, correspondingly, the common meaning of "nonestablishment" was simply nondiscrimination among theistic religions or "sect neutrality" (Bradley: 141). Not only did this understanding inform the Congressional proposal of the First Amendment but also and more importantly it was taken for granted in the state legislatures by which that amendment was ratified.

Ratification is the key event. Congress merely proposes amendments; the state legislatures enact them....The conclusion...is that the ratifiers understood their ratification of the Establishment Clause to interdict sect preferences by the national government. It is not that they intended it, connoting the presence in their minds of something not evident in the words they ratified. It is the meaning of the words. (Bradley: 136–37)[1]

Given that the present work is concerned principally with religious freedom as a principle in political philosophy and philosophy of religion, in distinction from its meaning in United States constitutional law, I will not attempt to review the extended debate about whether the Religionist interpretation of the First Amendment is appropriate. But it will be helpful to recognize why, according to Bradley and others, the United States of the eighteenth century could not understand nonestablishment to proscribe all aid to theistic religion or to prescribe legislative neutrality toward the difference between theistic religion and secularism. "The founding generation" of the Republic, we are told, commonly believed that theistic religion is necessary to morality. In his Farewell Address as the first president, George Washington gave expression to this conviction:

Of all the dispositions and habits which lead to political prosperity, Religion and Morality are indispensable supports,…. And let us with caution indulge the supposition, that morality can be maintained without Religion. Whatever may be conceded of the influence of refined education on minds of peculiar structure; reason and experience both forbid us to expect that national morality can prevail in exclusion of religious principle. (cited in Bradley: 123)

If the new Republic was a political experiment "conceived in liberty," as Lincoln would later say, this experiment could not succeed without a virtuous citizenry; liberty that is not disciplined by commitment to the common good but is simply a license to pursue self-interest would yield anarchy rather than political prosperity. But civic virtue required, excepting perhaps "minds of peculiar structure," theistic religious belief or adherence.

In the minds of the founding generation, moreover, this conviction was generally connected to the political importance of the Christian religion and, specifically, Protestant Christianity. The founders, Bradley asserts,

---

1. For an alternative reading of the meaning of "disestablishment" informing the drafting and ratification of the First Amendment, see Levy.

hoped and expected that the United States would remain
Christian,.....Legal efforts to that end were permissible so long as
they did not include test oaths, abridge free exercise, or violate
sect neutrality. Thus the constitution was a restrictive condition, and intentionally so, on the maintenance of a Christian
United States. (Bradley: 141)

For this reason, some of the contemporary advocates of the Religionist reading insist that the First Amendment allows governmental
recognition and encouragement of Christianity—or, if there is such a
thing, of the Judeo-Christian tradition. For Bradley and others,
however, the hope and expectation that accompanied nonestablishment cannot be read into "the meaning of the words." The
founding generation was well aware that the meaning of "theistic
religion" was not equivalent to Christianity or Judeo-Christian belief.
Whatever may have been the case in the United States of the
eighteenth century, then, it is clear in the twentieth century that
nondiscriminatory support for theistic religion cannot mean simply
sect neutrality toward Christian denominations. Given the contemporary plurality in the Republic, the latter would be preference for a
particular theistic religion.

But if this greater diversity of theistic religions is constitutionally protected, it remains, for many Religionists, that nondiscriminatory support of theistic religion is essential to political
morality. Even for the founders, on this interpretation, theistic
religion was important to the well-being of the Republic not because
politics should apply the principles distinctive of a particular theistic
religion but because theistic conviction provides the motivation or
commitment to pursue the common good. In other words, the
difference between encouragement of diverse Christian sects, on the
one hand, and of theistic religion as such, on the other, is not
germane because it is theistic religion in distinction from secularism
that promotes a virtuous citizenry. The point may be expressed by
saying that theistic religion does not properly determine *what*
political principles inform the activities of the state, but theistic
conviction is required to answer the question: *Why* be moral—in
distinction from amoral—at all?

So understood, the Religionist position is at least one way to
read the classic statement on religious freedom in the United States
given by John Courtney Murray, the Roman Catholic theologian
who, more than any other, is given credit for the endorsement of

religious freedom by Vatican II. Convinced that the activities of the state are properly determined in accord with universal moral principles that are accessible to or may be justified by reason alone, Murray also held that "the duty of government to the common good in the fullness of its realization necessarily includes a duty to religion in society—the duty of recognition and favor" (cited in McElroy: 94). Murray's formulation offers the opportunity to consider the Religionist understanding of religious freedom, and, therefore, I will seek briefly to review the logic of his proposal as it is presented in his volume *We Hold These Truths: Catholic Reflections on the American Proposition*.

Religious Freedom and Articles of Peace

Murray is lucid with respect to the political problem that pluralism presents. "By pluralism...I mean the coexistence within one political community of groups who hold divergent and incompatible views with regard to religious questions—those ultimate questions that concern the nature and destiny of man" (x). In the United States (at least at the time of his writing, the late 1950s), he continues, "there is no small political problem here" (x), because our contemporary experience of pluralism is not that of disagreement but, far worse, of confusion. Differing "views with respect to religious questions" have become "a plurality of universes of discourse" (15). Attending especially to Jewish, Catholic, Protestant, and secularistic convictions, Murray calls each a "conspiracy," that is, a "breathing together" of "those who think alike" and "join together in some manner of action to make their common thought or purpose prevail" (22); further, he believes that these conspiracies have become "incommensurable" (15), such that "one does not know what the other is talking about" (16). As a consequence, we experience "beneath the surface of civic amity" a "structure of passion and war" (19). The political problem, then, is whether "the four great conspiracies among us" can "conspire into one conspiracy that will be American society" (23), that is, whether there is some principle to which "common assent" can be given because it does not "infringe upon..., the freedom of consciences to retain the full integrity of their own convictions" (xi).

Murray's answer is, in principle, affirmative, even if, in fact, his "expectations are modest and minimal" (23). In principle, at least, "we could limit the warfare, and we could enlarge the dialogue. We could lay down our arms..., and we could take up argument" (23). A pluralist civil order is possible only if the diversity shares a commitment to political civility, and for the meaning of "civility" Murray recurs to "the mind of St. Thomas Aquinas, who was himself giving refined expression to the tradition of classic antiquity" (6). Civility means that "the specifying note of political association is its rational deliberative quality, its dependence for its permanent cohesiveness on argument among men" (6). It is, Murray holds, precisely "that exercise of reason which is argument" that constitutes "the distinctive bond of the civil multitude" (7) and the absence of which delivers public life to "the barbarian" (12). Thus, a pluralism of views with regard to religious questions cannot conspire together politically unless they agree that their common political life shall be constituted as an argument.

But if political civility is Murray's solution to the modern political problematic, he does not mean that diverse theistic and secularistic conspiracies will argue about their comprehensive convictions. On the contrary, Murray insists that "the root of the matter" is a distinction between "the spiritual and temporal orders and their respective jurisdictions" (65), such that political argument is about an aspect of the temporal order. What is required in a pluralistic society, then, is a common affirmation of just this distinction and, thereby, a consensus that the state is distinct from society or limited with respect to the matters properly subject to its jurisdiction, at least in the sense that politics has no authority with respect to ultimate questions. What is required, in other words, is common recognition of the traditional distinction between the natural law and the eternal law, such that the political process is bound by the natural law and limited by the distinction. This is to repeat that the body politic is properly constituted by civility or as an argument, because the natural law claims "no sanction other than its appeal to free minds" (30; see 109) or is accessible to human reason. In contrast, the eternal law or the valid answer to ultimate questions transcends, in the sense that it includes but is not exhausted by, that which reason can comprehend.[2]

---

2. On my understanding, Murray's distinction between temporal and spiritual orders is not equivalent to his distinction between the natural and the eternal law. The first distinction identifies the differing jurisdictions of political (or, at least, nonreligious) and religious institutions; the second distinction identifies the difference between universal moral laws that are

To first appearances, then, Murray's solution may seem to share with the privatist view the following feature: Comprehensive convictions or answers to ultimate questions are privatized in the sense that government has no authority with respect to them and they have no relevance to the civil discourse or argument by which the activities of the state are properly determined. So to understand Murray is, however, thoroughly to misunderstand him. What makes his interpretation of religious freedom Religionist rather than privatist in character is precisely the claim that the natural law must be understood as an aspect of, or as included within, the eternal law. In the classic formulation of Thomas Aquinas, "the natural law is nothing else than the rational creature's participation of the eternal law" (Aquinas: 618). So far from being subrational, in the sense that it expresses mere decisions, or nonreasonable, in the sense that justice is "political and not metaphysical" (Rawls 1993: 10), the comprehensive order of reflection, on Murray's account, includes but is not exhausted by the rational and in that sense transcends reason. The right exercise of reason, then, depends on relation to an ultimate reality that is, in some respects, rationally inaccessible or superrational.

For Murray, in other words, the principal threat to political civility is modern secularism. Because secularism denies any "eternal order of truth and justice" (51) and asserts that the temporal order is self-sufficient, it falsely accords to reason the authority fully to answer ultimate questions. Thus, the attempt to privatize religion is in truth an expression of the secularistic claim that the rational or natural law requires no transcendent or eternal ground. On this claim, "religion itself is not a value, except insofar as its ambiguous reassurances may have the emotional effect of conveying reassurance" (52), and secularistic answers to ultimate questions become a part of the political process. Because reason cannot fully answer ultimate questions, secularistic convictions lead, as they have all too pervasively in the United States, to the elevation of individual will or sheer individual utility in place of the "universal moral law" (51),

---

rational and the character of the divine governance that transcends reason. Still, the two distinctions are related. The proper understanding of temporal and spiritual orders depends on the distinction between the natural law and its divine ground. The jurisdiction of the temporal order is bounded by the natural law; the jurisdiction of the spiritual order concerns the answers to "ultimate questions" or the divine ground.

and, in politics, "soliloquy succeeds to argument" (16). In truth, only the conviction that the natural or temporal order has an eternal ground allows an individual or a society properly to affirm the limitations of reason and thereby to have a political life bound by the natural law.

In sum, commitment to political civility depends on theistic conviction. For just this reason, Murray did not believe that a body politic constituted as an argument *requires* religious freedom. On the contrary, "religious pluralism is against the will of God" (23); if in truth the United States includes a diversity of religions, "the truth is lamentable" (74). In principle, then, it is perfectly proper to a constitution or civil order that it establish a theistic religion, given only that this religion sanctions the distinction between the natural and the eternal law and, therefore, the distinction between temporal and spiritual orders (see 47)—and, ideally, the established religion would be Roman Catholicism, just because this religion is true. Still, Murray argues to the Roman Catholic community that precisely its distinction between the natural and the eternal law sanctions religious freedom in a society where religious pluralism so characterizes "the human condition" (23) that an attempt to establish one theistic religion would destroy the public peace. In those particular circumstances, "the policy of no establishment" (47) and freedom of religion follows because the principle of "public peace, the common good in its various aspects," is itself "the highest and most general norm" of the natural law (62). Religious freedom is "good law" (49) because any alternative constitutional stipulation would compromise more than it would advance the common good.

In America subsequent to European settlement, a plurality of religions has always been part of the human condition. An irreversible fact at the birth of the Republic, religious diversity in the United States has since become only more extensive (see 58–59). Moreover, two centuries of experience have proved "that political unity and stability are possible without uniformity of religious belief and practice, without the necessity of any governmental restrictions on any religion" (72). Perhaps preeminently in the United States, then, religious freedom not only may but also should be affirmed as one of the "articles of peace" (56). In so referring to it, however, Murray intends to underscore that religious freedom itself implies the importance of theistic religion to the body politic. Since "the policy of no establishment" (47) and freedom of religion is justified as a particular application of the natural law, this policy itself depends on the conviction that the temporal order has an eternal ground.

Precisely because of this dependence, Murray includes within the consensus that the Republic requires not only the affirmation of limited government bound by the natural law but also the affirmation of "the sovereignty of God over nations as well as over individual men" (28). If the latter is, in one sense, "a truth that lies beyond politics," it also "imparts to politics a fundamental human meaning" (28). Moreover, Murray can assert that this truth is properly a part of the national consensus, religious freedom notwithstanding, because he presumes "that God Himself belongs to the order of reason, in the sense that His existence and sovereignty as the Author of the universe are not inaccessible to human reason" (80). If I understand correctly, Murray here also appropriates the thought of Thomas Aquinas and, specifically, the respect in which he may be called a "natural theologian." Thomas believed and sought to show that the reality of God as the necessary source and end of all other beings can be rationally demonstrated. But his agreement with Thomas in this respect does not contradict Murray's conviction that the valid answer to ultimate questions cannot be fully redeemed by reason and is in that sense superrational. Thomas distinguished between proving the existence of God and knowing the essence or full character of the divine reality, and the latter, he held, is not a possible object of natural theology.

It is Murray's reliance on the distinction between the natural and the eternal law that allows one to read his proposal as a formulation of the view many have discerned in the founding generation of the Republic—namely, the conviction that theistic religion is essential to civic virtue. A body politic constituted as an argument depends on a consensus affirming this fundamental distinction because one cannot be motivated rationally to pursue the temporal or common good absent the conviction that it finds its ground in an eternal order that reason cannot fully comprehend. Because religious freedom is an application of the natural law to historically specific circumstances, it is not only consistent with but also essential to a body politic so constituted that the state support or encourage theistic religion, given only that this encouragement is nondiscriminatory. There cannot be genuine state neutrality to both theistic religion and secularism, in other words, because indifference to theistic religion compromises the very grounds on which a pluralistic society can maintain civility and, thereby, solve the modern political problematic. Neutrality to both theistic and secularistic convictions is, then, a denial of theistic religion or a secularistic principle, because it asserts that the body politic can be constituted as an argument without the common conviction that reason is limited with respect to ultimate questions. For Murray, as for Religionists generally, "the state must make a choice; not to choose is to opt for a vacuum of values" (McElroy: 95).

The Partisan View: A Critique

It should be apparent that the Religionist position, at least as it has been presented above, depends on separating the conviction that motivates a good citizen from convictions that identify the common good. Only this separation allows one to assert the constitutional importance of affirmations that transcend reason for a body politic that is bound to rationally justifiable principles. Were identification of the common good inseparable from the conviction motivating its pursuit, the former also could not be fully redeemed by reason. Absent the separation, to restate the point, nondiscrimination toward theistic religions would not solve the modern political problematic, because religious freedom would permit or encourage a plurality of partly superrational convictions regarding the principle or principles by which the state's activities are bound without providing a principle for political unification. It is, then, just this separation that allows Religionists to endorse religious freedom even while they insist that theistic religion should be affirmed by the political constitution.

As I suggested earlier, this Religionist understanding may also be formulated as follows: At least with respect to politics or the activities of the state, an answer to the question "what is moral?" or "what rules and principles distinguish between right and wrong activities?" is separable from an answer to the question "why be moral?" or "why should one choose the purposes that the rules and principles of morality prescribe?" On this account, the former question asks about the natural law or the political principles and rules that can be validated by appeal to reason, so that disagreements regarding what the state should do may be adjudicated by argument. In contrast, the question "why be moral?" does not have an answer that can be rationally redeemed. The answer to this question is the relation of human activity to a eternal order of reality that transcends reason. Thus, the commitment to civility or civic virtue that politics in accord with natural law requires is impossible absent some or other theistic conviction that is partly superrational, and the body politic is properly constituted by the support of theistic religion as such.

But there are good reasons to reject this separation between "what is moral?" and "why be moral?" One cannot justify by argument some claim about moral in distinction from immoral purposes unless the argument also justifies the claim that one ought to be moral—because moral in distinction from immoral identifies what one ought to be or do. Rationally to show *what* is moral is to show that some or all human activities are rationally required or obligated to choose some identified purpose. For instance, it might be argued that all eligible voters are obligated to vote. But no human is rationally required to choose anything at all unless a contrary choice is contrary to reason, and a contrary choice is never contrary to reason if reason does not require that one be moral. For instance, an eligible voter who chooses not to vote is not choosing contrary to reason if reason is not sufficient to require that she or he choose as morality prescribes. In other words, one cannot justify rationally any distinction between morality and *immorality* unless the argument also justifies morality in distinction from *amorality*.[3] "What is moral?" and "why be moral?" are, in that sense, inseparable, and the Religionist attempt to separate the content of the common good from the motivation to pursue it is incoherent.

So far as I can see, in any event, this separation is one that no adherent of a theistic religion could consistently accept. Given that a theistic conviction claims to identify the character of human authenticity as such, any such conviction is a comprehensive claim about *what* is moral. In the nature of the case, religious adherence affirms that the ground of all distinctions between moral and immoral purposes is identified by the valid answer to the comprehensive question. It follows that no adherent of a theistic religion consistently separates the source of moral commitment from the

---

3. In my judgment, clarity on this point is one aspect of Immanuel Kant's abiding contribution to our understanding of practical reason or the choice of purpose with understanding: An imperative is not moral in distinction from prudential unless it is categorical, that is, unless the exercise of freedom that it prescribes can be refused only by acting irrationally (see Kant). To cite Kant in this respect is not to say that we are bound to follow him in the further claim that moral activity is identified independently of inclination or desire. But if one holds that the commitment to do what reason prescribes depends in some specified way on desire, then it must be the case that action in accord with that desire can be refused only be choosing contrary to reason. I have sought to exposit and defend Kant in the relevant respect in Gamwell; see especially chapter 2.

identification of authentic human purpose. Since any such adherent asserts that "why be moral?" is answered by the relation of human activity as such to ultimate reality, properly understood, she or he also asserts that "what is moral?" is answered comprehensively by this same relation. But the Religionist position we are here assessing holds that all theistic religious adherents must separate the two answers. Diverse theistic religions are said to be politically legitimate because each theistic religion grounds the same rational moral enterprise, so that political civility may be independent of any given one.

Thus, any adherent of a theistic religion who also affirms this Religionist account of religious freedom thereby implies that the differences among theistic convictions make no difference to the body politic, that is, to *what* the state should do. But if it is absurd that any theist should accept the privatization of religion, it is equally absurd for her or him to believe that theistic differences are politically indifferent. Both claims deny what, in the nature of the case, is affirmed by every adherent of a theistic religion: The valid answer to the comprehensive question is the comprehensive condition or ideal of all human authenticity, including the authenticity of the state, and, therefore, the only valid grounds on which the activities of the state can be determined. Notwithstanding its assertion of governmental favor to theistic religion as such, this Religionist account, like the privatist view, denies that the comprehensive question has a valid answer. In that sense, the proposed meaning of religious freedom does not legitimate any religion.

We may also make the point by noting that Murray's resolution shares with Rawls's proposal the claim that justified principles of justice are authorized by an overlapping consensus. For Rawls, the consensus is among comprehensive doctrines that accept freestanding principles of justice, while, for Murray, it includes comprehensive convictions that affirm the eternal and partly superrational ground of temporal and rational politics. Both solutions thereby imply that the valid comprehensive conviction is one of many answers to the comprehensive question by which principles of justice are authorized, and that implication is inconsistent with all religious adherence because it denies that there is a valid comprehensive conviction.

But, of course, Murray intends to present an alternative to the privatization of religion. In his defense, it may be objected that theistic religion as such can be politically important and theistic differences can be politically indifferent because, for Murray, each theistic adherent is rationally bound to affirm the natural law and, therefore, a political order constituted as an argument. But if the valid understanding of the comprehensive purpose or of human authenticity as such transcends reason, then in truth the content of our temporal good cannot be identified solely by appeal to free minds. Accordingly, the conviction that reason is sufficient to the content of the common good can be only a particular and paradoxical conviction that is partly superrational. On Murray's own terms, in other words, every theist believes that valid claims about the content of authentic politics cannot be redeemed without a conviction that transcends reason, namely, the valid comprehensive conviction. There might be a particular theistic conviction in which the eternal order includes and, thereby, grounds a temporal order that is rational. But this possibility only serves to reveal that the putative separation of moral content (what is moral?) from moral motivation (why be moral?) is itself a particular answer to the comprehensive question—one that denies all differing understandings of the eternal order and, therefore, does not in truth separate the content of morality from what is taken to be the valid theistic conviction.

Murray holds, of course, that this *is* the valid comprehensive conviction and, in this sense, all are rationally bound to affirm the natural law. But this means that adherence to the valid theistic conviction is required in order to identify the respects in which human authenticity is accessible to human reason. So far as I can see, in other words, the distinction between aspects of human authenticity that are rational and those that are superrational could be only a *superrational* distinction, and this means that only the valid theistic conviction correctly identifies this distinction. In contrast, invalid theistic convictions may differ with respect to the part reason plays in the moral life, and all will not necessarily affirm that the content of our common good can be identified by argument. A political order constituted as an argument requires, then, common adherence to the particular theistic conviction in which rational and superrational are properly distinguished, and the differences among theistic religions are not politically indifferent.

To be sure, Murray also denies that the proper distinction between rational and superrational aspects of human authenticity is itself superrational. In keeping with his appropriation of Thomas Aquinas, Murray holds that "God himself belongs to the order of reason, in the sense that His existence and sovereignty as the Author of the universe," if not God's essence or full character, "are not inaccessible to human reason" (80). On this account, the possibilities and limits or reason and, therefore, the distinction between the natural and the eternal law, can themselves be rationally demonstrated or redeemed. So far as I can see, this account is not convincing. Whatever assessment one makes of Aquinas's arguments for the existence of God, one cannot demonstrate rationally that the valid comprehensive conviction is, even in some respects, superrational. So far as the way of reason goes, valid claims are those and only those that can be redeemed by reason.[4]

But even if we allow to Murray that reason identifies its own limits with respect to the comprehensive question, this concession will not redeem the Religionist position. On this Religionist account, the distinction between temporal and spiritual orders means that civility depends on some or other conviction about the eternal ground of the natural law, and it remains that differing theistic convictions may distinguish in differing ways between the rational and superrational aspects of human authenticity. Hence, even the arguments for the valid understanding of reason's capacities will not unite a plurality of theistic religions absent the particular theistic conviction for which argument constitutes the body politic.[5]

Having reached the conclusion that this Religionist view is not neutral to theistic religions as such but is, rather, the expression of a particular comprehensive conviction, we can account for a puzzle that the reader of Murray's proposal is bound to note. Political unity among adherents of diverse "conspiracies" or "universes of dis-

---

4. I will argue for this claim in chapter 5, because it will be important to an assessment of Greenawalt's position.

5. The point here may be formulated by posing for Murray the following dilemma: If the arguments for God's existence are sufficient to show that temporal civility depends on a spiritual ground, then the civil order does not require governmental favor to theistic religion as such but, rather, only to argument. If the civil order is required to favor theistic convictions, then the arguments for God's existence are not sufficient to overcome the differences among these convictions, presumably because some theistic convictions may not credit political argument. On the former alternative, the government of a body politic constituted as an argument should not encourage or support theistic beliefs. On this Religionist view, then, the arguments for God's existence will not unify the body politic unless citizens share the particular theistic conviction that includes Murray's distinction between the natural and the eternal law.

course" requires, we are told, a principle to which all can give common assent; but Murray then pursues political principles that, he says, are also consistent in other circumstances with the establishment of a theistic religion. Indeed, "religious pluralism is against the will of God" (23). Accordingly, these principles "approve themselves to the Catholic intelligence and conscience" (41), as the subtitle to Murray's book, *We Hold These Truths: Catholic Reflections on the American Proposition*, suggests. It is certainly true that a political principle to which all religious adherents can assent is one Catholics can also affirm. But the question that Murray's focus on "the Catholic view of this constitutional proviso" (46) raises is whether his understanding of religious freedom can be accepted only by Catholics—or, better, only by religious adherents whose answer to the comprehensive question agrees substantively with what Murray takes to be the Catholic faith. The critique of Murray's Religionist position can be repeated by showing, as I will now attempt to do, that his solution to the modern political problematic permits a religious establishment in other circumstances precisely because his view of religious freedom inconsistently implies an established religion.

Lucid in his description of the problem that pluralism presents, Murray is at least initially persuasive in his claim that the "great conspiracies" can conspire together if they "lay down arms" and "take up argument" (23), that is, if they affirm that civility is the constitutive feature of the body politic. To first appearances, in other words, this claim meets the condition that Murray himself sets down, namely, that the political solution should not "infringe upon..., the freedom of consciences to retain the full integrity of their own convictions" (xi). But Murray also insists that political civility cannot include an argument about the answers to ultimate questions, because the valid answers to these questions are not fully accessible to reason. Thus, one must distinguish between temporal and spiritual orders. It is this distinction that allows Murray to say that political civility is consistent in principle with an established religion, given only that the religion in question sanctions the distinction. Still, the same distinction also prescribes "the policy of no establishment" (47) and freedom of religion in certain historical circumstances—specifically, those in which the pluralism of answers to ultimate questions is so extensive that public peace would be threatened by the constitutional recognition of a single religion.

But if political civility is consistent in principle with both an established religion and with religious freedom and the proper constitutional provision depends on circumstances, then Murray's defense of religious freedom implies a moral principle that is independent of circumstances. A universal principle is required in order to evaluate the given situation and thereby decide which constitutional stipulation is proper, and the implied principle is moral because it identifies *what* character the political association should be given, that is, prescribes religious establishment in some circumstances and religious freedom in others. We may now ask about the status of *this* universal moral principle and, specifically, whether it is a principle that political argument or reason can validate. So far as I can see, it cannot be a rational principle, because political argument could never redeem as one of its own necessary conditions a particular comprehensive conviction that transcends reason—that is, could never justify a theistic religious establishment. To the contrary, then, the principle in accord with which Murray justifies religious freedom in certain circumstances must be itself a superrational moral principle.

The principle in question is, of course, the prescription that politics distinguish between temporal and spiritual orders in the manner that makes civility consistent with religious establishment. In other words, this distinction must itself transcend reason because it justifies in some circumstances the establishment of a conviction that is not fully accessible to reason. Nor is this conclusion avoided by Murray's claim, with Thomas Aquinas, that reason can identify its own limitations with respect to ultimate questions. Even if one credits that claim, it does not identify or imply a moral principle in accord with which religious establishment could ever be justified, since any such principle must assert the validity of some particular superrational conviction. We may now be told that no particular theistic religion is endorsed. Just as religious freedom supports theistic religion without discrimination, so any such religion could be established, given only that it affirms a political order constituted as an argument. But the qualification is in truth a principle distinguishing among theistic convictions and, therefore, is a particular one. If theistic convictions transcend reason, then any given theistic religion may or may not distinguish between temporal and spiritual orders in a manner consistent with a political order constituted as an argument. Since it is the distinction between temporal and spiritual orders that also prescribes nondiscriminatory support of theistic religions as such, at least in some circumstances, we arrive again at the conclusion that the meaning of religious freedom is a particular theistic conviction.

To be sure, Murray holds that the principle justifying religious freedom is not a particular theistic conviction but, rather, the natural law principle of peace. The point is, however, that this prescription is itself justified by Murray's distinction between the natural and the eternal law. On his account, the principle of peace requires that the Republic's plurality of legitimate theistic religions should never allow their differences to destroy political civility. But that prescription makes sense only if each theistic religion affirms the rational character of politics, that is, all theistic convictions give common assent to reason in the measure or respects Murray asserts. The principle of peace, then, is itself dependent on the superrational moral principle that prescribes adherence to just this understanding of the rational and the superrational.

In sum, the distinction between the natural and the eternal law on which Murray's Religionist view depends is itself a comprehensive moral ideal and, therefore, a religious conviction that reason cannot redeem.[6] It then follows that religious freedom cannot be consistently accepted by all citizens unless they also accept the comprehensive conviction in question. But citizens cannot be expected to share a conviction that transcends reason unless it is taught to all members of the political association. Contrary to his intention, then, Murray's proposal so understands the constitutional principle of religious freedom that the government is required explicitly to endorse a particular religious conviction—namely, the conviction that the rational and superrational aspects of human authenticity are so distinguished that the valid answer to ultimate questions affirms a political order constituted as an argument. Whether or not, as Murray suggests, this distinction "has found, and still finds, its intellectual home within the Catholic Church" (41), his solution to the modern political problematic is self-contradictory, because it implies the constitutional establishment of a particular answer to the comprehensive question.

---

6. It might be objected that this conclusion contradicts my previous claim that this Religionist position, because it separates the content of the common good from the motivation to pursue it, does not legitimate any religion. But the point is that both conclusions are correct because the comprehensive conviction on which the putative separation depends is self-contradictory. It claims to identify the valid comprehensive grounds of the separation, that is, both does and does not assert that the content of the common good is dependent on the theistic conviction that motivates its pursuit.

So far as I can see, the same implication will indict any view of religious freedom that prescribes governmental favor to theistic religions generally because one or another of their superrational convictions is a necessary condition of commitment to the common good. To separate the content of the common good, which is rational, from the motivation to pursue it, which depends on some or other superrational conviction, is to assert and, therefore, to establish a particular religious conviction. Indeed, the conclusion may be reached directly, given a view that seeks to avoid the privatization of religion even while it denies that theistic convictions can be publicly assessed: A plurality of religious convictions that cannot argue about their different understandings of human authenticity can only confront and conflict with each other, and a political resolution of this conflict can only be the coercive assertion of some particular religion.

The Religionist position, it may now be recalled, has been discussed here as one example of what I have called the partisan view. Given that religious convictions are in whole or part nonrational, the partisan view holds that the modern political problematic can be solved if some but not all religious or comprehensive convictions are important to politics, so that the state may support a specific class of comprehensive convictions given only that government does not discriminate among the differing convictions that belong to that specific class. It is important to note, then, that the incoherence of the partisan view in favor of theistic religion will also be present, *mutatis mutandis*, in any other exemplification of this view.

If, for instance, one asserts that religious freedom allows the state to support secularistic religion as such, given only that government does not discriminate among differing secularistic convictions, any formulation of this claim will by implication endorse the establishment of a particular answer to the comprehensive question, that is, a particular secularistic conviction. Any such formulation must include explicitly or implicitly the grounds on which differing secularistic convictions can be politically unified, notwithstanding that they are nonrational or superrational. In other words, there must be some claim that occupies in the logic of this formulation the same place occupied in Murray's by the distinction between the natural and the eternal law. But this means that the grounds advanced can only be themselves nonrational or superrational, just as is the case with Murray's distinction, and the consequence is that a particular secularistic conviction must be constitutionally endorsed.

More generally, then, any exemplification of the partisan view must include a principle in terms of which diverse comprehensive convictions belonging to the class that government may support are politically unified. Because these convictions, by hypothesis, cannot be rationally validated, this principle must be one of them. As a consequence, religious freedom cannot be consistently affirmed unless this principle is also explicitly accepted, and the state is bound to insure that the principle in question is taught to all citizens. Any exemplification of the partisan view, in other words, incoherently endorses governmental discrimination in favor of one member of the favored class, that is, endorses an established religion.

5

THE PLURALIST VIEW: KENT GREENAWALT

If we may say that the privatist view represents the separationists and the partisan view represents the Religionists in the Republic's recent discussion of religious freedom, then we are now in a position to see why the contention between them is perplexing. On the one hand, Religionists hold that the separationist understanding of religious freedom in fact denies all theistic convictions and, therefore, is not an understanding of *religious* freedom; and we have seen that the privatist view, on either its classic or its nonfoundational account, does imply a denial of the comprehensive order of reflection. On the other hand, separationists hold that the Religionist understanding of religious freedom in fact seeks to establish a particular religion and, therefore, is not an understanding of religious *freedom*; and we have seen that any exemplification of the partisan view does imply that some or other comprehensive conviction should be taught to all citizens.

"The pluralist view," as I will call it, seeks to overcome the apparent impasse between separationists and Religionists by offering a third alternative—and to do so without denying the theory of religion as nonrational. This third view, then, seeks to solve the modern political problematic by asserting that *all* of the religious convictions in the community are important to politics, notwithstanding that these convictions cannot be publicly or rationally assessed. For those who hold that religious claims are nonrational, this is the sole remaining alternative. Its logical alternatives, namely, that none or some of the religious convictions in the community is or are important to politics, identify respectively the privatist and partisan views I have sought to discredit.

One who affirms the pluralist view is, of course, required to clarify the sense or respect in which religions are important to politics. Absent such clarification, to affirm the political importance of a plurality of religious convictions is simply to express the modern political problematic. It is this requirement, then, that makes Kent Greenawalt's widely read volume *Religious Convictions and Political Choice* an especially apt illustration of the view we must now consider. Of course, this judgment assumes that Greenawalt's position is an illustration of the pluralist view, and I will attempt to redeem that assumption in the course of this discussion. Given the assumption, however, the point is that Greenawalt is especially careful to identify precisely the respect in which religious convictions properly inform political choice. Moreover, his proposal is also appropriate to our present inquiry because he takes the political thought of John Rawls to be a principal exemplar of the position Greenawalt intends to contest—namely, "that citizens in a liberal democracy should resolve both value and factual questions that are relevant to justice without relying on particular religious convictions" (53).

Religious Freedom and the Reliance of Citizens

As the title of his volume suggests, Greenawalt's principal concern is the proper character of citizenship. If religious freedom is in the first instance a proscription of a certain kind of governmental or state activity, Greenawalt rightly insists, this prohibition implies something about the relation between religious convictions and the political choices that citizens take. In other words, a constitution, because it consists in the explicit principles by which politics as such is defined in a given political community, prescribes the most general political commitment of the citizens.[1] The question he will address, Greenawalt underscores, is not a legal but a moral one, that is, not whether reliance on religious convictions should be legally proscribed but, rather, whether it is consistent with a "model of *good* liberal citizenship" (4; emphasis added). Similarly, Rawls insists that his

---

1. It is this implication that I had in mind when I said in chapter 1 that the modern political problematic may be formulated both politically and religiously. Politically, it is expressed in the question: How, if at all, is politics consistent in principle with a plurality of legitimate religions? Religiously, the same problematic is expressed in the question: How, if at all, may adherents of a plurality of legitimate religions consistently be citizens of the political community? If the focus of the political formulation is the meaning of religious freedom as a principle of political unity, the focus of the religious formulation is the meaning of religious freedom as a principle of citizenship or civic virtue.

conception of justice implies an "ideal conception of citizenship" (Rawls 1993: 213) in accord with which "public reason—citizens' reasoning in the public forum about constitutional essentials and basic questions of justice—is now best guided by a political conception the principles and values of which all citizens can endorse" (Rawls 1993: 10); but Rawls does not hold that failure so to reason about such matters should be prevented by governmental sanctions. Again, Murray's resolution of the modern political problematic implies that citizens as such should be adherents of some or other theistic religion, because only so can they be committed to civility, but Murray does not assert that government should punish those who adhere to secularistic convictions.

In clarifying his difference from Rawls, Greenawalt notes that one might distinguish between "personal grounds of decision and public justification," and he himself holds "that public justifications should often be more circumscribed than the entire range of considerations appropriate for decision" (51). But he also finds that "the line between grounds of decision and stated justifications is not explored by the theorists who propose the exclusion of religious grounds from political morality" (51). Accordingly, he understands Rawls's theory, I think rightly, "to embrace the ways in which a citizen justifies to himself the political positions that he takes, as well as the reasons he communicates to others" (53).[2] In contrast to Rawls, then, Greenawalt holds that good citizens may both affirm religious freedom and, in a respect to be clarified, rely on religious convictions in their political decisions.

The citizens who are the subjects of Greenawalt's discussion are those of the United States. "My perspectives for evaluation are the premises of our particular liberal democratic polity" (4). He specifies our liberal democracy as a "form of government" (22) whose premises include "indirect, democratic governance, extensive individual liberty" (26) and the First Amendment's guarantee of religious liberty

---

2. Greenawalt's volume appeared prior to the publication of *Political Liberalism*, so that his understanding of Rawls is based on *A Theory of Justice* and some of Rawls's subsequent essays. In *Political Liberalism*, Rawls formulates his own position in a manner that mitigates his difference from Greenawalt (see 240n.30, 244n.33). I judge, however, that a difference between the two remains, at least with respect to what Rawls calls "matters of basic justice" (240)—and, indeed, Rawls himself suspects that this may be the case (see 240n.30).

and disestablishment. Although he is impressed by historical arguments for the claim that "federal and state restrictions on establishment" in the eighteenth century did not mean to bar "aid to religion generally," Greenawalt holds nonetheless that "the present degree of diversity and nonbelief" in the Republic commend "the principle of nonsponsorship" as the proper understanding of the "relations between government and religion in a liberal state"—where this principle means that "liberal democratic government in the United States" should not support religion or "religious ideas, however broadly conceived" (19).

So defined, of course, the meaning of "nonsponsorship" depends on the meaning of "religion." Because "what beliefs and systems of beliefs count as religious" is a "perplexing topic" (30), Greenawalt does not attempt to defend a general definition. Instead he speaks of "religious perspectives of the kind familiar in our society" (73) and focuses especially on Judaism and Christianity as illustrative of the convictions with which he is concerned. Accordingly, he may say that such convictions include "a vision about the 'ultimate meaning' of human life and the place of humankind in the universe" (32) or "a comprehensive picture of the universe and people's place in it" (179). These descriptions allow us to assume that all religious convictions, on Greenawalt's usage, are, at least in all relevant respects, answers to what I have called the comprehensive question. Moreover, he might be taken to use "religion" in a broad sense, so as to include, in my terms, both theistic and secularistic convictions. It is apparent, however, that the phrase "religious perspectives of the kind familiar in our society" refers more or less closely to what I have called theistic convictions, since Greenawalt speaks of "individuals with pervasively secular attitudes" or "the nonbelieving minority" (19) in distinction from those with "religious views" (20).[3]

---

3. "I do not count as religious...every moral conviction that is accepted as an 'ultimate concern,' nor do I include as being religious the beliefs about people and what they should do that derive from comprehensive social philosophies like Marxism" (31). Given that "religion," on Greenawalt's usage, means, on my usage, "theistic religion," his understanding of nonsponsorship is ambiguously stated when he says that "the government may not...directly aim at furthering belief in some religious positions at the expense of others" (20). In this formulation, "others" could mean other "[theistic] religious positions," in which case government might directly aim at furthering belief in theistic religion generally, or "others" might mean

Given this usage, one might ask whether the principle of nonsponsorship, which proscribes governmental support of religious ideas, is consistent with governmental support of a secularistic answer to the comprehensive question, that is, an answer that denies the validity of any theistic religion. This question may seem all the more pertinent because Greenawalt does say that "one consistent aspect of liberal democratic political theory has been a secular justification of the state" (16) and that "laws adopted by the government should rest on some secular objective" (20; see also 87). But it is clear that his use of "secular" is to be distinguished from what I have called secularistic convictions. Were this not the case, "a secular justification for the state" would be patently inconsistent with Greenawalt's intent to defend the reliance of citizens on theistic religious convictions. For Greenawalt, then, "secular" means something like "not necessarily theistic"—and it will be important to an understanding of his solution to the modern political problematic to clarify this use of the term.

As I have mentioned, the position that Greenawalt is most concerned to refute is the claim that liberal citizens should exclude theistic convictions from the deliberations leading to their political choices. He also formulates this antagonist as the claim that political choices should be made solely on the basis of "shared premises and publicly accessible reasons" (57; see 23–25)—and he means this formulation to include Rawls's insistence that political choice, at least with respect to the basic structure of society, properly appeals solely to principles justified by the shared ideas of a modern democratic culture. As with the term "religion," however, Greenawalt does not attempt a general definition of "shared premises and publicly accessible reasons." Convinced that "the powers and boundaries of rational thought are...a deep and unending problem in philosophy and culture" (78n.36), he seeks to avoid "the immensely complex and controversial task" of proposing and defending a theory of rationality (24; see also 57). Instead, he stipulates that shared premises and publicly accessible reasons are "grounds of decision... [that] have an interpersonal validity that extends to all, or almost all,

---

other "positions" of the same order. But it is perfectly clear from his discussion as a whole that Greenawalt means so to understand disestablishment that it proscribes not only support for a particular theistic religion at the expense of other theistic religions but also support for theistic religion in distinction from secularism.

members of society" (56)—that is, grounds that are in fact generally acknowledged.

This stipulation is appropriate, he insists, because "for theories about political decisions in democracies, whether the decisions are backed by reasons whose relevance is generally acknowledged matters more than whether decisions are backed by reasons that may be defended as rational in some transcultural sense" (24). In this sense of "publicly accessible reasons," Greenawalt continues, "a great many people" think that such reasons "cannot anchor particular religious perspectives of the kind familiar in our society" (73), and he believes that the liberal premises of religious liberty and disestablishment "fit more comfortably with an attitude that for political purposes one religious view is as valid as another, at least as long as neither view itself conflicts with liberal premises" (72). Thus, the book "assume[s]" that claims about religious truth are outside the domain of publicly accessible reasons" (75) or that "reliance on religious grounds is not consonant with reliance on shared reasons" (56).

But given that "shared reasons" means "reasons whose relevance is generally acknowledged," to assume that a theistic conviction falls outside their domain does not settle the question of whether that conviction is valid. In other words, reasons that are shared may not be sufficient to answer all questions. Hence, to assert that something can be justified on "secular" grounds is not to deny the validity of theistic claims, because secular arguments are those "that rest on commonly accessible reasons" (90). Greenawalt identifies the two when he speaks of decisions "supportable on *rational secular* grounds" (90, emphasis added). Thus, when Greenawalt says that liberal democracy has a "secular justification" (16) or that "laws adopted by the government should rest on some secular objective" (20), he means that the proper purposes of the state are purposes that do not have to be understood theistically, are not necessarily theistic. "Laws should seek to promote some good that is comprehensible in nonreligious terms" (21), that is, some good that has "an interpersonal validity that extends to all, or almost all, members of society" (56) irrespective of whether they are adherents of theistic religion. In this sense, for instance, the relief of suffering is a secular good and cruelty is a secular harm, because these judgments can be defended on the basis of generally acknowledged forms of reasoning even while they beg the question of "religious truth" (16).

For Greenawalt, then, it is quite another thing to assert that the state should be informed by "*pervasively* secular attitudes" (19;

emphasis added), in the sense that religious freedom requires the government to promote secularism as the answer to the comprehensive question. If the proper purposes of the state are secular in the sense that they are "not necessarily theistic," they also are "not necessarily not theistic." In other words, the claim that "laws... should rest on some secular objective" intends to beg the question of whether the valid answer to the comprehensive question is theistic or secularistic. Were this not the case, to repeat the principal point, Greenawalt could not consistently defend the reliance by theistic religious adherents on their religious convictions as they deliberate about their political choices. But this is just to say that, for Greenawalt, "the principle of nonsponsorship" (19) proscribes governmental support not only of theistic religion but also of secularism.[4] It also follows that Greenawalt's defense of reliance on theistic religion simultaneously defends reliance on "pervasively secular attitudes" or secularistic convictions. Both are permitted precisely insofar as citizens are not bound to make political choices solely on the basis of publicly accessible or shared reasons. As we pursue Greenawalt's proposal, then, it will generally be irrelevant whether the term "religion" refers to, on my usage, "theistic religion" or to both theistic and secularistic answers to the comprehensive question; accordingly, except where the difference is pertinent, I will henceforth use "religion" without a qualifier.

Given his understandings of "liberal democracy," "publicly accessible reasons," and "religious convictions," Greenawalt's principal thesis is formulated as follows:

> When people reasonably think that shared premises of justice and criteria for determining truth cannot resolve critical questions of fact, fundamental questions of value, or the weighing of competing [secular] benefits and harms, they do appropriately rely on religious convictions that help them answer these questions. (12)

---

4. Greenawalt recognizes that the activities of the state may indeed have implications with respect to some theistic claims, at least in the sense that the former are inconsistent with the latter. A declaration of war, for instance, is a political decision inconsistent with commitment to a God "who demands pacifism" (20). What nonsponsorship means, then, is that government may not "*directly* aim at furthering belief" (20; emphasis added) in some theistic or secularistic position; that is, it may not explicitly affirm either.

Notwithstanding that laws should rest on some secular objective, in other words, decisions about the relative importance of differing generally acknowledged benefits or the relative evil of generally acknowledged harms, or predictions regarding the probable consequences of policies in pursuit or avoidance of such goods and evils, may require fundamental judgments or convictions regarding the human condition none of which is itself generally acknowledged—and it is at this point that citizens may rely on religion.

To "rely on" in its relevant sense is identified in relation to the "chain of evaluation" (35) in accord with which individuals make their ethical and political decisions, and Greenawalt holds that a citizen has relied on religious convictions if "their abandonment would force him seriously to reconsider the [ethical or political] position he takes" (37). To be sure, one may not be certain what position one would take in the absence of religious convictions, but, for Greenawalt, this means that one "is presently relying on those convictions to a degree" (37), that is, would need seriously to reconsider the position were the religious beliefs abandoned.

As the statement of his principal thesis makes clear, reliance on religious convictions is warranted only when shared premises and publicly accessible reasons are inconclusive, and this identifies the sense or respect in which religion is politically important. Thus, Greenawalt affirms "a constrained commitment to shared premises and ways of reasoning" (207) and suggests that "a good liberal citizen must remain open to publicly accessible reasons" (209). But this commitment is constrained or limited precisely because it does not completely exclude the political relevance of religion.

In his defense of this thesis, Greenawalt insists that the "critical line" is between publicly accessible reasons, on the one hand, and, on the other, a general class of "personal bases for decision" (156) of which religious convictions are a specific kind. This larger class of personal bases includes "personal perceptions, intuitions, feelings, and commitments, and deferences to the judgments of others that cannot be defended by persuasive reasons of interpersonal force" (156). In other words, the logic of the argument is that "common forms of reason are radically inconclusive for many public issues" (235), such that all citizens are then forced to rely on nonpublic grounds for decision. Given this situation, Greenawalt further contends, it would be simply unfair to exclude religious convictions from the personal grounds to which citizens might appeal. "If all people must draw from their personal experiences and commitments of value to some degree, people whose experience leads them to religious convictions should not have to disregard what they consider the critical insights about value that their convictions provide" (145).

To be sure, one might concede that some appeal to personal bases of decision is often inescapable and still hold that citizens should not rely on religious convictions—and this because there is something peculiar to the latter, for instance, they are peculiarly rigid, that makes them inappropriate in a liberal democracy. But Greenawalt finds no persuasive case for such a distinction between religious and nonreligious kinds of personal grounds. Indeed, given the distinctive character of religious convictions, namely, that they involve a "comprehensive picture" (179) and thus "bear pervasively" (30) on the ethical choices of religious adherents, it is perhaps impossible and at least "positively objectionable" that people should be required to "compartmentalize beliefs that constitute some kind of unity in their approach to life" (155).

Greenawalt presents his case against the sufficiency of "common forms of reason" through a detailed and impressive discussion of particular political issues. He gives extended attention to "borderlines of status" (98), that is, issues the resolution of which requires moral judgments regarding "entities that are in some ways like us and in others not like us" (148). Thus, for instance, political deliberation related to questions of "animal rights" or treatment of the environment cannot reach conclusions absent answers to "crucial questions" about "whether entities other than human beings intrinsically deserve protection and, if so, how much" (102). Again, "the abortion issue is so intractable because of the sharp divergence over the moral status of the fetus" (121), a vexing problem of evaluation because such worth as one might assign to the fetus seems to be based on a "mix of present characteristics and potential capacity" (132). Through an assessment of the alternative claims and the arguments for them that have been advanced within the relevant public debates, Greenawalt concludes that an appeal to shared premises and publicly accessible reasons is insufficient to validate moral judgments with respect to such questions of status. It is also insufficient, he contends, fully to resolve problems of distributive justice, evaluate alternative approaches to punishment, defend any given military policy, and determine in certain cases the proper relation between church and state (see chapters 9, 10). Hence, "with certain qualifications, an individual acts consistently with the spirit of political liberalism when...he gives weight to his religious convictions in resolving highly complex issues of fact and...of value" (231).

Having reached this conclusion, Greenawalt's book gives relatively brief attention to the proper character of political discourse or public argument, from which, in contrast to an individual's own "chain of evaluation" (35), appeal to religious grounds is, for the most part, excluded.

> The government of a liberal society knows no religious truth and a crucial premise about a liberal society is that citizens of extremely diverse religious views can build principles of political order and social justice that do not depend on particular religious beliefs. The common currency of political discourse is nonreligious argument about human welfare. Public discourse about political issues with those who do not share religious premises should be cast in other than religious terms. (216–17)

Greenawalt also attends to the deliberation of political officials, from which reliance on religious convictions cannot be excluded, and, finally, to relevant questions regarding the relation between reliance on religion and the constitutionality of legislation. As I have mentioned, however, the principal thesis concerns the political choices of liberal citizens generally or as such, and the previous discussion of this thesis is sufficient to clarify Greenawalt's solution to the modern political problematic.

With Rawls in particular and the separationist position generally, one might say, Greenawalt's view affirms religious *freedom* or the disestablishment of religion because any religious conviction at all is a proper "personal" basis of decision. With Murray in particular and the Religionist position generally, one might say, Greenawalt's view affirms *religious* freedom or the legitimacy of the comprehensive order of reflection because reliance on one's religious convictions is consistent with good liberal citizenship. Against both separationists and Religionists, then, Greenawalt so understands religious freedom that all religious convictions in the community are important to politics, precisely in the sense that any such conviction is a proper "personal" basis of political choice. On Greenawalt's view, moreover, religious freedom does not compromise the possibility of political unity because reliance on religious convictions is proper only when or insofar as "shared premises of justice and criteria for determining truth," including the premises of a liberal democratic form of government itself, "cannot resolve critical questions of fact, fundamental questions of value, or the weighing of competing benefits and harms" (12). In other words, a citizen's "constrained commitment" (207) to publicly accessible forms of reasoning makes this view of religious freedom a political principle and her or his qualified reliance on religious convictions makes this principle consistent with religious adherence.

The Pluralist View: A Critique

There is, perhaps, a construal of Greenawalt's principal thesis that is noncontroversial. It will be widely agreed that human reflection is partial or fragmentary, that many issues of public policy are complex, and that many if not most public policy decisions must be taken before there has been fully adequate insight, investigation, deliberation, and debate. At the time for decision, then, the attempt rationally to understand the relevant facts and values may be inconclusive, so that each citizen must make the best judgment she or he can in view of the fragmentary evidence and argument then available and, insofar as they are inconclusive, rely on whatever personal bases of decision she or he is prepared to trust. In support of this reading, one might appeal to a passage in which Greenawalt considers the claim that "whatever the capabilities of existing arguments in publicly accessible terms, further discourse and insight may make clear what is now debatable." In response, he argues: "The main difficulty is that such future prospects are essentially beside the point. The likelihood of future reasoned moral enlightenment is not much help for the person who must decide here and now. If that person rightly conceives the limits of his own reasoned understanding and that of others, is he to rely on other sources of guidance or not" (151)? An advocate of this reading will insist, then, that it provides the proper context in which to understand Greenawalt's suggestion that a liberal citizen "must remain open to publicly accessible reasons" (209).

Were this Greenawalt's point, however, he would simply assert that, as a practical matter, available evidence and argument can be inconclusive, and, if a decision is nonetheless required, a citizen must do the best she or he can. One has reason to expect, then, that something more is at stake for Greenawalt, and, in fact, it is readily apparent that his thesis cannot be exhausted by this initial construal. On the contrary, he intends to assert that reliance on religious "sources of guidance" is proper even if "future reasoned moral enlightenment" *in principle* cannot assess or validate religious convictions. So far as I can see, this is his point in seeking to avoid "the immensely complex and controversial task of developing a concept of rationality" and of determining whether decisions can be "backed by reasons that may be defended as rational in some transcultural sense" (24). In attending to "generally acknowledged" (24) forms of reasoning and assuming that "claims about religious truth are outside the domain of publicly accessible reasons" in this sense (75), he means at least to beg the question of whether religious convictions can be rationally assessed.[5] At least for purposes of the argument, then, Greenawalt is prepared to accept, with those whom he is most concerned to refute, the supposition that political rationality does not include the comprehensive order of reflection and, therefore, to defend the political importance of religious convictions even if religious convictions in principle go "beyond reason" (24).

That Greenawalt not only accepts this supposition for the sake of argument but also is inclined to believe it is at least suggested when he asserts the principle that "laws adopted by the government should rest on some secular objective" (20) in the sense that they "should seek to promote some good that is comprehensible in non-religious terms" (21), that is, in terms "whose relevance is generally acknowledged" (24). Given Greenawalt's intent to defend reliance on religious convictions, this assertion seems to make sense only if those convictions in principle cannot be rationally assessed. Were religious convictions subject to rational validation, then generally acknowledged terms or reasons would be subject to rational criticism in terms of the valid answer to the comprehensive question, and it would appear contradictory to stipulate that generally acknowledged reasons ought to be controlling. Unless religious convictions in principle cannot be rationally assessed, to rephrase the point, Greenawalt has not shown why reliance on them should be limited to situations in which secular or nonreligious forms of reasoning are inconclusive.

So far as I can see, in other words, Greenawalt can affirm that goods pursued by the state should be defensible on "rational secular grounds" (90) without implying that the state should be informed by

---

5. I have been aided in understanding Greenawalt's intent on this matter by personal correspondence with him, for which I am most grateful. Of course, this is not to say that he will consider my current understanding of that intent adequate.

"pervasively secular attitudes" (19) only if reason is limited in principle to generally acknowledged or culturally particular forms, and comprehensive convictions are understood to be nonrational. We might note that this understanding also seems implied by Greenawalt's distinction between the proper reliance on religious convictions in one's personal decisions and the generally improper appeal to religious claims in "public discourse about political issues" (217). Insofar as religious convictions can be rationally assessed, it does not make sense, absent some further consideration, to exclude them from public discourse. But to note this is in fact to repeat the previous point. For the distinction between personal decision and public speech is justified by the properly secular character of the latter. "The common currency of political discourse is nonreligious argument about human welfare" (217).

In any event, given that Greenawalt at least begs the question of whether religious convictions are subject to rational argument, his position is putatively consistent with the assumption that they are nonrational.[6] On this assumption, it is not only "presently existing" arguments that are inconclusive but also, at least with respect to some issues, "future reasoned moral enlightenment" (151) or rational argumentation as such. In the sense that it is consistent with this assumption, Greenawalt's proposal illustrates what I have called the

---

6. Another way to make this point is to say that a rational political theory cannot in truth remain neutral to or beg the question of whether comprehensive convictions can be rationally assessed. The claim "it *may be* the case that comprehensive convictions cannot be rationally assessed" is equivalent to "comprehensive convictions cannot be rationally assessed." For the first claim means that one cannot rationally assess whether or not comprehensive claims can be rationally assessed, and, if reason cannot determine whether it can assess comprehensive claims, then it cannot assess such claims. Thus, the attempt to beg the question is an answer to it. In this context, it is pertinent to note that Rawls, who seeks so to limit political thought as neither to assert nor to deny any comprehensive claim, finds himself bound to disagree with anyone who holds that her or his comprehensive doctrine is "open to and can be fully established by reason" (Rawls 1993: 153). In any event, Greenawalt's assumption that rational assessment *might be* limited in principle to "publicly accessible reasons" is the assumption that it is so limited. An address to the modern political problematic cannot avoid a theory of rationality in the manner that Greenawalt attempts, or, to say the same, the problematic is a philosophical matter in a sense that Greenawalt does not fully credit.

pluralist view: Notwithstanding that religion is nonrational, all religious convictions in the community are important to politics. As such an illustration, I will now try to argue, it is incoherent.

Precisely because he accepts that religion may be nonrational, Greenawalt's position becomes problematic when he considers the admittedly "thorny problem of religious convictions that are at odds with generally shared bases for judgment" (10; see chapter 11). Having shown to his own satisfaction that reliance on religious convictions is justified when shared premises and publicly accessible reasons are inconclusive, he asks whether such reliance is appropriate when it conflicts with claims that can be rationally established. Attention to one of his illustrations will help to display the problem: Assume "that common sense and scientific analysis yield no plausible basis to suppose that the earth will suffer a cataclysmic flood in three years"; assume also that "Thomas...believes that authoritative inerrant scripture indicates the certainty of such a flood" (204); is Thomas a good liberal citizen if he advocates that his government prepare for the cataclysm? Greenawalt answers in the negative, on the grounds that "a plausible theory of liberal democracy" (204) requires "a limited commitment to shared forms of reasoning" (205)—or, at the least, that commonly accepted methods of reasoning are constitutive of *our* liberal society (see 206). Let us grant that good liberal citizenship requires a commitment to shared forms of reasoning. Greenawalt also affirms religious freedom, and he does not address the question one expects Thomas to ask, namely, why should I be a good liberal citizen? Why should a religious adherent assume that conclusions justified by generally acknowledged or secular forms of reasoning are always valid? By definition, Thomas's religious conviction is comprehensive, "a vision about the 'ultimate meaning' of human life...in the universe" (32), so that one would expect him to resolve conflicts between liberal claims and his religious conviction in favor of the latter.

To be sure, Greenawalt may insist that this question is not pertinent to his inquiry. Since the book is about reliance on religious convictions *in this liberal society*, its "perspectives for evaluation are the premises of our particular liberal democratic polity" (4), and Greenawalt might assert that the priority of shared forms of reasoning is one of these premises. But Greenawalt also asserts that liberal citizens may rely on religious convictions, that is, comprehensive perspectives on fact and value that cannot be publicly assessed, and the question raised by the Thomas example is whether the second assertion defeats the first. Precisely because these convictions involve "fundamental frameworks" or claim to express "transcendent sources of truth" (180), they are, by definition, overriding in cases of conflict with other commitments. If our polity provides any space for reliance on overriding convictions that cannot be publicly assessed, why should its religious citizens maintain reliance on publicly accessible reasons when the two conflict? The guest for whom Greenawalt prepares a room in the mansion of liberal democracy seems willing to move in only if she or he can rule the house.

Greenawalt may now respond by arguing that liberal democracy is not consistent with any possible religious conviction but only with those that themselves affirm a "limited commitment to shared forms of reasoning" (205). Thus, "for political purposes one religious view is as valid as another, *at least as long as neither view itself conflicts with liberal premises*" (72; emphasis added). Just as one might insist that the political affirmation of religious liberty is inconsistent with intolerant religious beliefs, so Greenawalt might insist that religious liberty extends politically only to comprehensive convictions that include a limited commitment to public forms of validation.[7]

But now the question is: Why should good liberal citizens believe that public forms of reasoning so much as might be in prin-

---

7. Given Greenawalt's terms, one may argue that no religious adherent could accept this understanding of our liberal democracy. Because religions are nonrational, the political principle that permissible religions are limited to those consistent with liberal premises must itself be justified to citizens independently of any religion. Were its justification dependent on a particular religion, this constitutional principle could not be shared by all citizens unless that religion were taught to all citizens. But no religious adherent could consistently accept the claim that liberal democracy is justified independently of any particular religious conviction, because she or he affirms that the valid religious conviction is the comprehensive condition of all valid moral claims. In other words, no religious adherent could affirm that "for political purposes, one religious view is as valid as another, at least as long as neither view itself conflicts with liberal premises" (72), because any such adherent holds that authentic political premises can be justified only by *the* valid religious conviction. So far as I can see, Greenawalt's understanding of liberal democracy is troubled by the same inconsistency between freestanding liberal principles and comprehensive convictions that makes political liberalism on Rawls's formulation incoherent. In the text, however, I pursue another formulation of this critique.

ciple limited, so that reliance on convictions that in principle cannot be rationally assessed might be politically permissible? Why does liberal democracy not imply that all politically relevant claims can in principle be rationally assessed, so that good citizens are bound to deliberate rationally insofar as possible and then take their political decisions based on their best judgment regarding rationally justifiable facts and values? What justifies the liberal affirmation that nonrational convictions could ever have a public importance? The only aspect of Greenawalt's argument that might be taken as an address to this question is his assessment of the claims and the arguments for them that have been advanced with respect to particular political issues. In the nature of the case, however, this kind of assessment could only confirm the contemporary failure in fact, not the limitation in principle, of rational forms of validation.

If nothing in the book's argument redeems the claim that a liberal's commitment to public forms of reason can be in principle limited, this is because that claim cannot possibly be redeemed. In order to clarify this point, I begin by noting that any putative grounds on which a good liberal citizen might properly consider her or his commitment to reason limited must themselves be publicly accessible. Were one to claim that good liberal citizenship limits its commitment to reason on some basis that is not itself public, this basis could only be, in Greenawalt's sense, personal—and one cannot on personal grounds justify a claim about good liberal citizenship as such. With this point, Greenawalt seems clearly to agree, because he insists that his own proposal regarding religious convictions and political choice appeals to "secular" or publicly accessible reasons. "The analysis and conclusions I offer do not depend on the truth or falsity of particular religious positions" (5; see also 4, 6, 7).

But, now, it is self-contradictory to assert that one can redeem by appeal to reason a limit in principle to rational validation, such that some claims are or even might be nonrationally valid. This claim about claims says nothing or expresses no sensible understanding unless the term "nonrationally valid" is somehow fixed, that is, unless one can identify the conditions given which a claim could be so characterized. But if one could by appeal to reason identify the conditions of nonrational validity, claims so characterized could be rationally redeemed. In other words, reason cannot distinguish between the rational and nonrational validation of claims because doing so would require a rational validation of some criteria of nonrational validity.[8] On rational grounds, putative claims that are nonrational in principle can only be referred to in a negative manner, as simply *non*rational, and what is only negative cannot limit reasonable grounds for decision. Thus, it makes no sense to say that a good liberal citizen has a *limited* commitment to reason.[9]

I conclude that Greenawalt's position confronts an inescapable dilemma. Either (1) religious convictions are important to politics even if in principle they cannot be rationally assessed, in which case there is no reason why religious citizens should affirm an overriding commitment to publicly accessible or secular reasons, or (2) citizens as such should affirm some commitment to reason, in which case there are no grounds on which this commitment could be limited, such that nonrational convictions might be politically important. The dilemma may be restated with respect to the meaning of religious freedom: This term is either (1) a legitimation of a plurality of religions, as it must be, in which case there are no grounds on which to believe that the political community can be unified, or (2) a political principle, as it must also be, in which case there are no grounds on which to admit a nonrational basis for decision.

---

8. I recognize that my conclusion takes exception to a long tradition in Western religious thought, especially in Christian theology, in accord with which one may show rationally that knowledge of the character of God and, therefore, human authenticity as such depends at least in part on special divine revelation. I do believe that the tradition in this respect does not make sense. The putative distinction between rational and nonrational validity could only be, so far as I can see and for the reason given in the text, a nonrational distinction.

9. Even if we allow that limits to reason may be rationally identified, so that some valid claims are nonrational, it will not follow that a good liberal citizen can affirm the political importance of religious convictions. Since Greenawalt insists that liberal premises "do not depend on the truth or falsity of particular religious positions" (5), the distinction between rational and nonrational validity must be independent of any particular comprehensive conviction. But every religious adherent asserts that the valid answer to the comprehensive question is the only grounds on which any political principle can be justified. Hence, a rational defense of limits to reason would in truth deny that any religious conviction is valid, and a good liberal citizen could not consistently affirm that religious convictions have any valid relation to political choice. In other words, Greenawalt could rationally redeem the distinction between rational and nonrational validity only by contradicting the attempt to distance himself from Rawls or from the privatization of religion (see footnote 7, above).

Of course, Greenawalt may insist on the commitment to public forms of reasoning and then simply *stipulate* that these are limited in principle, so that, on some occasions, "critical questions of fact, fundamental questions of value, or the weighing of competing benefits and harms" (12) in principle cannot be answered or determined on rational grounds—and good liberal citizens cannot complete their political deliberation without relying on convictions that in principle cannot be rationally assessed. To the best of my reading, and however contrary to Greenawalt's intent, this is precisely what he has done. He is principally concerned to contest the claim that political thinking properly relies solely on reasons that are independent of religious convictions, in the "political and not metaphysical" (Rawls 1993: 10) or historically specific sense that Rawls advances. But Greenawalt is also concerned to avoid "the immensely complex and controversial task of developing a concept of rationality" (24). As a consequence, he is prepared to assume that reason, at least insofar as it is politically relevant, is limited in principle to historically or culturally specific forms, so that religious convictions in principle cannot be rationally assessed. He then finds that the historically specific forms of reasoning current in our society are inconclusive with respect to certain political issues, and he concludes that a good liberal citizen must insofar rely on personal bases, including religious convictions that in principle cannot be rationally assessed. But this means that the limits to reason informing Greenawalt's resolution of the modern political problematic have been simply assumed or stipulated.

If I am correct in this reading, the point to be underscored is that this stipulation itself cannot be defended. Because it is self-contradictory to claim that reason can redeem so much as the possibility of limits to rational forms of validation, the claim that nonrational convictions may be valid could only be a nonrational claim. Given that it purports to identify reason as such, moreover, it can only be a comprehensive nonrational claim; a liberal citizen's commitment to reason could be limited only if some nonrational comprehensive claim that identifies this limitation is valid. In other words, the meaning of religious freedom on Greenawalt's pluralist view itself relies on the validity of a particular nonrational comprehensive conviction. Whether this conviction is theistic or secularistic is immaterial. In either case, a nonrational comprehensive conviction could be constitutive of liberal citizenship as such only if it is taught to all, so that, on this view, the state has a duty to insure the teaching of this particular conviction. If Greenawalt is similar to Rawls because he is prepared to limit reason in its politically relevant sense to historically specific forms, he gains distance from Rawls's privatization of all comprehensive convictions only by sharing Murray's problem: The distinction between rational and nonrational validity entails an established religion.[10]

It also follows that this same problem will invade any formulation of the pluralist view. To hold that all of a plurality of nonrational religious convictions are important to politics can only be to limit in principle the rational grounds for political choice. So far from a third alternative that solves the modern political problematic, the implied consequence is either a plurality of comprehensive claims for which no principle of political unity is possible or the establishment of a particular comprehensive conviction that contradicts a plurality of legitimate religions. As with the privatist and partisan views, a coherent formulation of religious freedom must be something other than pluralist.

10. This way of putting the matter suggests that Rawls may be similar to both Greenawalt and Murray in that his distinction between the reasonable and the rational also implies an established religion. That conclusion follows if, as I will argue in chapter 7, the denial that any comprehensive conviction is valid implies a comprehensive conviction. Rawls's political liberalism, I argued in chapter 3, in truth denies the comprehensive order of reflection.

PART 3
THE PUBLIC VIEW

6

The Enlightenment Rationale: Sidney E. Mead

Part two of this work sought to show that the modern political problematic cannot be solved if religious convictions are immune to public debate or assessment. The argument proceeded by reviewing privatist, partisan, and pluralist views of the relation between politics and comprehensive convictions. In each case, I sought to show that the interpretation of religious freedom advanced by a representative of the view in question is incoherent—and, further, to show that the incoherence must, *mutatis mutandis*, characterize any formulation of that type of view. Success in those critical reviews is sufficient to demonstrate that, on the theory of religion as nonrational, religious freedom has no coherent meaning, because the three views criticized formally exhaust the alternatives consistent with that theory: The privatist view asserts that none of the religious convictions in the community is important to politics; the partisan view asserts that some of the religious convictions in the community are important to politics; the pluralist view asserts that all of the religious convictions in the community are important to politics; and the trichotomy "none, some, all" is logically exhaustive.

On the privatist view, exemplified by John Rawls's political liberalism, religious freedom denies the legitimacy of all religions because it asserts political principles that are said to be independent of the comprehensive order of reflection. On the partisan view, exemplified by John Courtney Murray's Religionist position, religious freedom establishes a religion because it means the assertion of a comprehensive conviction that unites a specified class of religions. On the pluralist view, exemplified by Kent Greenawalt's proposal, religious freedom either denies the legitimacy of all religions, because it asserts a commitment to public forms of reasoning that cannot be limited, or it establishes a religion, because its limitation on rational assessment stipulates a comprehensive conviction. The incoherence of religious freedom on the theory of religion as nonrational may be summarily stated: A plurality of religious convictions is a plurality of claims regarding the comprehensive condition of the activities of the state. On the assumption that the differences within this plurality cannot be rationally assessed, political conflicts among adherents of differing religions cannot be resolved except by a principle that denies the validity of all comprehensive claims or coercively asserts one of them. Either the legitimacy of all religions is proscribed or some given religious conviction is established, and the modern political problematic cannot be solved.

The widespread assumption that religious convictions do not belong to a rational order of reflection and, therefore, cannot be publicly assessed, I conclude, introduces inescapable confusion into the understanding of religious freedom. A coherent understanding of religious freedom requires that answers to the comprehensive question *are* public in the sense that their claims to validity can be assessed or validated by appeal to human experience and reason. Just because this requirement is so widely thought to be inappropriate with respect to religious adherence, our understanding of the relation between politics and religion in America, both in academic discussion and in that of the wider public, is so perplexed.

In my judgment, no student of this problem has appreciated this conclusion as clearly as has Sidney E. Mead, even if, as I also believe, he too finally fails to formulate a fully adequate understanding of religious freedom. Accordingly, I will now seek to approach a constructive statement regarding the logic of religious freedom through a conversation with him, especially with his classic volume *The Lively Experiment*. In doing this, I should note at the outset that Mead is a historian of religion and of religion in the United States in particular. Thus, his discussion of religious freedom is a historical review of the events leading to the religion clauses in the First Amendment and of the meanings given to those clauses by their advocates. My purpose here is not to assess the merit of his historical interpretations, any more than my purpose generally is to discuss the First Amendment as an issue in United States constitutional law. It is also apparent, however, that Mead intends to endorse an understanding of religious freedom that he takes to be included more or less clearly in the historical record. Hence, my purpose is briefly to review the history that Mead presents in order to arrive, with him, at his proposal regarding the proper resolution of the modern political problematic.

The Essentials of Religion

Mead is fond of the saying of W. E. Garrison that "the declaration for religious freedom in the American constitution was 'on the administrative side' one of the 'two most profound revolutions which have occurred in the entire history of the church'" (Mead 1963: 59–60). Religious freedom may be so described, Mead believes, because it reversed the relation between the political community and the church that had characterized European civilization since the first profound administrative revolution, namely, the recognition of Christianity as the official religion of the Roman Empire by the emperor, Constantine, in the fourth century C.E. The point is not simply that the United States Constitution broke with a practice that had endured for some thirteen centuries. More importantly, religious freedom was a profound change because it rejected what to European civilization had seemed more or less self-evident—namely, "that the stability of the social order and the safety of the state demanded the religious solidarity of all the people in one church" (Garrison, cited in Mead 1963: 60). This claim had commanded enduring assent for the reason that we have already had more than one occasion to cite: A conflict among diverse religions could never be resolved by appeal to a common political commitment, since the religious convictions would be, by definition, overriding; hence, a political community inclusive of religious plurality would be ever threatened by schism.

Mead is, of course, fully aware that some European political communities prior to the later eighteenth century had not been able to prevent internal religious plurality and had in greater or lesser measure experimented with religious toleration. Still, one might say that this experiment only confirmed the inherited wisdom. Toleration was entertained because religious plurality had indeed been profoundly divisive—and, moreover, toleration, assuming as it did the persistence of an official or established religion, was a merely pragmatic solution, in the sense that it did not purport to include an understanding or theory of the body politic in accord with which religious conflict could be resolved in principle. The turn to full religious freedom in the United States at least suggested that such a theory had been advanced, and it is in this regard that the profound "administrative" revolution occurred in America. Accordingly, Mead's attempt to understand America's "lively experiment" is an attempt to understand why those who advocated religious freedom believed nonetheless that the integrity of the new Republic would be secure.

This is not to say that, for Mead, the lively experiment was solely or even primarily the historical consequence of a theory that had been advanced. On the contrary, the causes were many, including the presence in the colonies of Christians (especially Baptists and Quakers) who advocated religious freedom as a matter of Christian principle and the more extensive presence of pietistic or revivalistic expressions of Christianity, born with the Great Awakening, that sought to be free from the domination of colonial religious establishments (see 1963: 19, 41f.). Above all, Mead contends, religious diversity was constitutionally affirmed because it was already present in the nation to be created. Although there were established churches in most of the colonies, settlement had drawn on the diversity of the Protestant Reformation, and different churches were established in different colonies. At the time of national independence,

> no one of them...was in a position to make a successful bid for a national establishment....On the question of religious freedom for all, there were many shades of opinion in these churches, but all were practically unanimous on one point: each wanted freedom for itself. And by this time it had become clear that the only way to get it for themselves was to grant it to others. (1963: 35)

If Western history argued that a nation could not have integrity *without* an established religion, the facts in the colonies dictated that they could not be united *with* one. "If there was to be a *United States*....the new nation's central authority had to be neutral, neither favoring nor hindering any sect's beliefs or practices except where the latter might violate socially acceptable conduct" (1975: 58).

It is true that all of the numerically significant communities were Christian, and it might be argued that the establishment of Christianity or even Protestant Christianity was a possibility. This would not have allowed an official church in the sense that includes some unified institutional expression, but a Christian test for public office might have been stipulated and all citizens might have been required in some specified way to support the activities of some or other Christian church. Moreover, the concept of "multiple establishment" was thoroughly familiar in the colonies. Because such multiple establishment was a possibility, Mead believes, it is all the more remarkable that the First Congress rejected this alternative, suggesting that at least some of those within it were persuaded that political stability could be secure in the presence of full religious freedom (see 1963: 61).

In any event, particular historical circumstances do not provide answers to philosophical questions, and Mead asks whether a coherent rationale for the First Amendment was included in the conditions leading to religious freedom. As I have noted, he insists on the role that support from certain expressions of Christianity played in the outcome. But the pietistic belief that the Christian church should be voluntary, like the Baptist conviction that it should be free from governmental interference, could not serve as a coherent rationale for religious freedom. For neither of these convictions was religiously neutral; that is, both were explicitly understood to be distinctively Christian and, therefore, neither could identify a meaning of religious freedom that could command the assent of all religious adherents.[1] To the contrary, then, it is Mead's conviction that a coherent understanding of religious freedom was present only in the minds of a relative minority of its supporters whom Mead calls "rationalists" and for whom he takes Jefferson, Madison, and Franklin to be the principal voices.

Rationalists were a relative minority because they constituted something of a cultural elite in the colonies. Schooled by the European Enlightenment, they were typically convinced that individuals fulfill their potential and the body politic is perfected insofar as people are guided by reason. With respect to the political process, this conviction implied that opportunities for full and free rational discussion and debate should be provided and protected. The errors or prejudices of irrational claims could be disclosed by the light of criticism and the truth could be approached by common reflection.

Rationalists like Jefferson concluded that reform depended upon the freeing of man's natural reason from...enslavement—largely by opening all the channels of communication through freedom

---

1. These are, of course, ecclesiastical beliefs or claims about the proper form of the Christian church. Hence, it might be thought that they are not claims about the valid comprehensive self-understanding and, in that sense, not religious beliefs. But Christian ecclesiastical convictions have often been asserted as a necessary part of human authenticity as such. This is, perhaps, especially the case when confession of the decisive event of the Christian religion, the putative revelation of God in Jesus as the Christ, is thought to be essential to salvation. Given that christology, the proper form of the church's continuing witness to that event may also be included within an answer to the comprehensive question.

of speech, freedom of the press, freedom to assemble and petition, so that every opinion could have a hearing. Errors, they believed, would cease "to be dangerous when it is permitted freely to contradict them." This is the theory that lies back of the great zeal for freedom developed during the eighteenth century. (1963: 46)

One should not conclude, however, that the rationalists sought to constitute secularistic politics. Although it is commonplace that the Enlightenment was relentless in its critique of allegedly superstitious elements within traditional Christianity, it can hardly be characterized as inherently anti-religious in the sense of repudiating all theistic convictions. On the contrary, it was more typical of eighteenth-century Enlightenment thinkers to be deists. In any event, Mead insists that each of the rationalist founders formulated his own more or less clear statement of deistic belief (see 1963: 42). But this belief was thoroughly consistent with their rationalism because they were also convinced that the existence of God and the character of the divine will were accessible to or could be understood by human reason without the aid of special divine revelation.

> Rationalism fostered the idea of individual human autonomy guided by the light of Nature and Nature's God, through Reason. "Reason," of course, did not mean merely the process of reasoning, but a basic principle of human nature through which man, the creature, was enabled to read the great revelation of the Creator in His works and to shape his conduct accordingly. (1963: 61)

It is because the relevant founders were deists that their writings about the Republic frequently refer to its dependence on divine providence and its obligation to a divine commission. It is because their deism was rationalist, Mead continues, that they were able to distinguish between the "essentials" or universal truths "of every religion" (1963: 65), which are accessible to human experience and reason, and the peculiar or particular convictions or inessentials, which are "irrelevant for the general welfare" (1963: 65) and the affirmation of which depends on some putative special revelation (see 1963: 49). In this context, Mead cites especially the autobiographical statements of Franklin:

Perhaps "essential" does not imply "inessential"

I never doubted, for instance, the existence of the Deity; that he made the world and govern'd it by his Providence; that the most acceptable service of God was the doing of good to men; that our souls are immortal; and that all crime will be punished, and virtue rewarded, either here or hereafter. These I esteem'd the essentials of every religion; and, being to be found in all the religions we had in our country, I respected them all, tho' with different degrees of respect, as I found them more or less mix'd with other articles, which, without any tendency to inspire, promote, or confirm morality, serv'd principally to divide us, and make us unfriendly to one another. (cited in Mead 1963: 64)

On Mead's reading, then, this distinction between the essentials of all religions, which are accessible to reason, and the inessentials of diverse religions, which are not, permitted a rationale in accord with which the stability of the Republic could be consistent with religious neutrality by the state. Religious freedom meant neutrality toward the several religious communities wherein the universal truths of religion are mixed with inessentials, but the integrity of the body politic would be secured by a common adherence to religious essentials. "I conclude" Mead says, "that what is commonly called the relation between church and state in the United States ought to be resolved into the theological issue between the particularistic theological notions of the sects and the cosmopolitan, universal theology of the Republic" (1975: 69). Of course, it might be asked how the common adherence would be maintained in the midst of religious diversity. But Mead claims that the rationalist founders did not in this respect perceive a problem, precisely because they believed that the universal truths are rational. Since the essentials of religion are accessible to human experience and reason, they are, in Franklin's words, "found in all the religions," however mixed they may be with "other articles." Accordingly, the teaching of all religious communities would include inculcation of the essentials, and the latter would constitute the common religious convictions of the body politic. Thus, Thomas Jefferson, when he argued for the Virginia Statute for Religious Freedom, directed the attention of his fellow Virginians to the practice of religious freedom in "our sister States of Pennsylvania and New York" and observed that there "religion is...of various kinds, indeed; but all good enough; all sufficient to preserve peace and order" (cited in Mead 1963: 59). "Good enough" and "sufficient," Mead interprets, because the various churches all taught the beliefs essential to the well-being of the body politic.

In sum, then, Mead appropriates the affirmation that essential religious convictions are accessible to reason in order to distinguish between the "religion of the Republic," as he sometimes calls it (see 1975: 5 and passim), and the religions that are disestablished. The former consists in those universal religious truths that can be known by reason alone; the latter consist in the various mixtures of those "essentials" with inessentials. On this distinction, neutrality by the state, "which is often referred to as 'secularization,' is more accurately described as de-sectarianization of the civil authority" (1975: 58–59). Accordingly, Mead can also offer a distinction between the religion of the Republic and a religious establishment. Establishment, he summarizes, "rested upon two basic assumptions: that the existence and well-being of any society depends upon a body of commonly shared religious beliefs...and that the only guarantee that these necessary beliefs will be sufficiently inculcated is to put the coercive power of the state behind the institution responsible for their definition, articulation, and inculcation" (1963: 63). Religious freedom, he continues, did not mean a denial of the first assumption; "it meant only the rejection of the second" (1963: 63). What permitted the rationalists coherently to divorce the two was precisely their conviction that the commonly shared religious beliefs on which society depends are accessible to human reason and experience and, therefore, will be taught or inculcated by all of the disestablished religious communities.

But Mead himself, notwithstanding that he appears to credit the solution, warns that there is a "troublesome lacuna" in the founders' theory. The problem lies in the assumption that disestablished churches or free religious communities will indeed "define, articulate, disseminate, and inculcate the basic religious beliefs essential for the existence and well-being of the society" (1963: 65), an assumption that does not follow from the affirmation that religious essentials can be known by reason alone. It is one thing to assert that the truth of certain religious beliefs is accessible to human experience and reason; it is another to claim that all religious communities teach them. From the former, one might conclude that those truths are *potentially* included in the teaching of all religious communities, but the latter claims that they are *actually* taught. The theory did not "envisage a time when some or even all the religious groups might not teach...[the basic religious beliefs] at all" (1963: 65).

Beyond the assumption that basic religious beliefs are actually taught, moreover, the founders' theory also assumes that each of the several free religious communities will distinguish those essentials that it has in common with all other religions and will understand the beliefs that are peculiar to it as inessential to the well-being of the Republic. "It is hard to escape the conclusion that each religious group accepted, by implication, the responsibility to teach that its peculiar doctrines, which made it distinct from other sects and gave it its only reason for separate existence, were...irrelevant for the general welfare of the nation-community" (1963: 66) Quite apart from the question of whether or in what sense the distinction between essentials and inessentials could make sense to particular religions, it certainly seems possible that differences between religions will seem to some sufficiently substantial in their import for politics that believers would not ignore them.

In other words, the theory assumes that all religions not only actually teach the essentials but also actually agree on what aspects of their several teachings do and do not belong to the convictions that can be redeemed by appeal to human experience and reason. But even if both of these conditions obtain in fact, the rationalist founders also assumed that the several disestablished religions would together command sufficient allegiance throughout the American citizenry that the essentials would indeed continue to be commonly shared religious beliefs. The theory did not "envisage a time when" the religious communities might be no longer adequate to the teaching necessary "for the support of the public welfare" (1963: 65).

Having noted the "troublesome lacuna," Mead asks about the implications of the rationalist theory for a situation in which the free religious groups did not accept or could not sufficiently serve the political purpose that is assigned to them. In response, he at least wonders whether institutions of the civil order must then "guarantee the dissemination and inculcation...of the beliefs essential to the existence and well-being of the democratic society" (1963: 67), and he finds provocative the proposal of J. Paul Williams that "governmental agencies must teach the democratic ideal *as religion*" (cited in Mead 1963: 69). Mead has in mind especially the public schools, and he even suggests that "the rise of compulsory free public education" (1963: 67) was due in part to the failure of the churches with respect to teaching the religion of the Republic. "In other words, the public schools in the United States took over one of the basic responsibilities that traditionally was always assumed by an established church" (1963: 68).

At this point, we may recall the two assumptions that together defined traditional religious establishment and that, on Mead's account, the rationalist theory of disestablishment divorced—first, the existence and well-being of any society depends on a body of common religious beliefs, and, second, sufficient adherence to these beliefs will be guaranteed only if the coercive power of the state is placed behind their inculcation. The rationalist founders rejected the second even while they embraced the first because beliefs accessible to human experience and reason would be taught by diverse, disestablished religious communities. But even on this theory, as we have now seen, there might be circumstances in which governmental agencies must take on the religious education of the citizenry, because voluntary religious groups are inadequate to the task. It now follows that the putative difference between establishment and disestablishment is not a matter of political principle but, rather, of accidental fact. In both cases, the state has a duty to insure that the relevant religious convictions are adequately taught, even if, in the latter case, there may be situations in which, as a matter of fact, nongovernmental agencies are sufficiently effective that no state action is required. In both cases, then, the required religious character of the citizenry is guaranteed by the coercive power of the state, so that, as a matter of theory or principle, the founders' theory implies a religious establishment.

It is now apparent, in other words, that the first of the two assumptions by which establishment is defined is sufficient to identify it. To assert that the existence and well-being of the body politic depend on a body of commonly shared religious beliefs is to imply religious establishment, because this assertion implies that the teaching of these beliefs must be guaranteed by the state. It is, then, beside the point to insist that the religious convictions commonly adhered to should be those that are accessible to reason. Since adherence must be common, the question of *which* religious beliefs are indeed accessible to reason cannot be a matter of public disagreement but must be authoritatively answered. The fact that a given claim can be redeemed by reason does not guarantee that all will agree on this fact, and the requirement that it be explicitly affirmed by all can be fulfilled only if the duty to insure agreement is given to the state. Their rationalism notwithstanding, the rationalist founders, on this reading, share with Murray and Greenawalt the implied commitment to an established religion. If religious establishment is to be avoided in principle, then the first and, therefore, both of its defining assumptions must be rejected.

[handwritten marginal note:] But it is not an "institution" that is established, rather a "theology".

The Conflict of Opinions

But if Mead's formulation of the founders' theory shares with other positions previously examined the implied affirmation of an established religion, this does not cancel the singular importance of his attention to the Enlightenment affirmation of the rationalists. As the remainder of this work will seek to argue, it is just Mead's attempt to make this affirmation central to the rationale of the First Amendment that provides the resources for an interpretation of religious freedom that is coherent, that is, an interpretation that does reject both defining assumptions of religious establishment without denying the validity of any religious conviction. If this entails a revision of the theory that Mead attributes to the founders, the revision only pursues without compromise the affirmation that religious convictions can be assessed by appeal to human experience and reason. It is, moreover, a revision that Mead himself comes close to completing when, in another chapter of *The Lively Experiment*, he at least suggests a view of the First Amendment substantially different from the theory we have just reviewed. It will be helpful, then, to pursue further the conversation with him.

In discussing Abraham Lincoln's expression of the religion of the Republic, Mead underscores Lincoln's conviction that the nation stands "always under the judgment of the infinite God" and, therefore, is bound in all of its striving "to stand 'with firmness in the right as God...gives us to see the right'—the 'right' being conformity with the ultimate purposes of the infinite God" (1963: 73). Because one "can never be absolutely sure that he rightly senses the will of the infinite God" (1963: 73), however, Lincoln also insisted that each citizen "must approach all the complex problems of human existence finally 'with malice toward none; with charity for all'—always with the realization that in the sight of God he may be wrong" (1963: 74). Accordingly, the nation's attempt to conform to God's purposes must proceed through "government of the people, by the people, for the people," and Mead summarizes Lincoln's "profound statement" (1963: 74) as including the nation's "destiny under God" and "the democratic way" (1963: 80).

To first appearances, Lincoln's formulation may seem to be a restatement of the founders' theory that we have previously examined. The nation's destiny under God and the way of democracy might be seen as the particular religious convictions or commonly shared beliefs on which, according to that theory, the existence and well-being of the Republic depend. Mead is not entirely clear whether he intends so to be understood. But more detailed attention offers another reading. The belief in God "is equivalent to" no more than "the assertion that there is order and ultimate meaning in the universe which is discoverable at least in part by man" (1963: 80). In other words, a common belief that the nation has a "destiny under God" does not necessarily include agreement about what the divine purpose is. Moreover, this must be the case if "the democratic way" follows from the recognition that each citizen "in the sight of God... may be wrong" (1963: 74). Accordingly, "the democratic way" means "the belief that the will of the people which is finally the surest clue to the will of God, can really be known only when all the channels of communication and expression are kept open" (1963: 81). In other words, Mead's reading of Lincoln suggests that "the religion of the Republic" is simply the common commitment to seek through democratic discussion and debate the "order and ultimate meaning in the universe" (1963: 80) to which the nation should conform but any proposed formulation of which may be wrong.

With the reading so stated, one is reminded not so much of Franklin's distinction between religious essentials and inessentials as of the rationalist commitment that Mead attributes to Jefferson: "Jefferson concluded that reform depended upon the freeing of man's natural reason from...enslavement—largely by opening all the channels of communication through freedom of speech, freedom of the press, freedom to assemble and petition, so that every opinion could have a hearing" (1963: 46). Indeed, Mead explicitly says that Lincoln's "democratic way" presupposed the rationalist commitment. Only if the truth about the "order and ultimate meaning in the universe" (1963: 80) is accessible to human experience and reason does it follow that democratic discussion, in which every opinion has a hearing, is the appropriate pursuit of the nation's destiny under God. Thus, Mead cites in this context the singular words in Jefferson's "Act for Establishing Religious Freedom" in Virginia: "Truth is great and will prevail if left to herself;...she is the proper and sufficient antagonist to error, and has nothing to fear from the conflict unless by human interposition disarmed of her natural weapon, free argument and debate; errors ceasing to be dangerous when it is permitted freely to contradict them" (cited in Mead 1963: 82). On this revised reading, then, the rationalist commitment informed an affirmation of continuing public discussion and debate as the only proper source of whatever purchase on the truth the

7

THE RATIONALITY OF RELIGION

Our public discussion of religious freedom, I have suggested, has been widely invaded by confusion because it is widely believed that religious (or, at least, theistic) convictions are nonrational. This belief, I judge, persists for many reasons. Many theistic religious adherents assume that religious faith relates humans to something that cannot be rationally understood because it transcends everything else that exists. Some who adhere to secularistic convictions equate religion with theistic religion and, therefore, deny the rationality of religion. In addition, both theistic religious adherents and secularists often separate questions of morality and justice from those of religion. On this understanding, religion is nonrational because it involves personal beliefs that are independent of our common moral enterprise. Finally, there are some, perhaps especially in the contemporary academy, for whom the comprehensive question itself simply is not sensible, that is, does not have a valid answer. In contrast to these several understandings of religion, the public view of religious freedom presupposes the possibility of public debate about human authenticity as such. The purpose of the present chapter is to redeem the claim that the comprehensive order of reflection is rational and to pursue some of the implications of this Enlightenment affirmation for the meaning of religious freedom.

The Necessity of Comprehensive Convictions

One mode of thought in which the possibility of comprehensive debate is not affirmed is the so-called nonfoundational or neo-pragmatic approach to understanding that many have recently endorsed. Advocates of this approach hold that the long tradition in Western philosophy addressed to the character of reality and human purpose as such has been a series of failures. Every expression of this tradition has in truth escalated some culturally or historically specific characteristic or characteristics to supposedly ahistorical status. Moreover, the consequences have not been merely intellectual. Identifying the possibilities specific to some particular culture or society with human authenticity as such, this philosophical project has often led to politically oppressive responses toward dissent and imperialistic attitudes and actions toward people of other particular cultures or societies. The history of failure, we are told, discredits the project, at least in the sense that we do not have to accept its definition of the philosophical task. In other words, we may think "without foundations," and the claim should be formulated as a permissive rather than an imperative, because advocates of this approach typically intend simply to refuse the significance of the comprehensive order of reflection rather than refute or deny its claim to validity. So Richard Rorty, for instance, holds that the "pragmatism" he endorses does not deny what he calls "Philosophy" but, rather, simply chooses to "change the subject" (Rorty 1982: xiv).

It is, we may now recall, just this nonfoundational approach that informs the political liberalism of John Rawls, and it is to the point that Rorty endorses Rawls's proposal (see Rorty 1988: 261f.).[1] In his defense for a modern democracy of political principles that are freestanding or "political and not metaphysical" (Rawls 1993: 10), Rawls simply refuses either to affirm or deny the comprehensive order of reflection and appeals to historically specific ideas implicit or latent in the political culture of modern democratic society in order to justify his conception of justice. But my critique of Rawls argued that this putative distinction between refusal and denial is untenable. Because a comprehensive conviction claims to identify the comprehensive condition of all valid moral claims, no religious adherent could consistently accept that principles of justice may be validated on historically specific grounds alone. In other words, Rawls's claim that principles of justice for a modern democracy may be justified by appeal to historically or culturally specific ideas and, in this sense,

---

1. Some may object to the implication that Rawls explicitly refuses the significance of comprehensive reflection, since he holds that the problem of justice is important only because citizens pursue some or other conception of the good, and he allows that at least some of these conceptions are comprehensive. But Rawls does claim that we may refuse the significance of comprehensive reflection with respect to the conception of justice, and that is the sense in which the nonfoundational approach informs his political liberalism.

"without foundations" implicitly denies the validity of all comprehensive convictions and, thereby, denies the order of reflection that the comprehensive question identifies.

The incoherence in Rawls's proposal betrays, I believe, that nonfoundational thought generally cannot simply refuse the comprehensive order of reflection; that is, every such refusal is implicitly a denial. Thus, when Rorty claims that he simply chooses to "change the subject," this choice at least implies that one can make that choice consistently. Simply to choose Rorty's neopragmatism implies that it is rationally permissible, in the sense that one is not inconsistent in choosing to think without "Philosophical" implications or comprehensive presuppositions. As I sought to clarify in chapter 2, however, the comprehensive order of reflection asks and answers the question of human activity or self-understanding as such. No comprehensive claim could possibly be valid unless it refers to characteristics or conditions implied or presupposed by all human thought or understanding. Hence, to say that thought without such implications is rationally permissible is to imply that there are no such characteristics or conditions. The refusal is a denial that any comprehensive claim is valid.

But if Rawls's political proposal in particular and nonfoundational or neopragmatic thought in general implicitly deny all religious or comprehensive convictions, this conclusion does not itself confirm that there can be a public discussion and debate about human authenticity as such. Some might hold that the denial is valid. To be sure, a political constitution that expresses this denial does not solve the modern political problematic or, to say the same, cannot coherently affirm religious freedom. But this is the case, one might say, because the problem has been ill-conceived. The stipulation that a plurality of religions is legitimate means that constitutional principles must be consistent with religious adherence, and it is mere confusion to seek a coherent understanding of that stipulation if religious adherence as such is not rational.

Those who seek to revise Rawls in this direction might not advocate that all religious activity should be illegal and, therefore, coercively proscribed. Individuals and groups in the political community might still be permitted to engage in what they take to be religious activity on the mistaken belief that the comprehensive question has a valid answer. But this political permission must be qualified by the priority of the constitution. Putative religious activity is allowed as long as it does not violate the principle or principles of political unity stipulated in the constitution and, in this sense, religious adherents are required to affirm the "priority of right to good." So to affirm is, of course, to make politics prior to religion in a sense that no religious adherent could consistently accept, and, in that sense, one might say that religion is illegal or, at least, not legitimate. But this is just to repeat that the political theory now advanced denies the comprehensive order of reflection.

In assessing this denial of religious freedom, we may begin by underscoring that any constitutional principles endorsed can only pretend to be neopragmatic or, in Rawls's sense, political and not metaphysical. Since his intent is to apply "the principle of toleration to philosophy itself" (1993: 10) and, thereby, simply to refuse the comprehensive order of reflection, it is just this nonfoundational intent that is contradicted by the implicit denial of all comprehensive convictions. But this means that the denial is itself a philosophical or, in Rawls's sense, metaphysical claim, that is, a claim of the same comprehensive scope as the claims it denies. One who insists on the denial may well wish to distinguish between a comprehensive claim that is negative, that is, the claim "there are no valid understandings of human authenticity as such," and the positive convictions that assert such an understanding. But this does not gainsay that the denial is a claim about human activity as such, namely, that no human activity includes a valid comprehensive self-understanding, and, at least in that sense, the denial is as philosophical or comprehensive as the convictions it denies.

This point is confirmed by the recognition that one cannot validate a denial of all positive comprehensive claims by appeal to historically specific conditions; that is, one cannot show by such an appeal that *no* historically general understanding of human authenticity could be valid. An appeal to the conditions of some particular time and place implies that the claim one thereby seeks to defend has been validated only insofar as those conditions obtain. To argue, for instance, that slavery is wrong because it is inconsistent with the fundamental affirmations of modern democratic culture is to show, if one has, that slavery is wrong wherever the public culture is modern and democratic. So far as the argument goes, then, the claim one has sought to defend may not be valid given other conditions. Similarly, to argue by appeal to specific historical or cultural conditions that no positive comprehensive claims are valid would be to imply, so far as the argument goes, that some or other such claim may be valid given alternative circumstances. It now follows that the argument cannot be successful even for the specific conditions to which it appeals. If there is ever a valid understanding of human authenticity as such under any conditions, then that understanding is valid under all conditions, precisely because it is comprehensive. Hence, to validate the denial of all positive comprehensive claims, one must show that no such claim could ever be valid, so that the denial is itself a (negative) comprehensive claim.

Because a denial of all religious or comprehensive convictions is itself a (negative) comprehensive claim, it prevents the validation or justification of *any* positive beliefs about human authenticity, comprehensive or otherwise. In other words, no moral claim, even one highly specific to circumstances, can be validated on historically specific grounds alone. This is because historically specific conditions could be sufficient conditions of validity only if no positive comprehensive conviction is valid, and the denial of all such convictions cannot itself be defended on historically specific grounds. If one argues, to repeat the example, that historically specific ideas of modern democratic culture are sufficient to validate that slavery is wrong, this argument could be successful only if there is no comprehensive condition of all valid moral claims. Since the denial of all religious or comprehensive convictions cannot itself be validated by appeal to the specific conditions of modern democracy, neither can the moral claim that slavery is wrong.

This point may be reformulated by noting that a moral theory in which all comprehensive understandings of human authenticity are denied is, at least implicitly, an example of moral relativism. Because Rawls's conception of justice, for instance, implicitly denies the comprehensive order of reflection, he implicitly asserts that the character of authentic political activity is always and in all respects relative to given historical and cultural conditions. If there is no character or positive principle of human authenticity that is valid under all historical conditions, then all valid understandings of human authenticity must be relative to some or other specific circumstances. But, then, no moral claim could be justified without validating moral relativism, and moral relativism is a *positive* claim about human authenticity, the validity of which cannot be relative to specific circumstances. To assert that the moral norms of every actual and possible human activity are in all respects relative is to make a positive claim about human activity that is comprehensive. In other words, moral relativism is self-refuting because it implies the comprehensive moral condition that it denies, and, therefore, the denial of all comprehensive convictions prevents the validation of any moral claim.[2]

If one doubts that moral relativism is a comprehensive moral claim, one need only consider that it asserts a comparison of all human activities. To assert that the authenticity of every human activity is in all respects relative to specific conditions is to compare all human activities. Moreover, a comprehensive comparison, the consequence of which is a moral conclusion, must be itself a moral comparison. Only the moral character of human activity as such could justify the claim that authenticity is always and in all respects historically specific, and the comprehensive moral norm of moral relativism may be formulated: Always choose in accord with the solely relative norms appropriate to your particular setting. But, then, no moral claim could be justified without appeal to this comprehensive norm; that is, no such claim can be justified on historically specific grounds alone. Contrary to its denial of all religious or comprehensive convictions, moral relativism is itself an answer to the comprehensive question and, therefore, self-refuting. It is, I judge, their recognition that this denial has this self-refuting character that leads both Rawls and Rorty simply to refuse the comprehensive order

---

2. Some may object that this argument assumes the conclusion it seeks to defend—namely, that some positive comprehensive claims are valid. On this objection, "moral relativism" is a sensible term only in contrast to or distinction from "moral universalism," and one who denies all positive comprehensive claims does not credit the distinction between universal and relative. In truth, however, this distinction does not assume the validity of positive universal claims but only the validity of some universal claim, and the denial of all positive comprehensive claims grants that some universal claim is valid because that denial *is* a universal claim, even if a negative one. Hence, one who makes moral claims and denies all positive comprehensive claims credits the distinction. The argument is, then, that moral relativism is self-contradictory, because that position has positive implications that are also universal. To the best of my reasoning, in other words, one could refuse to credit the distinction between universal and relative only if one could simply refuse the comprehensive order of reflection. But, as I have previously argued, a refusal is a denial. It is true, then, that the argument I advance presupposes the conclusion it seeks to defend, because the comprehensive order of reflection is implied by all reflection. But that is not to say that the conclusion is *assumed*, that is, arbitrarily posited. On the contrary, the conclusion is shown to be presupposed by showing that moral relativism is self-contradictory.

of reflection. As we have seen, however, this putative refusal *is* a denial; the distinction between the two is merely verbal.

But if no moral claims can be validated on historically specific grounds alone, then the denial of all religious or comprehensive convictions reduces to the denial of all moral claims and, therefore, all principles of justice. Absent a valid answer to the comprehensive question, there can be no valid distinction, general or specific, between authentic and inauthentic human activity. The embrace of this conclusion is, we may recall, expressed in the theory of human activity on which all ultimate ideals and, therefore, all evaluative affirmations are subrational. In chapter 3, I associated this theory with the privatist view of religious freedom on what I called its classic account, which is illustrated especially in Max Weber's understanding of Western "rationalization." Alternatively stated, the denial of all comprehensive convictions implies the classic amoralist claim, also expressed in some forms of nihilism, logical positivism, and existentialism: The choice of a purpose by which human activity is constituted is always merely a choice and never an exercise of reason; that is, the choice is never bound by a norm that identifies what one is rationally required or ought to choose. It may be apparent from what has been said, however, that this too is a self-refuting claim. To assert that one's choice of a purpose is never bound by a norm is also to assert a norm and, moreover, a comprehensive one—namely, that human authenticity as such is always and in all respects particular or relative to the activity in question.

To this criticism, it may be objected that a negation of all moral claims is hardly itself an assertion about human authenticity. So far from this assertion, the objection holds, amoralism claims that there is no such thing as human authenticity, because all human activity expresses merely a choice or decision. To the best of my reasoning, however, this objection is not convincing. In truth, amoralism itself implies a moral principle, because a human activity may choose contrary to the self-understanding amoralism asserts. Contrary to the claim that all choice of purpose is merely a decision, one may choose so to understand oneself that one affirms some understanding of human authenticity as such. One may believe, for instance, that all human activity ought to pursue the democratic ideal or ought to conform to the will of God—and may choose one's particular purposes accordingly. Indeed, it seems undeniable that most human individuals throughout most of human history, even among those who have been explicitly aware of amoralism, have at least explicitly believed that some ideal binds their choices and those of all other humans.

To be sure, the amoralist claims that all such beliefs are invalid. In doing so, however, she or he formulates a belief about human activity as such or a comprehensive self-understanding that purports to be valid. Thus, she or he cannot consistently hold that whether we understand ourselves in accord with *this* comprehensive belief is itself merely a choice. On the contrary, every human activity ought not to understand itself in terms of any moral norm because all such understandings are invalid. In other words, the amoralist asserts an understanding that every human activity ought to choose or to exemplify without duplicity, and the implied comprehensive norm might be formulated: Always choose arbitrarily. It is a norm because it identifies a self-understanding that an activity may choose against, and it is a self-refuting norm because one cannot be rationally required always to choose arbitrarily.[3] I conclude that the denial of all

---

3. An amoralist might seek to avoid this conclusion by saying that "one ought not to understand oneself in terms of any putative moral norm" is solely a theoretical or cognitive imperative and, therefore, neither is nor implies a moral imperative. On this defense, no activity whose comprehensive self-understanding affirms a moral norm is an immoral activity because no purpose is immoral. Hence, the imperative to choose the valid comprehensive belief neither is nor implies a moral imperative. But if an imperative is solely theoretical, then obedience to it can make no difference to one's choice of purpose. To the contrary, an activity whose comprehensive self-understanding affirms a moral norm may or may not choose the same purpose that it would have chosen had it believed that there is no moral norm. Accordingly, whether or not one chooses what the amoralist claims to be the valid comprehensive self-understanding at least may make a difference with respect to the choice of purpose, and the imperative to choose this self-understanding is not solely theoretical or cognitive. The imperative to choose a comprehensive self-understanding that so much as may make a difference to one's choice of purpose is a moral imperative.

Moreover, a difference in one's comprehensive self-understanding must make a difference to one's choice of purpose in the following respect: To believe that some comprehensive self-understanding is valid is to choose that any subsequent activities in which that belief is remembered or to which that belief is communicated (as when, for instance, the amoralist advocates amoralism) should also affirm its validity—at least in the absence of convincing reasons to the contrary. To this extent, at least, the imperative to choose the amoralist's comprehensive self-understanding identifies a required character of one's purpose and is a moral imperative.

religious or comprehensive convictions, whether in the name of moral relativism or of amoralism, could never be valid; it is self-refuting because it always implies an understanding of human authenticity as such.[4] In other words, the distinction between a negative comprehensive claim and the positive comprehensive claims that it denies is no distinction at all or is merely verbal.[5]

If the considerations I have presented serve to show that the comprehensive order of reflection cannot be consistently refused or denied, then they also confirm the understanding of human activity with which religion and politics were formally identified in chapter 2. Because humans lead their lives with understanding, every human activity chooses, at least implicitly, a comprehensive understanding of reality and authentic human purpose. The refusal or denial of all comprehensive convictions is self-refuting just because all understandings of or claims about the distinctive character of our lives imply the comprehensive order of reflection. Whatever else one may say about the religious history of humankind, the diverse attempts explicitly to represent human authenticity as such express irreducibly the singular character of the human adventure: Human

---

Conceding that human activity is morally required so to understand itself that its choice of a purpose is arbitrary, an amoralist may now assert that this is what is meant in the denial of all positive claims about human authenticity as such. But the point is that this assertion is self-contradictory precisely because the amoralist's claim about human activity as such is a positive claim about human authenticity as such. In other words, arbitrary choice among purposes is now advanced as the comprehensive purpose of human activity, and the amoralist cannot consistently hold that the choice of this comprehensive purpose is arbitrary.

4. In saying that both moral relativism and amoralism are "self-refuting," I use this term in the sense of "absolutely self-refuting" that is clarified by John Passmore: "The proposition *p* is absolutely self-refuting, if to assert *p* is equivalent to asserting *both p and not-p*" (Passmore: 60). The proposition "human authenticity is in all respects historically specific" and the proposition "no distinction between human authenticity and inauthenticity is valid or invalid" are both, I have argued, absolutely self-refuting because both imply a comprehensive understanding of human authenticity as such. Either is, therefore, equivalent to asserting both *p* and *not-p*. Alternatively, one may say that both claims are, by implication, logically self-contradictory.

5. That it is self-contradictory to deny all moral claims is, on my reading, the singular contribution of Kant's critique of practical reason, and I have elsewhere called this Kant's insight. For an extended discussion, see Gamwell: especially chapter 2.

activity as such is constituted by asking and answering the comprehensive question. We are bound to conclude, in other words, that this question identifies a rational order of reflection. At least in the respect that it presupposes the possibility of discussion and debate whose purpose is to determine which among diverse religious or comprehensive convictions should inform the body politic, the public view of religious freedom is coherent.

To conclude that a public discussion and debate can be identified by the comprehensive question is to imply that there is a criterion or norm for argument in accord with which comprehensive convictions can be assessed. Because a rational question has a valid answer, every rational question has a criterion or norm for the argument by which valid and invalid answers may be distinguished. If we ask, for instance, who was elected to the office of President of The United States in 1992, the meaning of the question, including as it does the stipulations with respect to presidential elections given in the United States Constitution, thereby includes the norm for argument. Should one assert that someone other than Bill Clinton was in fact elected, one would be bound to show that the votes cast by eligible voters, weighted according to the electoral votes allotted to the several states, were somehow miscounted and that an accurate accounting would in fact confirm the election of another candidate.

If the considerations we have already reviewed successfully show that the comprehensive question is rational, then they have also suggested, at least by way of illustration, the proper norm for the comprehensive order of reflection. The denial of all comprehensive convictions, I argued, is in truth the claim that human authenticity is always relative to historically specific conditions or to the decision of each human activity, and this answer to the comprehensive question is invalid because it is self-refuting. I now wish to show that all invalid answers to this question are similarly self-refuting, so that a comprehensive conviction is redeemed by argument when one shows that it is self-consistent or coherent.

Of course, no answer to any question can be valid if it is not self-consistent. With most questions, however, coherence in this sense is only a necessary and, therefore, not a sufficient condition of a valid answer. In contrast, coherence is also a sufficient condition of validity in the comprehensive order of reflection, and this criterion of validity is implied by the comprehensive question itself. Because the question asks about human authenticity as such, the valid answer is implied by every human activity, and, therefore, any claim at all about any human activity. Thus, an invalid answer to the comprehensive question implies the valid answer that it also denies, so that all invalid answers are self-refuting.

Let us, assume, for instance, that John Dewey is correct when he asserts that the "all around growth" of all human individuals is the comprehensive telos of human action (see 1957: 186), so that activity is authentic when or insofar as it pursues this telos. It follows that any contrary answer to the comprehensive question, for instance, the hedonist claim that human authenticity consists in maximizing the sensual pleasure of all human individuals, is self-refuting. Because the latter is a claim about human activity, it implies the comprehensive telos of all around growth and, therefore, refutes its own hedonism. But if all invalid comprehensive convictions are self-refuting, then an answer to the comprehensive question that is not self-refuting must be valid. Self-consistency or coherence is a necessary and sufficient condition of a valid comprehensive conviction and, therefore, the norm for argument about human authenticity as such, and the fact that this question does imply a norm with respect to which valid and invalid answers may be distinguished confirms that the question is a rational one.[6]

The Full Debate

Having sought to redeem the comprehensive order of reflection and insofar the public view of religious freedom, we may now return to the suggestion, noted at the close of the previous chapter, that Religionists might seek to appropriate Mead's reading of religious freedom. The Religionist position, we may recall, holds that religious freedom prescribes governmental neutrality to all theistic religions but does not prohibit nondiscriminatory governmental aid to theistic religion as such. We may also recall that theistic religion as such is said to be a subclass of the primary form of culture in terms of which comprehensive question is explicitly addressed, and I have proposed that we may identify this subclass in the following way: Human authenticity is said to derive from or be authorized by ultimate reality. Thereby, theistic religion as such is purportedly distinguished from secularistic answers to the comprehensive question, all of

---

6. The logic of the comprehensive question is discussed in greater detail in the Appendix to this work. See the section entitled "The Criterion of Comprehensive Reflection."

which hold that ultimate reality is indifferent or hostile to, even if it must permit, human authenticity.

On the appropriation of Mead that I have suggested, then, Religionists concede that a plurality of legitimate religions can be politically unified only if public argument among their adherents is possible—and, in this respect, Religionists now agree that the rationalist founders of the Republic provided the rationale for religious freedom. But Religionists also insist that this public discussion and debate is properly limited to theistic convictions. On this reading, in other words, the United States is constituted as a nation "under God," in Mead's sense; the Republic constitutionally affirms its responsibility to an "order and ultimate meaning in the universe." "The democratic way" (Mead 1963: 80), then, means a persisting public debate about the character of this order and ultimate meaning and, thereby, about the nation's responsibility. Accordingly, it is at least permissible for the state to encourage or support theistic religion as such.

To first appearances, this understanding of the public argument may seem to be perfectly sensible, because it is clearly possible to pursue many debates within the limitations of agreed on or hypothetical assumptions. For instance, a debate about the best institutional form of education might assume that it should be coeducational, so that argument about the other proper institutional characteristics proceeds on the condition that they be consistent with a coeducational setting. To be sure, some may denounce the entire discussion because, on their view, the intent to educate in the best possible manner is compromised by an arbitrary refusal to consider gender-specific institutions. Whatever the merit of that objection, however, a debate constituted by this refusal is not senseless; that is, answers to the question as posed can be rationally assessed and, therefore, the debate resolved. Similarly, then, it may seem possible to identify a public debate with the assumption that some actual or possible theistic religion is valid.[7] Whether or not it is wise to posit that the universe has "an order and ultimate meaning," to recur to Mead's phrase, that stipulation may seem perfectly sensible.

---

7. I mean by a "possible theistic religion" some appropriate answer to the comprehensive question that does not in fact function religiously but could be so represented. Given that religions are particular forms of culture, it is possible that all theistic religions are invalid, notwithstanding that human authenticity as such is authorized by ultimate reality. Similarly, we may speak of actual and possible religions.

But there is good reason to reject this understanding of the public debate about comprehensive convictions. Given the logic of the comprehensive question, it is not possible to assess candidate theistic answers without asking critically whether the valid answer is theistic or secularistic. This follows from the fact that all invalid answers to the comprehensive question are self-refuting. If human authenticity is not in truth authorized by reality as such, then all theistic convictions are incoherent, and it is not possible successfully to show that one incoherent claim is more credible than another. If, to the contrary, some actual or possible theistic religion is valid, it remains that a successful argument for this comprehensive conviction will invalidate all substantively different answers to the comprehensive question, theistic or secularistic. A debate limited to actual and possible theistic religions is either a futile debate or a debate not so limited.

In other words, a discussion and debate limited to theistic convictions is not a sensible argument because it cannot exclude critical reflection on the assumption it makes—namely, that some or other theistic conviction is valid. We may sensibly argue about the best institutional form of coeducational learning precisely because answers to this question can be redeemed while merely assuming that coeducation is better than gender-exclusive schooling. But if one cannot argue successfully in answer to a given question without simultaneously defending the supposed assumption with which it is asked, then in truth the question does not identify a sensible debate. The relevant question is one that also puts in question the assumption. Because all invalid answers to the comprehensive question are incoherent, one cannot successfully argue that a given theistic conviction is superior to others without including an argument for the claim that human authenticity is not secularistic. Thus, a debate limited to theistic convictions is not sensible, and a Religionist appropriation of Mead is not convincing. The question identifying public debate among any comprehensive convictions can be only the comprehensive question itself.[8]

---

8. Moreover, one cannot identify a more inclusive debate by including within the question an incoherent assumption. Some might propose that in fact the state should be explicitly neutral to *whether* the comprehensive question has a valid answer, so that religious freedom constitutes a discussion and debate in which the denial of all comprehensive convictions is one of the parties. On this proposal, the identifying question would be

Indeed, we are now in a position to discredit the very distinction between theistic religion and secularism, in the sense that is essential to the Religionist position. Perhaps nothing is so striking in the literature endorsing nondiscriminatory state support of theistic religion than the measure in which advocates take for granted that theistic and secularistic beliefs, as classes or kinds of comprehensive convictions, each of which includes differing convictions, are real alternatives. To be sure, there is sometimes a concession that theistic religion, at least for purposes of constitutional interpretation, is difficult to define with precision (see, e.g., Adams and Emmerich:

---

formulated: Is there a valid understanding of human authenticity as such and, if so, what is that understanding? As an alternative view of religious freedom, however, this proposal is also unconvincing, because its question assumes that the comprehensive order of reflection may not be sensible, and that assumption is self-refuting. One cannot constitute a more inclusive debate by adding a self-refuting assumption. In truth, there is a valid answer to the comprehensive question, so that this question identifies the debate. As a party to this debate, the denial of comprehensive reflection can only be represented as what in truth it is, namely, the comprehensive claim that human authenticity is always in all respects relative, either to given cultural of historical conditions or to the decision of each human activity.

We may formulate the same point with respect to the political process by underscoring that the objects of the debate are politically important convictions the state may not explicitly affirm or deny. The denial of all religious or comprehensive ideals is not itself a politically important conviction, because it is a solely negative claim, and the determination of the state's activities requires some or other positive moral principle. Those who insist on this denial advocate politically only insofar as they also assert some or other noncomprehensive or historically specific ideal as the grounds for political decision—for instance, the two principles of justice advocated by John Rawls. But any noncomprehensive moral principles might be asserted as the alternative to all comprehensive convictions. Thus, if religious freedom means state neutrality in the debate among comprehensive convictions and the denial of them all, the state could not explicitly affirm or deny any moral claims, that is, could not legislate at all. For this reason, as Rawls's proposal illustrates, political theorists who deny the comprehensive order of reflection typically do not identify religious freedom with a public debate about whether any comprehensive conviction is valid. On the contrary, this denial typically informs a political theory in which religions are privatized, at least with respect to basic principles of justice. If religious freedom means a free discussion and debate, its identifying question can only be the comprehensive question, and it is this question that identifies the kind of explicit claim proscribed to the state.

88–93). Still, the manifest burden of the position is to oppose the view that religious freedom prescribes state neutrality to the distinction between theistic religion and its denial. As a consequence, the possibility in principle of that distinction is an essential premise, and the discussion often proceeds without acknowledgment, much less examination, of that supposition.

To be sure, I too have distinguished between theistic and secularistic kinds of convictions. The former and not the latter, I have said, assert that human authenticity is authorized by ultimate reality. But this difference is, as I will try to show, merely verbal or has no real meaning. In contrast, the distinction essential to Religionists must be a real or substantive one; that is, the difference between theistic religion as such and secularism as such must make a difference to human life and, therefore, the body politic. Were this not the case, it would be pointless for the government to encourage or support theistic religion on a nondiscriminatory basis.

To say that the Religionist distinction between theism and secularism is merely verbal is not to say that comprehensive convictions are all really the same, as if it makes no difference which one we choose. On the contrary, they differ substantively in two senses, but neither sense allows the distinction that the Religionist position requires. Most obviously, there is a real difference between the valid answer to the comprehensive question and all others, and this difference identifies the all-important choice between authentic and inauthentic activity as such. But this is not a difference between classes or kinds of answers to the comprehensive question, where each class includes more than one answer. To distinguish theistic religion and secularism in that sense, we must be able to identify real differences between some invalid answers and others, such that some invalid answers belong in a class with the valid one and others do not. But invalid answers to the comprehensive question are all self-refuting or incoherent; each affirms by implication the valid answer that it also denies. Hence, there is no way to identify substantively which invalid answers do and which do not belong in the same class with the valid comprehensive conviction—and, therefore, no way to distinguish theistic religion as such in the manner that the Religionist position requires.[9]

---

9. In contrast, answers to any other question about human activity (excepting "yes or no" questions) may be distinguished into classes, each of which has more than one member. For instance, answers to the question "what is the best institutional form of education?" may be classified so that

We may also speak of real differences between invalid comprehensive convictions in the sense that particular purposes in which those beliefs are expressed may differ. Inauthenticity, in other words, may appear in differing ways as a consequence of differing duplicity in comprehensive self-understandings. Let us assume, for instance, that the pursuit of white supremacy and the pursuit of Aryan supremacy are both invalid understandings of human authenticity as such. At least in some circumstances, individuals who believe the former corrupt human activity in differing ways than those who choose the latter. White supremacists in the United States opposed Nazi Germany even while they sought to maintain a racist society in their country. But however different their expressions, such invalid convictions cannot be classified in the manner that the Religionist position requires. Since every invalid comprehensive belief is duplicitous, real differences in the particular purposes they inform do not allow some of these beliefs, in distinction from others, to be classified with the valid or authentic answer to the comprehensive question.[10]

---

one set of answers is identified by the common claim that education is best if its institutionalization is coeducational, and a second set is distinguished by the common claim that education should be gender-specific. Clearly, there may be more than one answer in each class, the members of which differ from each other in terms of the other characteristics that each attributes to the best institutional form of education. In each class, for instance, there might be one answer that endorses relatively small classrooms and another that endorses relatively large classrooms. Given that the valid answer belongs to one or the other of the two classes, that answer is classified with some invalid answers. But this classification is possible because coherence alone is not the criterion in accord with which the valid answer is validated; more than one answer to the question of the best institutionalized form of education is coherent. *Mutatis mutandis,* the same is the case with any question about human activity (excepting "yes or no" questions) whose valid answer is not determined by coherence alone

10. Invalid answers to the comprehensive question assert that one or more *non*comprehensive characteristics of human activities identify human authenticity as such; that is, these answers differ in terms of which particular or noncomprehensive characteristic each claims to be comprehensive. Thus, for instance, white supremacy and Aryan supremacy as comprehensive convictions each asserts that pursuit of dominance by a specific race is comprehensive, although they differ in which race is said to identify human authenticity as such. In contrast, the valid answer to the comprehensive question asserts only the comprehensive characteristics of human activity. Hence, the differences among invalid comprehensive convictions do not

Another way to approach this conclusion is to recognize that *all* invalid comprehensive convictions could be included in the class of theistic beliefs or, alternatively, the class of secularistic beliefs, depending only on how adherents choose explicitly to identify themselves. Since an invalid understanding of human authenticity as such implicitly affirms even as it also denies the valid answer to the comprehensive question, any such understanding could be explicitly represented as theistic or secularistic without making a real difference. In other words, no invalid comprehensive conviction is rationally bound to assert or, alternatively, to deny that human authenticity is authorized by ultimate reality. One cannot say, for instance, that a comprehensive commitment to white supremacy or to Aryan supremacy must be explicitly formulated as theistic or, alternatively, secularistic, because both convictions are incoherent. It is to the point, then, that both white supremacists and Aryan supremacists have in fact asserted their convictions on both theistic and secularistic grounds.

In sum, nothing real or substantive is at stake in asking whether those whose comprehensive conviction is invalid call themselves theistic or secularistic, and this is what I mean in saying that the classification the Religionist position requires is merely verbal. Only a valid religion is bound to be theistic, if in truth authentic human

---

allow some to be classified with the valid answer to the comprehensive question.

Someone might propose that all invalid answers to the comprehensive question can be roughly divided into those that are more and those that are less inauthentic, that is, those that do and those that do not corrupt human activity more fully, and that the latter may be classified with the valid comprehensive conviction. Let us grant that some invalid answers to the comprehensive question corrupt human activity less than others in most situations. On the assumption that human authenticity as such is, with Dewey, pursuit of the all around growth of all human individuals, it may be that a quietistic answer to the comprehensive question (for instance, the conviction that human authenticity as such seeks to maximize contemplation of nonhuman nature) does not, in most situations, corrupt human activity as seriously as does religious adherence to white racism. Even if invalid comprehensive convictions can be graded in this respect, the attempt to choose the less corrupting and classify them with the valid answer to the comprehensive question requires that one already know the valid answer. In other words, a class of theistic religions defined in this way is simply the assertion that some given answer to the comprehensive question is valid.

activity is authorized by ultimate reality, or is bound to be secularistic, if in truth ultimate reality is indifferent or hostile to our authenticity. Assuming that Religionists do not mean by "theistic religion" the class of all invalid religions, the only real meaning the term can have is either the class of all religions or the particular religion that a Religionist takes to be valid. Because all invalid religions represent duplicitous convictions, in other words, it is absurd for any adherent of a theistic religion to believe, as a matter of principle, that others who call themselves adherents of theistic religions are somehow more important to the authenticity or well-being of the body politic than those who call themselves secularistic. Precisely that belief is, however, what the Religionist position implies.

It now follows that nondiscriminatory state support of theistic religion could be politically significant only if it means either support for religious associations and activities as such, theistic or secularistic, or aid to a particular theistic religion that is taken to be valid. On the former alternative, theistic religion is not supported in the sense that Religionists intend; on the latter alternative, the aid is discriminatory. In a similar way, nondiscriminatory state support of secularism identifies a significant governmental purpose only if it means support of all religions or aid to a particular secularistic conviction that is taken to be valid. In other words, state support of some rather than all comprehensive convictions has no real meaning other than support of one such conviction and, therefore, the establishment of a religion. This result is, I judge, merely a reformulation of the earlier conclusion that a debate among some limited class of comprehensive convictions is not a sensible debate. Since a limited class of comprehensive convictions cannot be substantively distinguished, either the debate includes all answers to the comprehensive question or one must assume that a particular conviction is valid.

At the outset of this work, I argued summarily that the plurality of legitimate religions defining the modern political problematic should be considered *indeterminate*, and we are now in a position to redeem this claim more completely. As a matter of fact, the diversity of religions within some modern political communities has been decidedly limited. Numerically minor exceptions aside, for instance, the religious communities within the English colonies in America were all Christian, and it might be thought that the problem of modern politics could be so formulated that it asks about political unity among such a determinate plurality. But if a plurality of substantively differing religions can be politically unified only through a full and free public discussion and debate, and if this public debate cannot be coherently limited to a specific class of comprehensive convictions, then it follows that religious freedom legitimates an indeterminate plurality of religions. To legitimate debate about human authenticity as such is necessarily to legitimate adherents of all actual and possible religions, because a more limited class of participants cannot be substantively distinguished or does not constitute a sensible debate. It is this necessity that makes a theistic or secularistic interpretation of religious freedom incoherent. Political unification of an indeterminate plurality of religions through free discussion and debate is, then, what I mean by the public view of religious freedom.

The First Amendment

Although my principal purpose in this work is to pursue religious freedom as a philosophical principle rather than a provision of the United States Constitution, the public view of religious freedom has implications for judicial interpretation of the First Amendment. In order briefly to pursue this matter, let us assume that the Religionist reading of the First Amendment is historically correct in this respect: To the Congress that proposed and the several States that ratified that amendment, "no establishment" explicitly meant no state preference for one theistic religion in distinction from others, and, therefore, the amendment permitted governmental aid to theistic religion in distinction from secularism. Let us also accept the conclusion that nonpreferential state support of theistic religion makes no sense because religious freedom can coherently mean only a public discussion and debate among all answers to the comprehensive question. How shall the First Amendment be understood judicially? It will not help to say that the courts are bound by "the meaning of the words" (Bradley: 137), that is, by the meaning that the founding generation explicitly intended. This meaning is incoherent and, therefore, cannot coherently inform activities of the state.

I suggest that the courts have no alternative except so to interpret the Amendment that its proscription allows for coherent state activity. The prohibition against establishment of a particular comprehensive conviction is, it seems clear, the one aspect of the founding generation's intent that cannot be sacrificed. If, as I have argued, the only coherent alternative to such establishment is a public discussion and debate among all comprehensive convictions, then it follows that the courts have no alternative except so to interpret the First Amendment that it prescribes state neutrality toward all religions, whether theistic or secularistic. Even if we grant that most in the founding generation did not agree with the rationale for religious freedom more or less adequately expressed by rationalist founders such as Jefferson and Madison, the courts are bound to this rationale because there is no other coherent principle for judging the activities of the state.

The point might be restated in the following way: Many Religionists believe that most in the founding generation not only intended state aid to theistic religion but also connected this purpose with the hope that Christianity or even Protestant Christianity would dominate the religious life of the Republic. Still, such Religionists concede that this connection does not allow preferential state support of Christianity, because the founding generation clearly meant by "religion" something that was not exhausted by Christianity (see, e.g., Bradley: 141). In other words, preferential state support of Christianity would be inconsistent with the clear meaning of "no establishment of religion." Now grant, as I have argued, that nondiscriminatory state aid to theistic religion is also inconsistent with the clear meaning of "no establishment." However connected the former may have been to the latter in the intent of the founding generation, it follows that state neutrality toward all comprehensive convictions is the only clear meaning that the words can have.

This conclusion might be restated once more: Although the founding generation used the word "religion" to mean a broader class of convictions than the diversity of Christian denominations, it seems apparent that most people in that generation nonetheless equated religion with a belief in God, that is, belief that ultimate reality is a supreme being or individual. With the recognition that all religions do not affirm a divine being or individual, most interpreters agree that this equation is not consistent with the disestablishment of religion. Thus, some have proposed that the founders' use of "God," as my use of "theistic" throughout this work, must be understood in a formal sense, so that it means the authorization of human authenticity by ultimate reality but allows disagreements among religions regarding the character of ultimate reality. On this proposal, in other words, "God" does not necessarily refer to a supreme being or individual, and religions that affirm no such divine reality may be said nonetheless to include a belief in God. This, I take it, is Mead's point in saying that a debate "under God" is a debate about the "order and ultimate meaning in the universe" (Mead 1963: 80). But consistency with disestablishment also requires, I suggest, that the term "religion," whatever restricted intent may have been current in the eighteenth century, must now be understood in a strictly formal sense: Its meaning includes both theistic and secularistic convictions. If no other meaning allows a coherent disestablishment of religion, then the strictly formal sense of the term is the meaning the courts are not only permitted but also bound to assert.

Some who are persuaded by this conclusion may still object that it interprets only the establishment clause of the First Amendment, "Congress shall make no law respecting an establishment of religion," and, therefore, leaves underdetermined a proper understanding of the free exercise clause, "or prohibiting the free exercise thereof." This objection implies the widespread judgment that the two clauses are not coextensive. If the establishment clause proscribes state teaching or support for the teaching of any particular answer to the comprehensive question, the free exercise clause, it might be argued, also places religious activities in a special category. The state may not interfere with them except, perhaps, when some compelling public interest so requires—and, in that sense, religious practices are specially protected.

It has been said, for instance, that the state has no right to enforce the authority of historical perservation commissions against the freedom of religious communities to control their places of worship, or to coerce attendance at state authorized schools for children (at least children beyond a certain age) whose religious communities seek to withdraw from participation in the larger society. Similarly, the state ought to exempt from otherwise justifiable proscriptions activities that are part of the cultic practices of religious communities—for instance, exempt from a proscription on consumption of drugs the use of peyote in religious rites of the Native America Church or from a proscription on the service of alcoholic beverages to children the use of wine in Christian or Jewish worship. In this sense, the First Amendment prescribes nondiscriminatory state support of religion (in distinction from theistic religion) as such. As a reading of the First Amendment, then, the public view of religious freedom is said to be incomplete because it does not include, even if it does not preclude, the special protection of religious activity.

If the current work is not meant to sustain an argument in United States constitutional law, even less is it designed to address the relation between the two religion clauses of the First Amendment. Still, I am inclined to believe that special protection of religious practices may be justified as a necessary condition of the full and free debate religious freedom constitutes. On the public view, specifically religious activities are assigned a distinctive place in the political community. The state is denied the right to teach or support the teaching of any answer to the comprehensive question in order that the grounds for evaluating all of the state's activities may be left to the public debate alone. In the absence of special protection of religion, there is the ever-present danger that some may use the coercive power of the state to hinder the teaching of certain religions and, thereby, bias the public debate in accord with their own convictions or purposes. For instance, a law might require that all children attend state authorized schools. Although this law does not itself deny any religious convictions, some may support it because, say, they hope to hinder the pacifist teaching of certain religions that seek to withdraw from the larger society. Given this danger, one may defend as a practical condition necessary to full and free political assessment that state interference with religious teaching must be justified by a more demanding standard.

It might be said that interference with the teaching of a religious conviction is one thing and interference with other practices prescribed by that conviction (for instance, cultic activities) is something else. But we must remember that the function of specifically religious activity is so to represent an answer to the comprehensive question as to cultivate in the lives of religious adherents comprehensive self-understandings that are authentic. As a consequence, the modes of religious expression are highly symbolic or figurative and include symbolic practices.[11] The specifically religious activities of religious communities, in other words, *are* modes of religious teaching, and to interfere with these, absent special cause, is to compromise the full and free debate through which the state's interference with any activity is properly determined.

Still, virtually any particular activity is one that some or other individual or community could purport to be specifically religious, and, therefore, the special protection assigned to religious activities cannot be automatically granted to anyone who claims it. The state

---

11. See the section entitled "Religion and Politics" in chapter 2.

does have the right to insist that activities exempted from otherwise justified legal prescriptions are indeed those in which an answer to the comprehensive question is explicitly represented. This may require that the judiciary formulate guidelines in accord with which religious associations and activities are formally identified. In the end, there may be no escape from certain pragmatic tests, for instance, that the practices in question are those of an identifiable community or association and that those who claim exemption can reasonably articulate the relation of a given practice to the comprehensive conviction it is said to cultivate. To be sure, there is the danger that any such guidelines will themselves lead to bias in favor of some answers to the comprehensive question. But the alternative is the absence of special protection of religion, which would permit legislation that compromises the public debate, and the danger of judicial bias is preferable because the matter is then subject to the separation of powers.

In some such terms as these, I suspect, the free exercise clause may be so understood that it is in principle consistent with and required by the prescription of religious freedom. Both are expressions of the intent to constitute a full and free public debate. To be sure, it may be another question whether judicial decisions commended by each clause will in every particular set of circumstances be complementary, but it is the matter of constitutional principle on which I have sought to comment, and I will not here pursue the discussion of particular cases. In any event, it is important to underscore that any distinctive place proper to religious associations and activities is, on the public view of religious freedom, distinctive to *religious* associations and activities; that is, the government is bound to neutrality toward the difference between theistic and secularistic answers to the comprehensive question.

The completion of Mead in the public view of religious freedom may now be stated as follows: Religious freedom is nothing other than a political expression of the comprehensive question. Because a legitimate plurality of religions cannot be politically unified in principle unless religious convictions can be publicly debated, and because that debate cannot be coherently limited to some comprehensive convictions, the only solution to the modern political problematic is a free discussion and debate about alternative understandings of human authenticity as such. As a political principle, of course, such discussion and debate concerns the relevance of religious claims to what the state should do, that is, to the assessment of actual and possible activities of the state, and we may now include this point by saying that religious freedom means nothing other than a full and free political discourse. Because a modern political community cannot establish an answer to the comprehensive question, religious freedom constitutes the body politic by the question itself.

PART 4
THE DEMOCRATIC RESOLUTION

8

RELIGIOUS FREEDOM AND DEMOCRATIC DISCOURSE

On the public view, I have said, religious freedom means a free political discussion and debate among answers to the comprehensive question. In the previous chapters, I have sought to argue for this view by showing that (1) religious freedom cannot be coherently affirmed absent the affirmation that comprehensive convictions can be assessed in free discussion and debate; that is, religious freedom is not consistent with the theory of religion as nonrational; and (2) a free discussion and debate among answers to the comprehensive question cannot be coherently denied; that is, one cannot coherently deny that the comprehensive question identifies a rational order of reflection. But success in redeeming both claims is not a sufficient defense of the public view. One may agree that a free discussion and debate among comprehensive convictions is a necessary condition of religious freedom and also concede that this discussion and debate is possible—and yet remain unpersuaded that religious freedom is a coherent political principle. This is because the previous discussion has offered relatively little with respect to a theory of a modern political constitution, including therein the meaning of good citizenship that a modern political constitution entails.

I have previously noted that the modern political problematic may be formulated either politically or religiously. On the former, the question is: How, if at all, is politics consistent in principle with a plurality of legitimate religions? On the latter, the question is: How, if at all, may adherents of a plurality of legitimate religions consistently be citizens of the political community? Precisely because religions represent comprehensive convictions and, therefore, claims about the comprehensive condition of authentic politics, the modern political problematic is constitutional in character. Accordingly, the question in which it is expressed may now be restated in order to make explicit the importance of a constitutional theory. Politically, the problematic may be formulated: What constitutional principle, if any, is consistent with a plurality of legitimate religions? Religiously, the problematic may be formulated: What constitutional principle, if any, can be consistently affirmed by adherents of a plurality of legitimate religions? Of course, the two formulations are only verbally different, so that an answer to either question is an answer to the other. Still, objections to the public view of religious freedom may focus on its claim to unite the political community or, alternatively, on its claim to be consistent with adherence to any religion. In this final part of the work, then, I will pursue a constitutional theory in the measure required to address what are, so far as I can see, the relevant objections. In the present chapter, I will seek to sustain the public view against objections that it is not a principle of political unity, and, in the next chapter, I will address objections that this view cannot be consistently affirmed by at least some religious adherents.

As we pursue this task, it is important to note at the outset the constitutionally *definitive* character of religious freedom. This principle cannot be merely one constitutional principle among others; all implications taken into account, it is the *only* constitutional principle. One may even say that religious freedom *is* the constitution, in the sense that other constitutional prescriptions are, properly speaking, stipulations necessary to the full and free political discourse that religious freedom constitutes. This follows because it is the comprehensive question that the state is not permitted to answer. If the character of human authenticity as such and, therefore, the comprehensive grounds for evaluation are to be publicly contested, then all activities of the state are to be assessed by this discussion and debate, and the only prescriptions proper to the constitution are those required to make this assessment possible.

I assume here the definition of a constitution that I offered in chapter 2—namely, those explicit principles in accord with which the state as such and, therefore, politics as such are defined in a given political community. On this assumption, the other constituting prescriptions of a body politic identified by religious freedom can be only the necessary conditions of the full and free political discourse. In other words, the constitution should answer those questions and only those questions that must be answered in order to have this kind of political process. In saying this, however, one must underscore that the process in question is *political*, that is, consists in activities through which an association explicitly asks and answers the question of the state it includes. Decisions must be made and, since they are associational decisions, executed; and this is what I mean in calling the discussion and debate a full and free political discourse.

Accordingly, it might be argued that the constitution must identify the body politic or the participants in the discussion and debate, the rights of participants or citizens without which the discourse could not be full and free, a procedure in accord with which the discourse informs decisions about the activities of the state, a procedure for executing such decisions and for enforcing the prescriptions of the constitution itself, and a procedure for adjudicating differences with respect to the meaning of such decisions or of the constitutional prescriptions themselves. Whether or not these examples exhaust the necessary conditions of a full and free political discourse, political questions that are not about such conditions are not properly answered in the constitution but, rather, are properly debated within the body politic so constituted. If the discourse is to be full and free, moreover, the constitutional conditions themselves must be subject to continual assessment in the body politic; that is, they should include a procedure for changing or amending the constitution. Given religious freedom, in other words, "the distinctive bond of a civil multitude" is, to recall John Courtney Murray's proposal, "that exercise of reason which is argument" (Murray: 7). The body politic is constituted as an argument. What not only allows but also requires one to say this without qualification is the affirmation, in contrast to Murray, that comprehensive convictions themselves can be assessed or validated only by appeal to human experience and reason.

Political Discourse and Democratic Decision

Given that a constitution defined by religious freedom can consistently prescribe only the necessary conditions of a full and free political discourse, it may be objected that the public view of religious freedom does not in fact resolve the modern political problematic because a body politic so constituted cannot be expected to make the decisions that its unification requires. Debates, after all, can be interminable, in the sense that explicit agreement among the participants never occurs. Its absence may be all the more probable when the debate includes answers to the comprehensive question and all but inevitable when the argument includes many differing answers, each of which commands a large number of adherents. In contrast, political unification requires explicit agreement, in the sense that the body politic must decide for one course of action by the state rather than another, even if the course of action is not to have a policy with respect to some particular aspect of the common life. But, the objection concludes, if full and free public debate does not imply a common conclusion and political unity requires one, then the former cannot be a political discourse, and the public view of religious freedom is not a political principle after all.

Alternatively stated, the issue is whether the principle of religious freedom is consistent with any procedure by which the activities of the state are in fact decided, and the objection holds that there is no such procedure, other than, perhaps, that of unanimous agreement.[1] Participants in a full and free debate have no reason in principle to accept a decision with which they disagree; hence, a political community constituted by religious freedom cannot be expected to make the decisions its unification requires. Of course, a decision may be coercively imposed on those who disagree, but the objection is that such coercion contradicts the constitutional affirmation of full and free debate.

One might wonder whether, on this objection, it is possible for politics to include any legitimate debate at all, even one that is not inclusive of a plurality of legitimate religious convictions. Let us suppose that a body politic is constituted by an established religion, meaning that (1) citizens are bound in principle to assess possible activities of the state in accord with the understanding of human authenticity identifying that religion, but (2) are free to debate whether some or other particular course of action is prescribed or permitted by that common conviction. Significant disagreement about particular activities of the state might still obtain, and the question remains: What reason do citizens have to accept a political decision with which they disagree? But the objection will maintain that an established religion at least may include a general principle authorizing some decision-making procedure other than unanimous agreement. For instance, the authority of kings or priests, or, alternatively, of an elected legislature may be religiously legitimated, given only that those so empowered should be informed by whatever public debate occurs within the convictions of the established religion. Because it is authorized by the religion in question, the decision-making procedure is overriding, in the sense that citizens who debate particular political policies are bound to accept a decision legitimately taken even if they disagree with it.

---

1. Some may contend that even unanimous agreement is an unacceptable decision-making procedure, given full and free debate. Participants must always be free to change their minds and, therefore, cannot be bound to any decision, even one with which they previously agreed.

Thus, this first objection to religious freedom is directed specifically against the constitution of a political discourse inclusive of argument about human authenticity as such. Absent common adherence to some explicit answer to the comprehensive question, the objection maintains, it will not be possible consistently to prescribe a political decision-making procedure. One's disagreement may be a consequence of the comprehensive conviction that one affirms, even after debate, and a comprehensive conviction cannot be overridden. The specter of conflict among a plurality of legitimate religions that is irresolvable except by force reappears. The modern political problematic persists.

Since the objection holds that a commitment to a full and free debate cannot require commitment to common decisions with which one disagrees, its point may be expressed by saying that such debate may in fact be anarchistic. With this formulation, however, the objection displays its own inconsistency, because no full and free debate can be anarchistic. Any such debate must be ordered. It cannot proceed without, for instance, an agreement regarding participants and some commonly accepted rules of their association. All participants cannot speak at the same time, and, if the argument includes a large number of individuals and groups, so that it cannot occur in a common assembly, the rules for communication become highly complex. But if some or other commonly agreed conditions are *necessary* to any full and free debate, then the commitment to such a debate requires an overriding commitment to decisions about the rules that may not receive unanimous consent. As we have seen, the participants in a full and free debate may not unanimously agree on anything.

It is true that the rules in accord with which a debate is ordered are logically prior to the debate itself, in the sense that some such rules are its necessary condition. They constitute the debate. Thus, one might assume that some such rules have been decided, because in their absence there is no debate to talk about, and that continued participation in the debate is itself an expression of consent to these rules, so that they continually receive the unanimous consent of those who participate. But the constituting rules of the debate are, if the debate is in truth full and free, themselves a possible subject of debate, that is, of assessment toward the possible end of change or reformulation. To be sure, this debate about the proper rules of the debate must proceed in accord with the given rules, but, in that case, participants who advocate a change are in fact accepting rules with which they disagree. For these participants, the given rules represent a previous decision, commitment to which overrides disagreement. In this sense, at least, a commitment to decisions that overrides disagreement with those same decisions is not inconsistent with but, rather, required by commitment to a full and free debate.

It now follows that commitment to a full and free debate also requires a commitment to a procedure through which decisions are taken. This latter commitment is implied because decisions must be taken about the ordering rules of the debate itself when those rules are the object of disagreement. One might insist that this decision-making procedure should be that of unanimous agreement; only decisions about the rules unanimously taken can subsequently override disagreement. But this too is a rule of the debate subject to disagreement and possible change. If the ordering rules of a given full and free debate include the stipulation that the rules can be changed only through unanimous agreement, then the merit of this rule can itself be debated, and the participants can decide unanimously to substitute for unanimity some other procedure. Commitment to that full and free debate then requires overriding commitment to subsequent decisions about the rules that are taken through a procedure other than unanimous agreement.

Once we recognize that participation in a full and free debate requires commitment to a decision-making procedure that overrides disagreement with the decisions taken, it becomes apparent that the decisions to be taken need not be limited to the ordering rules of the debate itself. For this limitation also represents a decision subject to disagreement and change. Participants in the debate may decide, in accord with their decision-making procedure, to make other kinds of decisions and to stipulate a procedure, not necessarily that of unanimity, for those decisions—and continued participation in that debate then includes an overriding commitment to those decisions. The kind of decisions that a given full and free debate will decide to make and the associated decision-making procedure will, or at least should, depend on the purpose for which an association engages in the debate. Some may hold, for instance, that a university, properly understood, is an association whose purpose is critical reflection as such and, therefore, an association that is constituted as a full and free debate about whatever subjects its participants judge to be important. Summarily speaking, then, the kind of decisions that this association should take concern membership in the university, the ordering of its debate, and the maintenance of the association given the social and political context in which it exists—and its procedure for making these decisions should be appropriate to its purpose.

But, now, one of the possible purposes of a full and free debate is political. The association is constituted in order explicitly to decide the activities of the state it includes. Thus, there is no inconsistency in the claim that such a debate constitutes the body politic, meaning that commitment to this full and free debate includes commitment to a political decision-making procedure that overrides disagreement with the decisions taken. When the association constituted is political, moreover, a viable constitution is not likely to prescribe unanimity as the decision-making procedure, at least if, as with most political associations, the community to be governed includes a large number of members.

Still, if a body politic is constituted as a full and free political discourse, the kind of decisions it takes are limited in this respect: The state should not engage in any activities that compromise the necessary conditions of full and free debate. Among other things, this limitation implies that the state should not teach or support the teaching of any religion or answer to the comprehensive question. Given that the relation between politics and the comprehensive order of reflection is properly a constitutional matter, the state could properly teach or support the teaching of a religion only if the constitution endorses some comprehensive conviction. But a constitutional stipulation identifying the comprehensive condition of good politics is inconsistent with the constitution of a full and free political discourse. The fact that constitutional provisions are themselves subject to debate does not alter this conclusion. For the constitutional establishment of a religious conviction identifies the comprehensive purpose in terms of which even constitutional debate properly occurs. In other words, it would be self-contradictory for a constitution to identify the comprehensive grounds of evaluation and simultaneously affirm debate about those grounds. A body politic constituted as a full and free discourse must be constituted by religious freedom.

In a political community so constituted, there is also the following limitation on the decision-making procedure that it includes: The procedure must be of such a kind that decisions are maximally informed by the political discussion and debate. Were this limitation transgressed, the constitution would again be inconsistent; the political discourse is constituted in order that better and worse alternatives for the state's activities may be determined by it. Given conformity with this prescription, however, one may say that commitment to the decision-making procedure overrides one's disagreement with the decisions that it yields. Contrary to the objection to which we have been attending, then, a plurality of legitimate religions is not inconsistent with the decisions by which the political process unifies the political community if all religious adherents are united in a free debate about human authenticity as such in its relevance to the decisions of the state. But just this union is what religious freedom, on the public view, constitutes. The legitimacy of a religion *is* the right of its adherents to advocate its claims in the political discourse.

It now follows that all individuals governed by the state who could be participants in the political process should be citizens. The discourse should be *free* in the sense that all members of the community whose natural capacities permit political participation should be free to participate.[2] Moreover, political freedom means equal freedom. All individuals whose capacities permit political participation should be equal in whatever respects freedom to participate requires. Political freedom in this sense is a necessary condition of the discourse precisely because it is full, that is, includes a discussion and debate about human authenticity as such or is constituted by religious freedom. Because no particular comprehensive conviction is constitutionally prescribed, the disagreement of any individual with decisions that are taken can be overridden in principle only because the decisions were maximally informed by a discourse in which she or he, along with all others, is equally free to participate. Religious freedom means that government "of the people" is "by the people," just as, because it intends to be consistent with human authenticity as such, it is "for the people."

In contrast, a provision that limits citizenship to a certain class of possible participants or in some other manner favors its part in the body politic (for instance, a stipulation that only owners of landed property enjoy the franchise) contradicts religious freedom. Any such stipulation asserts that other possible citizens are obligated by decisions the favored class takes or has an undue opportunity to deter-

---

2. Children, for instance, may not yet have developed the natural capacities that political participation requires. I here beg the question of how to identify the relevant capacities, although it follows from what has been said that any individual who has the capacity to choose a religion also has the capacity to be a participant in the political process.

mine, and this decision-making procedure cannot override the religious convictions of those who are less favored participants unless some comprehensive conviction authorizing the discrimination is taught to all members of the community. A political discourse that is not free is, in other words, consistent only with an established religion. We may say, then, that the phrase "full and free political discourse" is redundant, even if a useful redundancy, because "free" makes explicit the equal participation of all possible citizens that "full political discourse" or religious freedom implies.[3]

In this context, we may recall that, on Mead's account, Abraham Lincoln recognized religious freedom as "the democratic way." It is appropriate, in other words, to define democracy as the constitutional form of political association that prescribes political decision making maximally informed by a full and free discourse, and we may say that political communities are more or less democratic insofar as they approach that ideal. I will not attempt here to pursue

---

3. It does not follow, so far as I can see, that any association whose purpose is a full and free debate ought to be so constituted that its members are equal participants in all decision making. If a university may be understood as a full and free debate about whatever subjects its members judge important, the "constitution" or statutes of this association may nonetheless assign certain decisions to, say, a board of trustees, thereby expressing the judgment that, for practical reasons, this full and free debate is better protected and enhanced in this way. This "constitutional decision" is not inconsistent with the character of a university because the university is a voluntary association, so that those who disagree with its statutes or with decisions that its board of trustees takes may choose not to become members or to withdraw. In contrast, a political association has as its purpose the governance of all activities and associations within the political community, so that membership in this community has traditionally been called involuntary; one does not choose to become a member or to withdraw. To be sure, emigration is, at least for some, not impossible, as exemplified by those who chose to move to Canada rather than obey the selective service laws of the United States during its prosecution of the war in Vietnam. But renouncing one's political membership is a decision the consequences of which are generally so profound that the political association cannot be considered voluntary. Thus, the withdrawal of one's commitment to the political community has traditionally taken the form of rebellion or revolution rather than emigration. It is, then, because the political community is involuntary that a political association constituted as a full and free debate must include as an equal participant in the political process any member of the community who could participate.

in detail a theory of democratic decision-making procedures but simply use this term to mean the manner of decision making proper to a body politic constituted as a full and free discourse.[4] All implications taken into account, then, we may say that religious freedom is the necessary and sufficient constitutional principle of democracy, and this principle unites politically a legitimate plurality of religions just because it prescribes that political decisions be taken through democratic discourse.

On Mead's revised account, moreover, the Republic chose democracy because, citing Jefferson, "truth...is the proper antagonist to error, and has nothing to fear...unless by human interposition disarmed of her natural weapon, free argument and debate" (cited in Mead 1963: 82). Religious freedom, says Mead, "was clearly envisaged as the deliberate creation of a situation where every religious opinion and practice, having the right to free expression, would continually contend with all others in order that error might be exposed to view and the truth be recognized" (1963: 82–83). On this account, the United States Constitution chose democratic discourse as the proper way for the body politic most fully to approach the truth or to be authentic. As defined by religious freedom, in other words, democracy is a political expression of the rationalist or Enlightenment affirmation that the truth about human life and the world in which it is set is accessible to reason and, therefore, that all human understandings are properly assessed only by appeal to human experience and reason or by argument.[5]

---

4. In doing so, I do not intend to imply that there is a single, detailed decision-making procedure that alone is properly democratic. Alternatives for aspects of such a procedure may well be a matter of preference. It may also be the case that a constitution properly stipulates differing kinds of decision-making procedures for differing kinds of decisions, because the difference may be required in order to help insure that decisions are maximally informed by full and free political discourse. It might be argued, for instance, that decisions about the constitution itself are so profound in terms of their consequences for the political community that a necessary condition of an amendment being maximally informed by full and free political discourse is a more demanding decision-making procedure. Again, the differing circumstances of differing political communities—including their size, composition, and particular political history— may well commend differences with respect to procedure without violation of the general prescription that this procedure be democratic.

5. To say that all understandings can be rationally assessed does not imply, some may object, that all understandings can be assessed *only* by appeal to

The democratic resolution, then, means that no politically relevant claim can be redeemed or validated by appeal to the fact that some individual, community of individuals, or tradition of thought and practice asserts or makes the claim. The commitment to human experience and reason is the denial of every such authoritarian affirmation. The fact that some understanding has been accepted by some who have gone before us, no matter how widespread that adherence or how long it has endured, is not a sufficient condition of its validity. On the rationalist account of democracy, this is the case with respect to all claims about the activities of the state because it is also the case with respect to all answers to the comprehensive question, each of which purports to identify the comprehensive condition of authentic politics. In sum, democracy expresses politically the affirmation that "free argument and debate" are, finally, the only "natural weapon" of truth.

Since the democratic discourse is full and free, continuing debate about the merit of decisions that have been taken must be constitutionally protected. One might formulate this point by saying that not changing a decision is itself a decision, and this latter decision too should be maximally informed by full and free debate. Thus, the overriding commitment to decisions that are constitutionally taken is not a commitment to agree with those decisions but, rather, to respect or comply with the law—and those who disagree with a legislative enactment must have full and free opportunity to persuade the body politic that the law should be changed. It also follows, of course, that the constitutional stipulations identifying necessary conditions of the political discourse must themselves be subject to continuing assessment and, therefore, open to change. As we have mentioned, a body politic constituted as a democracy requires constitutional provision for amending the constitution.

---

reason. On this objection, one might hold that a certain claim is accessible to reason *and* can be redeemed by appeal to something else, for instance, a sacred text. But this objection is not convincing. The appeal to a sacred text seeks to validate a given claim by appeal to some other claim or claims, and, if all understandings can be rationally assessed, then this is true of the claims expressed in the text. In contrast, the appeal to reason is not the appeal to another claim, since rational argument as such is not itself a claim but, rather, the general form of validation in distinction from assertion. Thus, appeal to a text is valid if and only if the claims of the text can be redeemed by appeal to reason, but not vice-versa.

Political Discourse and the Democratic Constitution

The reassertion that democracy must provide for constitutional amendment may renew, now on another level, the objection that religious freedom on the public view is not a political principle or cannot unify the body politic. Commitment to full and free political discourse, I have said, includes an overriding commitment to comply with the state's decisions, given only that the body politic, including its decision-making procedure, is in truth democratic. It then follows, the renewed objection runs, that one's overriding commitment to constitutionally taken decisions disappears if one is convinced that the current constitution is not authentically democratic. In other words, one is bound to respect or comply with the decisions that have been taken only if they are maximally informed by full and free debate; but one may hold that the constitution does not in fact prescribe the necessary conditions for a body politic constituted as an argument and, thereby, consistently claim that one has no obligation to obey the law.

For example, a given United States citizen may believe that full and free political discourse in this country is significantly compromised by the substantial social and economic inequality, or at least the toleration of substantial poverty, that characterizes the United States political community. This citizen agrees that certain political rights (for instance, rights to the franchise; to freedom of speech, press, and assembly; to due process; and to equal protection of the laws) are necessary conditions of full and free political discourse. But she or he also holds that all participants in the political process are not relevantly free, and, therefore, decision-making cannot be authentically democratic in the absence of a constitutional right to certain social and economic resources. Accordingly, this citizen may deny any obligation to obey the laws, or, at least, those laws the debate about which has been significantly compromised by economic inequality or by the unequal opportunity of the poor to participate.

Moreover, it seems apparent that disagreement about the constitutional conditions proper to a democratic political community at least may be a consequence of the difference between or among comprehensive convictions. An assessment of the constitution is itself an evaluation of human activity and, therefore, implies some understanding of authentic human activity as such. For instance, the difference, roughly characterized, between those who hold that certain political rights are sufficient to establish a full and free political discourse and those who assert that democracy also requires a right to certain social and economic resources at least may derive from differing understandings of authentic human freedom as such. Religious freedom, in other words, at least permits disagreement among adherents of differing comprehensive convictions about whether the current constitution is democratic. Since this is disagreement about the constitution, the objection maintains, those who dissent from the current constitution are not bound to comply with constitutionally taken decisions. Thus, the objection concludes, the putative coherence of religious freedom as a political principle disappears when one raises the level of disagreement from decisions within the constituted political process to those about the constitution itself. At the latter level, the modern political problematic reappears, notwithstanding that all religious adherents are committed to democratic discourse, and political unification cannot be achieved in principle except by force.

A response to this objection may begin by underscoring the distinction between political debate that does not include constitutional dissent and disagreement about the constitution itself. In the former, a participant may properly advance and defend any political decision consistent with the constitution that she or he believes to be authentic. If the participant is a religious adherent, she or he may properly advocate any political decision consistent with the constitution that she or he believes to be required by her or his comprehensive conviction. With respect to constitutional disagreement, however, the decisions that are properly advanced and defended are in principle limited, because these decisions are about the necessary conditions of a full and free political discourse. In other words, constitutional decisions properly identify the optimal conditions in which any political claim, including any comprehensive conviction, may be publicly assessed as a part of the political process.

I use the term "optimal conditions" to express the fact that the necessary conditions of a democratic discourse may be, in some respects, historically variable and, therefore, may change over time. For instance, the social and economic resources, if any, to which citizens should have a constitutional right of access may differ from one period to the next in the history of a democratic political community—due, say, to a change in the wealth of the community and the technology available to it. This fact complicates the possibility of constitutional disagreement, because some citizens who earlier agreed that certain political problems were legislative in character may subsequently believe that they have become constitutional issues. But if it is complicated, the distinction between constitutional disagreement and political contention exclusive of it is not confused. It is one thing to identify the necessary conditions of a full and free political discourse and another to participate in the discussion and debate those conditions establish.

This distinction is analogous to that between the rational criteria in accord with which argument occurs and the claims that are assessed by appeal to those criteria. This latter distinction is required in order to identify what an argument for the relevant kind of claim is. Of course, the relevant criteria may themselves be subject to argument, but that fact also presupposes and, therefore, does not confuse the distinction. Absent the distinction between criteria of validation and claims to validity, in other words, claims could not be argued but only asserted. Similarly, then, argument within a political association requires a distinction between the necessary conditions of political argument and the practice of arguing for claims. This distinction is necessary in order to identify what the practice is. That the association may also argue about the character of these necessary conditions also presupposes and, therefore, does not confuse the distinction. Absent the distinction, then, political interaction could not be argument but only the assertion of claims, and the political process would be solely a matter of force.

We may identify the distinct character of an authentically democratic constitution by saying that its provisions are politically formal or that they articulate formal principles of justice. The term "formal" here means that these provisions properly identify or establish the political practice in which all claims about justice may be fully and freely debated. To insist on this distinction is not to deny that the provisions of an authentically democratic constitution are themselves claims about justice and, therefore, imply some understanding of the comprehensive grounds for evaluation or some comprehensive conviction. The point is, rather, that these constitutional claims are distinct and may be called formal because they identify the conditions in which these very claims—and, therefore, all claims about justice—may be assessed in full and free political discourse. The constitution might stipulate, for instance, that every member of the political community should have access to economic and social resources that are sufficient to insure "freedom from want." The constitution thereby asserts that the right to such resources is necessary to equal participation in the political association and, therefore, to the practice in which all political claims, including this constitutional stipulation, are assessed in full and free political discourse.

It follows, then, that every religious adherent committed to democracy is bound by that commitment to draw the distinction between formal and material claims about justice, even if, in doing so, every such adherent will be informed by what she or he takes to be the valid answer to the comprehensive question. In other words, this distinction limits the proper object of constitutional dissent. With this limitation, I will now try to show, the public view of religious freedom solves the modern political problematic notwithstanding the possibility of constitutional disagreement.

Since a legitimate plurality of religions may result in differing convictions about the proper character of a democratic constitution, the public view of religious freedom does imply the possibility of constitutional dissent that releases the dissenter from the overriding commitment to constitutionally taken decisions. Notwithstanding that religious adherents are all committed to democratic discourse, then, a political community may not be unified without force, one form of which is revolution—where revolution here means the process through which the constitution is changed by nonconstitutional and (since democracy is a constituted political process) nondemocratic means.[6] But the limitation in principle on the proper character of constitutional disagreement is pertinent to whether or not one is released from one's commitment to obey the law. Given that such disagreement is properly about the conditions of full and free political discourse, constitutional dissent does not remove one's overriding commitment to constitutionally taken decisions unless one believes, all relevant things considered, that the ideal of democracy itself prescribes revolution.[7] Constitutional dissent only *may* release one from obedience to the law. One is consistently outside

---

6. I will not discuss the possibility of civil disobedience as a course expressing constitutional dissent. The proper understanding of civil disobedience is, to be sure, important to clarity about the relation between democratic politics and constitutional disagreement. But the question our current discussion seeks to address is more general, namely, whether or not the possibility of constitutional disagreement contradicts the claim that religious freedom is a political principle.

7. This use of the term "ideal of democracy" differs from Dewey's term "democratic ideal," which I have previously cited illustratively. For Dewey, the democratic ideal is equivalent to the all-around growth of all human

the law only with the considered conviction that the current constitution so compromises democracy that one's commitment to democracy itself proscribes participation in the body politic. Properly speaking, revolution is itself an expression of the commitment to democratic discourse, that is, commitment to constituting a political community in accord with the public view of religious freedom.[8]

This constraint is all the more severe because, as we have emphasized, a democratic constitution properly stipulates a procedure through which the constitution itself may be changed. Given such a procedure, a conviction that the current constitution is not fully democratic (because, for instance, it does not stipulate certain social and economic as well as political rights) does not overcome one's obligation to the law unless the following condition also obtains: It is probable that pursuit of a political revolution will result in a more democratic constitution, or will do so more quickly, than will a constitutional attempt to amend or change the current one. In making that judgment, those who consider revolution are bound to take into account the differing constitutional convictions of all other religious adherents, who are informed by their comprehensive convictions. I do not mean to say that this condition is a sufficient condition for revolutionary activity. The political instability and possible violence that revolution involves must also be assessed. But the greater probability that a more democratic constitution will result or result more quickly from the pursuit of revolution is a necessary condition of justified release from constitutionally taken decisions.[9]

---

individuals and, therefore, identifies the comprehensive purpose of human activity. As specified to politics, then, it identifies the most general material principle for evaluating the activities of the state. On my usage, "the ideal of democracy" identifies neither the comprehensive purpose nor a material principle of political evaluation. On the contrary, the term identifies a formal political principle in accord with which the comprehensive purpose and, therefore, all material principles for political evaluation are subjects of full and free discussion and debate.

8. In formulating this point, I have been greatly assisted by Karl R. Popper's argument for "the open society." See Popper, especially 1: chap. 10, and 2: 149–52.

9. This does not mean that a commitment to democracy entails the conviction that all political communities should be constituted by religious freedom. Democracy may not be possible in some historical circumstances. For instance, democratic participation may be impossible absent access in a

It follows, so far as I can see, that an enduring democratic community requires a constitutional consensus, that is, a consensus among citizens, notwithstanding their diverse comprehensive convictions, that the constitution is acceptably democratic. To believe that the constitution is acceptably democratic is to judge that the ideal of democracy will be more fully realized by accepting the conditions for political discourse stipulated by the current constitution, including its procedure for constitutional change, than by the pursuit of revolution. This need for a constitutional consensus makes the persistence of any political community constituted by religious freedom uncertain, even if all citizens are committed to full and free political discourse.

Nonetheless, the outcome is not simply accidental. Because some answer to the comprehensive question is valid, some constitution is, given the historical circumstances of the community, authentically democratic. That this is so is presupposed in the distinction between formal and material claims about justice and, therefore, also presupposed in the constraint on revolution, namely, that it should be itself an expression of the commitment to democracy. Insofar as the current constitution approaches the authentic conditions of democratic discourse, then, there is reason in principle to hope that political discourse about the constitution will approach the truth about the constitution, and its acceptability will be widely affirmed. This is not to say that one hopes for consensus about the valid answer to the comprehensive question. The constitution is limited to formal principles of justice, that is, necessary conditions of a full and free political discussion and debate. Hence, there may be consensus that the constitution is acceptable notwithstanding substantial disagreement within the practice it defines.

------

certain measure to certain material and social resources, including education, that simply cannot be secured in situations of massive and unavoidable poverty. Since "ought implies can," religious freedom is not a coherent political principle unless circumstances are such that there can be full and free political discourse or, at least, some significant approximation thereto. In this work, I have assumed that democracy is, in this sense, possible. Still, commitment to democracy implies, I believe, that democracy is the formal telos of all political life. Insofar as present conditions prescribe some other constitution, its proper purpose is so to define politics that the community may pursue whatever change in conditions is required to make democracy possible. But the argument for this claim is not germane to the present work.

Introducing the term "constitutional consensus" reminds us that, for John Rawls, a stable democratic society requires an "overlapping consensus."[10] But the meanings of these two terms differ in a way that expresses the difference between the public view and Rawls's privatist view of religious freedom. Participants in an overlapping consensus, on Rawls's usage, commonly endorse a freestanding conception of justice, such that the differences among comprehensive doctrines are irrelevant to the basic structure of society; or, to say the same, the freestanding principles of justice set the limits to permissible comprehensive doctrines. The object of an overlapping consensus, in other words, is a material conception of justice, meaning that the task of political deliberation and decision is to specify these material principles, at least so far as the basic structure is concerned. Precisely because the object of agreement is material, it sets material limits to permissible comprehensive doctrines and its justification must be freestanding. The basis on which one may hope for an overlapping consensus, then, is historically specific. Given the endurance of free institutions, which initially may have been accepted as a modus vivendi, the comprehensive doctrines that command larger numbers of adherents may become adjusted to the concept of freestanding principles of justice and may in fact overlap on particular principles, since they are justified by appeal to the very political culture that is implicit in the tradition of free institutions.

Because a religious conviction identifies the comprehensive condition of all valid moral claims, no religious adherent could, I sought to show, accept a freestanding justification for material principles or limits on what is permissible. In contrast, then, the object of a constitutional consensus, on the public view of religious freedom, is a formal conception of justice, meaning that it identifies the necessary conditions for full and free political discourse about all proposed principles of justice, including, therefore, its own identification of the necessary conditions of full and free political discourse. Accordingly, the differences among comprehensive convictions are integral to politics, and all comprehensive convictions are permissible, given only that their adherents judge the current constitution acceptably demo-

---

10. Indeed, I appropriate the term "constitutional consensus" from Rawls, who himself appropriates it from Kurt Baier. Precisely because Rawls uses the term to identify one aspect of what he calls an "overlapping consensus," however, my use of "constitutional consensus" differs from his. See Rawls 1993: 149, 158f., and Baier.

cratic. The basis on which one may hope for a constitutional consensus, then, is precisely that human reason as such includes the comprehensive order of reflection. A constitution may be authentically democratic, and, insofar as the current constitution is so, argument in defense of it may be persuasive.

Still, the objection may insist, we have not shown how, on the public view of religious freedom, political unity is consistent in principle with a strictly indeterminate plurality of legitimate religions. Because any given democratic constitution depends on a constitutional consensus, the body politic does set a limit, however minimal, on permissible comprehensive convictions. Since any democratic state will resist revolution, religions are impermissible if they require adherents to judge the constitution, including its provisions for constitutional change, unacceptably democratic, so that, strictly speaking, the constitution does not legitimate all actual and possible religions.

But we have said that some set of constitutional provisions is authentically democratic or, given historical circumstances, does in truth establish the necessary conditions for full and free political discourse and only these conditions. Given that the current constitution is in truth democratic, it identifies formal conditions of justice on which adherents of all actual and possible religions at least should agree, given only that they are committed to full and free political discourse. An authentically democratic constitution is, we may say, worthy of a consensus among an indeterminate plurality of religions. Any religious adherent who judges this constitution unacceptably democratic thereby contradicts her or his own commitment to democratic discourse. Thus, all actual and possible religions are permitted or legitimated by an authentically democratic constitution, even if some religious adherents may not recognize and, therefore, may resist the conditions of their own legitimacy—and this is just to repeat that the public view of religious freedom includes a basis on which to hope that the political community will be enduring. Notwithstanding the possibility of constitutional disagreement, then, an authentically democratic constitution and, therefore, the public view of religious freedom solve in principle the modern political problematic.

Political Discourse and Practical Politics

Even if a plurality of legitimate religions may in principle be unified politically through a full and free debate, it may now be objected that such a political process is simply not practical. In the nature of the case, answers to the comprehensive question are or include the most general and abstract claims about human activity as such and about reality as such. As a consequence, I have argued, comprehensive convictions can be rationally assessed only in terms of their self-consistency or coherence. Thus, the objection holds, the public view of religious freedom seems to require that all citizens become sophisticated philosophers and, even were this practical, the time and training required properly to engage in political discourse about human authenticity as such would preclude the kind of experience and wisdom about particular problems that is generally agreed to characterize good political judgment.

But nothing that has been said above implies that public argument about human authenticity as such is necessarily the most important aspect of full and free political discourse. Democratic discourse as such addresses the question "what should the state do?" and, therefore, discusses and assesses understandings of the comprehensive purpose only insofar as that is required in the given circumstances to reach a democratic decision about particular activities. The principle of religious freedom, then, does not imply that the political process has failed if the comprehensive question is not explicitly addressed in the public's deliberations regarding every issue of state policy. Given that the human capacity for reflection is fragmentary, and given the need within some relatively limited period of time to take a decision, the political process must often choose to which aspects of a political issue it will direct its attention. The character of human authenticity as such is only one such aspect, others having to do with the particular conditions relevant to the problem, including the consequences that alternative courses of action are likely to yield.

When there is widespread agreement at some relatively general level regarding the values relevant to a given decision, the public is likely to focus debate on more particular aspects of policy, and that may well be the proper thing to do. Still, doing so does not gainsay that any policy has comprehensive implications. Thus, when political discourse does not attend to the comprehensive question, the political process asserts implicitly that the general values commanding widespread agreement themselves imply the valid understanding of human authenticity as such. Moreover, the principle of religious freedom means that citizens should from time to time attend explicitly to the comprehensive implications of widely-held general values. The body politic is constituted as a full discourse in order to approach political authenticity through discussion and debate, and the general values commanding widespread agreement can themselves be redeemed only through assessment of their comprehensive implications.

It is true that political discourse regarding answers to the comprehensive question is or includes the exercise of a philosophical capacity. But this does not imply that all citizens must be professional philosophers, any more than democratic governance of economic activities implies that all citizens should be professional economists. In the nature of the case, professional vocations pertinent to the political process are not those that citizens as such can pursue. It is, then, perfectly appropriate that the public generally should include some who specialize in critical thought about the relation between religious convictions and contemporary political issues—and, therefore, equally appropriate that religious associations should support theologians who have a political vocation. In the end, however, those who so specialize must persuade democratic citizens generally. Hence, one may say that modern democracy requires of citizens as such a general or nonspecialized philosophical capacity. Religious freedom is indeed demanding on the citizens of a body politic so constituted. But there is no reason to think that the demand for a nonspecialized capacity to discuss and debate human activity and reality as such is any greater than the demand for a nonspecialized capacity to discuss and debate activities of the state with respect to the economy or the environment or foreign relations. Democracy as such is demanding on its citizens, because a democratic state relies on full and free political discourse.

Alternatively, then, the understanding of democracy asserted by the public view of religious freedom may be rejected as impractical in the sense that it is hopelessly idealistic. In the real life of communities we call democratic, some may insist, the decisions of the state are not informed by a full and free public discussion and debate which seeks purchase on authentic politics by appeal to human experience and reason. On the contrary, government occurs in large measure as a consequence of personal and group interests strategically and often deceptively advanced; decisions are taken in favor of those who have dominant control of wealth, the definition of success or prestige, and the channels of communication; and what passes for public debate is in large measure sophistic rhetoric or systematically distorted communication. But the validity of the public view does not turn on whether the democratic discourse that religious freedom constitutes is realized without fault in modern politics. A constitution must include an ideal that identifies the authenticity of the political process if that constitution is to command the reflective allegiance of its citizens—and it is the ideal of democracy that the principle of religious freedom expresses.

To be sure, a constitution cannot be hopelessly idealistic, in the sense that it allows the vices of political life so to command the political process that its ideal has no significant relation to politics in fact. Generally speaking, a constitution that affirms religious freedom can avoid this consequence not by compromising the commitment to full and free political discourse but in its design of the procedure by which the political process yields decisions or activities of the state. Whatever its inadequacies, for instance, the United States Constitution seeks through such forms as the secret election of officials, the separation of powers, and the variety of "checks and balances" to provide protection against political corruption. Moreover, as I suggested in the previous chapter, the "free exercise" clause of the First Amendment, in the sense that it prescribes special protection for religious activities, may be justified as a condition that protects democratic politics. By insisting that the state must meet a more demanding standard in order to prohibit activities that teach a religion, the constitution resists the danger that some will use the coercive power of the state to hinder certain views or convictions.

Still, "realistic" forms of decision-making, that is, those that seek to contain the failure of citizens to be good citizens, cannot themselves create democracy. Without effective public assessment of the state's activities in some measure, the mechanisms intended for democratic decision would be impotent to prevent more or less tyrannical coercion or anarchic conflict. Reinhold Niebuhr, perhaps better remembered for saying that our "inclination to injustice makes democracy necessary," preceded this by saying that our "capacity for justice makes democracy possible" (Niebuhr 1944: xi).

Because the failures of political life may overwhelm any democratic constitution, however realistic it may be, the government may become so corrupt that the political process is democratic only in pretense and is in fact controlled by force. If one concludes that the current situation is so characterized, commitment to the constitution may entail that one seek to overthrow the regime by nonconstitutional means. We may speak of this course as that of rebellion against the regime, in distinction from the revolutionary attempt to reconstitute the political community. Thus, if an enduring democracy requires a consensus that the constitution is acceptably democratic, it also requires a consensus that the regime is acceptably constitutional. "Acceptably constitutional" means that, all things considered, reforms in the actual political process that are themselves authorized by the constitution are properly pursued within constitutionally stipulated procedures rather than through rebellion. But the fact that rebellion may be justified has no relevance to whether the public view of religious freedom is coherent. Since it properly occurs in order to effect a regime that better accords with a democratic constitution, rebellion presupposes the possibility of democracy and, therefore, the full and free political discourse religious freedom constitutes.[11]

So far as I can see, then, objections to the public view of religious freedom on the grounds that political argument cannot itself unite a political community are unconvincing. At least until some more telling objection is advanced, I conclude that full and free political discourse is indeed a coherent constitutional principle, and, assuming that we may call this principle democratic, the democratic resolution to the modern political problematic is successful.

---

11. So far as I can see, this practical objection can deny the coherence of the public view of religious freedom only if the objection denies that humans have, in Niebuhr's phrase, a capacity for justice. In that event, the objection is no longer practical, in the sense in which I have here used that term, but, rather, philosophical. Moreover, the required philosophical claim denies the possibility of *justified* revolt because it denies that politics is bound by a principle or principles of justice. To deny the capacity for justice is, in other words, to assert that the political process is solely the conflict of forces. Were that the case, religious freedom on the public view, as well as any other moral theory of politics, would indeed be incoherent. But I argued in chapter 7 that all human activity is bound by a moral principle, because it is self-refuting to deny the comprehensive order of reflection. If the argument there was successful, then every human activity chooses between authentic and inauthentic purposes, and all humans have a capacity for justice.

9

RELIGIOUS FREEDOM AND DEMOCRATIC CIVILITY

In the previous chapter, I sought to sustain the public view of religious freedom against objections that it is not a principle of political unity and, thereby, to sustain the claim that this view solves the modern political problematic on its political formulation. We must now consider objections that the public view of religious freedom cannot be consistently accepted by adherents of at least some religions and, thereby, seek to sustain the claim that this view solves the modern political problematic on its religious formulation. Given that the two formulations express the same problematic, of course, any objection in either chapter could be considered an objection to either claim, so that, if any objection is successful, both chapters must fail to achieve their purpose. Still, there are objections that focus on the religious formulation.

Religious Adherence and Democratic Decision

Generally speaking, those who deny that the public view of religious freedom can be consistently accepted by all religious adherents hold that even this view cannot avoid the establishment of some religion or some answer to the comprehensive question. In one of its forms, this objection may be presented as follows: Since the intent of political debate about human authenticity as such is to inform the activities of the state, those activities will be, just insofar as that intent is fulfilled, informed by some or other comprehensive conviction. Just in the measure that any given political decision is taken through a democratic procedure, in other words, it will express the persuasiveness of some comprehensive conviction or, at least, the unpersuasiveness or denial of others and, in that sense, will establish some or other such conviction.

In order to illustrate this point, we may recall that American politics in the later 1930s included a substantial debate regarding the possible participation of this country in the European war—and, moreover, a debate that included the assertion of differing religious convictions. Some argued on religious grounds for pacifism and made common cause with others who supported an isolationist policy. Some argued on religious grounds for the doctrine of a just war and made common cause with others who supported engagement in the resistance to the Axis powers. In the end, the body politic decided (whether or not it was through a democratic procedure is not germane to the illustration) to declare war. The point is, then, that this decision was inconsistent with and, therefore, implicitly denied any understanding of human authenticity as such that requires political pacifism. Accordingly, the objection holds, the state established comprehensive convictions that authorize the doctrine of a just war. *Mutatis mutandis*, the objection continues, all other state activities, even if they are informed by a debate about human authenticity as such, cannot fail implicitly to deny some comprehensive convictions and, therefore, implicitly to affirm another or others—and, thereby, implicitly to violate the prohibition of establishment.

But the apparent contradiction with which the public view is now charged is merely apparent, because the objection fails to distinguish between convictions that are *implicit* in the activities of the state and the state's *explicit* prescriptions. Given that the character of human authenticity as such is presupposed by all human activity, it follows that all human activity and, therefore, the activities of the state implicitly affirm some answer to the comprehensive question. A given activity is either authentic and so implies only the valid comprehensive conviction, or it is inauthentic and so implies a comprehensive self-understanding that is incoherent. Thus, an understanding in accord with which religious freedom proscribes to the state any implicit answer to the comprehensive question would proscribe to the state any activity at all. As the previous chapter insisted and the objection itself suggests, moreover, religious freedom constitutes a democratic discourse precisely in order that the political association may in this way approach the truth and, thereby, the activities of the state may imply as fully as possible only the valid understanding of human authenticity as such.

The explicit prescriptions of the state are, however, quite distinct from their comprehensive implications. On the public view of religious freedom, what is proscribed to the state is the explicit affirmation of any comprehensive conviction, that is, the teaching or support for the teaching of any answer to the comprehensive question. It is one thing for the state to declare war against the Axis powers and, thereby, to imply that human authenticity as such does not in principle require political pacifism; it is something quite distinct for the state to teach that a just war is required by the divine purpose to which the country is bound or, alternatively, by the comprehensive moral norm of the greatest happiness of the greatest number.

The distinction is allowed as a matter of political principle because the question of the state is not the comprehensive question. As I mentioned in chapter 2, religious activity differs from political activity because the former addresses explicitly the question of the comprehensive human purpose, whereas politics addresses explicitly the question of a noncomprehensive purpose—namely, that of ordering or governing the activities and associations within a given society. As a consequence, the question of the state may be explicitly and decisively asked and answered, that is, particular prescriptions ordering a society may be politically fixed, without explicit address to the comprehensive question. A prohibition against racial discrimination, a requirement that citizens pay income taxes, rules regulating the market for securities, and a declaration of war, for instance, are noncomprehensive prescriptions. Each has as its purpose to order the political community in a certain way and, thereby, to achieve in part the state's noncomprehensive purpose. Each of these noncomprehensive prescriptions or purposes does indeed have implications regarding the character of human authenticity as such or the comprehensive purpose, but none of the laws I have mentioned explicitly identify what those implications are.

All governing legislation, of course, is or involves teaching, in the sense that it explicitly prescribes for individuals and associations in the political community. To promulgate a law that prohibits racial discrimination, for instance, is to teach that racial discrimination is, in the given political community and in the respects prohibited, wrong. In addition, the content of a law may be that some teaching occur, as, for instance, in laws prescribing the education of children. Thus, one of the noncomprehensive prescriptions of a given state might have as its explicit purpose that a particular understanding of the comprehensive purpose is taught. Precisely this possibility, however, is proscribed by religious freedom, which prescribes that the state be explicitly neutral with respect to religious convictions. Any law may, therefore, be challenged as unconstitutional on the grounds that it requires or supports the teaching that some or other religious conviction is valid or invalid. If challenged, the state is bound to show that the explicit purpose of the law does not include an address to the comprehensive question.[1]

The distinction between the explicit prescriptions or purposes of the state and their implicit claims regarding the comprehensive purpose permits the public view of religious freedom to appropriate the term "civil religion," whose relevance to the American body politic has been debated at least since the appearance of Robert N. Bellah's now classic essay "Civil Religion in America" in 1967. There are, it seems to me, two meanings with which this term has been used that are pertinent to the present discussion, on only one of which civil religion in America is consistent with religious freedom. On the first meaning, "civil religion" refers to certain affirmations regarding human authenticity as such that are different than those of any single disestablished religion present in the political community and that are explicitly constitutive of the Republic.

I take Mead's first reading of the rationalist founders, in accord with which they distinguished between the essentials and ines-

---

1. We may, I think, speak of a legislative purpose in both strict and broad senses. In the strict sense, the explicit purpose of a legislative prescription is that individuals and associations in the body politic should conform to it, that is, should choose their purposes accordingly. A law prohibiting theft has as its explicit purpose that people in the community should not steal from each other. But legislation may also have a broader purpose when obedience to the law in question has other effects in the political community that one has reason to believe would not occur absent the legislation. Thus, for instance, a tax on industrial firms that release pollutants into the atmosphere or the nation's waterways may have as its explicit purpose not only the paying of taxes but also the protection of the natural environment. The broader effects of a law are certainly a part of its explicit purpose if they are cited in the legislation and, further, may be so considered when they are more or less directly related to the legislated prescriptions. For instance, a law that provides for public reimbursement to children for the costs of transportation to accredited primary and secondary schools operated by theistic religious groups might be said to have as part of its explicit purpose support for the teaching of theistic convictions. On the other hand, this conclusion might be defeated if the reimbursement is provided for transportation costs to any accredited private school. But I will not seek here further to answer the difficult question of how the explicit purpose of a law is properly identified.

However that question is answered, the fact that legislation may not have as its explicit purpose an address to the comprehensive question is at least

sentials of religion and believed that civic virtue depends on explicit adherence to the former, to include a civil religion in this first sense. It is, therefore, appropriate that Mead referred to the essentials of religion as "the religion of the Republic." Although Bellah's classic essay is not completely clear in this regard, some of his formulations therein at least suggest that he also had this first meaning in mind. His oft-cited statement, "there actually exists alongside of and rather clearly differentiated from the churches an elaborate and well-institutionalized civil religion in America" (Bellah 1974: 21), may not necessarily mean that the government may teach this religion. But his later claim that relevant founders envisioned a "quite clear division of function between the civil religion and Christianity" (and, by extension, other disestablished religions), such that the President, "whatever his private religious views, operates under the rubrics of the civil religion as long as he is in his official capacity" (Bellah 1974: 29–30), more or less clearly suggests that this religion is politically equivalent to Mead's religion of the Republic. In any event, the principal point here is that, on this first meaning, a civil religion is inconsistent with the public view of religious freedom, since the latter prohibits to the state the teaching or support for the teaching of any answer to the comprehensive question.

---

one understanding of the United States Supreme Court's stipulation in *Lemon v. Kurtzman* that legislation must have a "secular purpose." We may interpret "secular" here to mean "nonreligious," rather than "secularistic." On this understanding, the teaching of a comprehensive conviction is the distinctively religious purpose. This way of putting the matter reminds us that, for Greenawalt, "laws adopted by the government should rest on some secular objective" (Greenawalt: 20). But his meaning of "secular objective" is different than the meaning of "secular purpose" I suggest here. For Greenawalt, secular considerations are prior to religious ones, in the sense that publicly accessible reasons are prior to personal bases in the political decision-making of a good liberal citizen. Thus, a secular objective refers to benefits to be pursued or harms to be avoided, the identification of which as benefits or harms can be justified independently of any theistic or secularistic conviction. On my usage, a "secular purpose" cannot be justified independently of the valid comprehensive conviction and is secular because the purpose does not include teaching or support for the teaching of any comprehensive conviction. Of course, particular cases may be complicated by the fact that legislation having a secular purpose may also have as its more or less direct effect support for a particular address to the comprehensive question. The other aspects of the so-called Lemon test might be understood as an attempt to identify when such effects should be considered a part of the explicit purpose of the legislation.

On a second meaning, however, "civil religion" refers to those comprehensive convictions that are implicit in the activities of the state. To be sure, if "religion" is used to mean theistic religion, then it may be that there is no civil religion at all. This will be the case if the valid comprehensive conviction is secularistic, and the state's activities are authentic. On the definition of religion for which I have argued, however, all activities of the state may be said to endorse some or other civil religion, because every claim about human authenticity implies an understanding of human authenticity as such.[2] Moreover, it may be the case that several civil religions obtain at some particular time; that is, differing political policies imply differing answers to the comprehensive question. Notwithstanding that this result ought not to be intended, there is no factual necessity that all public policies will be consistent in their comprehensive implications. In another writing, for instance, Bellah himself has argued that the Republic's legislative expressions of a commitment to equality have long implied the conviction that a national covenant with the divine requires this commitment, even while other public policies have systematically oppressed certain peoples and thereby implied that Anglo-Saxons or Europeans or whites are the "chosen" within the divine providence or purpose (see 1975: chapters 1, 2).

Again, one might argue that a given civil religion has been more or less dominant in a given period of the nation's history, because most public policies have implied it. Thus, for instance, Mead contends that the state's implied religious commitments changed as the Republic moved into the post-Civil War period. In the earlier half of the nineteenth century, he argues, the nation sought a political order jealous of each person's freedom and opportunity "to develop his every latent possibility or natural power" (Mead 1963: 92), including especially the power to contribute to the common good, with the implicit affirmation that this was the Republic's "destiny under God." After the Civil War, however, the understanding of freedom narrowed. Due principally to the emerging capitalist industrial order, public policy was increasingly directed toward securing and protecting the liberty to

---

2. If we do speak in this way, we use the term "religion" to mean "actual or possible religion." It may be that the comprehensive implications of the state's activities are not in fact those of any actual religion.

pursue economic self-interest, with the implicit affirmation that in this pursuit each participates in the progressively greater economic rewards for all that constitute God's plan for the United States (see Mead 1963: chapters 5, 8).

On the public view of religious freedom, then, "civil religion" properly refers only in this second sense, and, in this sense, one may say that the purpose of the public debate about answers to the comprehensive question is nothing other than to determine what the civil religion should be. That debate properly includes, of course, attention to the comprehensive claims that *are* implicit in the policies of the state, in order that the validity of those claims and, therefore, the authenticity of those policies may be assessed, as well as the comprehensive convictions that *ought to be* implicit in the state's activities, in order that authentic policies may be identified.[3] But one policy that can never properly be enacted is the state's own teaching or support for the teaching of what the civil religion is or should be. That proscription is the explicit meaning of religious freedom, even if its own implicit meaning is the comprehensive conviction that can be redeemed by appeal to human experience and reason, because religious freedom establishes a full and free political discourse in order that the state's activities may be informed by the valid answer to the comprehensive question.

Although the explicit meaning of religious freedom prohibits the state's explicit affirmation of a civil religion, it is another thing for the state to teach the constitutional principle itself. Indeed, the state has not only the right but also the duty to insure the teaching to all political participants of the explicit meaning of religious freedom, including therein the constitutionally stipulated conditions of a full and free political discourse, because explicit affirmation of this meaning constitutes the body politic. To prescribe religious freedom is, in other words, to prescribe for all citizens explicit commitment to a democratic body politic.

---

3. Among Christians in our century, probably no individual has made a greater contribution in this regard than did Reinhold Niebuhr. With singular clarity and power, he sought through several decades to expose what he took to be the secularistic convictions implied in various aspects of domestic and foreign policy, especially the conviction that authentic human activity consists in participation in the progress of history, and to advocate in relation to a diversity of political issues what he took to be the valid claims of the Christian faith. See, for instance, Niebuhr 1949.

Religious Adherence and the Democratic Constitution

The claim with which the previous section concluded may raise in a new and more subtle form the objection that religious freedom on the public view cannot be consistently accepted by adherents of a plurality of religions. The mere teaching by the state that the body politic should be democratic is, it might be argued, not neutral to this plurality. Democracy is a particular kind of body politic, and, the objection holds, it is certainly possible that the teaching of a democratic constitution is itself inconsistent with one or more religious convictions. For instance, it might be argued that democratic politics in America is inconsistent with a religion in which human authenticity as such is identified as pursuit of white supremacy. However reprehensible such a religion may be, governmental teaching that politics should be democratic is, in effect, the teaching that this religion is illegitimate, and, therefore, a state that has the duty to guarantee the teaching of the public view of religious freedom is not neutral to an indeterminate plurality of religions.

In this context, we may recall again Mead's first reading of the rationalist founders of the American Republic, in accord with which the state would not be required to teach the essentials of religion because the teaching of these by all of the disestablished religious communities would be "good enough" (Mead 1963: 59). Mead himself recognized, however, that the state would be required to assume the task, should it occur that the several religious communities were unwilling or unable sufficiently to inculcate the beliefs on which the well-being of the Republic depended. In other words, the state retained as a matter of principle the duty to guarantee the teaching of religious essentials, and this duty is, I argued, an establishment of religion. The public view of religious freedom, I have now said, implies that the state has a duty to guarantee the teaching that the political order should be democratic, and the objection is that this too is governmental endorsement of a civil religion, at least in the sense that it denies legitimacy to any religion with which democratic politics is inconsistent.

But this form of the objection may also be answered by insisting on the distinction between the explicit prescriptions of the state and their implications with respect to human authenticity as such. Granting that the teaching of democracy is the teaching of a particular political constitution, this claim does not explicitly address the comprehensive question. To say that the political association should be constituted as a full and free political discourse is not explicitly to identify human authenticity as such and, therefore, not explicitly to deny the legitimacy of any religion. A democratic constitution may indeed be implicitly inconsistent with the comprehensive conviction of a given religion, for instance, a religion in which human authenticity is identified by the pursuit of white supremacy. Indeed, an authentically democratic constitution is implicitly inconsistent with all answers to the comprehensive question except the one that can be redeemed by appeal to human experience and reason. But just because these implications are not themselves claims whose teaching the state may effect or support, teaching democratic politics is explicitly consistent with any religious conviction.

Assuming that the constitution includes, for instance, provisions similar to the Civil War Amendments to the United States Constitution, the state is required to guarantee the teaching of these provisions, just as the state is also required to guarantee the teaching of statutory law that prohibits forms of racism. But the principle of religious freedom proscribes state support for the teaching that such constitutional provisions or laws are or are not authorized in accord with any given understanding of human authenticity as such. To be sure, teaching constitutional or statutory prohibitions of racism more or less obviously implies that a religious assertion of white supremacy is false. But the fact that constitutional or statutory prescriptions have more or less obvious implications does not gainsay the distinction in principle between a noncomprehensive purpose that is explicitly affirmed or taught and a comprehensive conviction that is only implied. In principle, the state is prohibited from teaching any such implication, however transparent it may be.[4]

Still, those who advance the objection we are now considering may insist that its burden has not been addressed. Granting that the state does not explicitly teach the comprehensive implications of a

---

4. One might imagine a public school classroom in which constitutional provisions and laws prohibiting racism are being taught and a child who asks if they mean that his friend's parents, whose religion affirms white supremacy, are wrong. I judge that the teacher's proper response is something like the following: You must eventually decide for yourselves which religious convictions are right or wrong, true or false, but I can tell you this: Any citizen of this country is wrong if she or he acts in a manner that violates the constitutional provisions and laws we have been discussing.

democratic constitution, we may be told, it remains that democratic discourse may be implicitly inconsistent with a given religion. If this is so, an adherent of this religion cannot consistently commit herself or himself to democratic politics. Adherents of a religion relevantly similar to the religion of white supremacy, in other words, are inconsistent if they accept a body politic that is constituted as a full and free political discourse. In principle, then, it remains that a democratic constitution cannot be consistently accepted by adherents of a plurality of legitimate religions.

Clarity may be served if I note that the question I here have in mind is not whether commitment to a full and free political discourse is consistent with an overriding principle of political decision-making. I argued in the previous chapter that a full and free debate requires some such overriding principle and that the kind of decisions properly taken depends on the purpose for which the debate is constituted. Nor is the question here whether a common commitment to democratic discourse solves the problem of constitutional disagreement regarding the necessary conditions of democracy. I also argued in the previous chapter that constitutional dissent by some who are committed to democracy may lead them to pursue revolution, but the proper purpose of revolution can only be an authentically democratic constitution. The objection to which we are currently attending asks whether adherents of all religions can consistently commit themselves to full and free political discourse. Which commitments a religious adherent can consistently accept would seem to depend on the character of her or his religious conviction. Even if the state's teaching of democracy does not explicitly deny the legitimacy of a religion with which democracy is inconsistent, it remains that adherents of this religion cannot consistently accept religious freedom, and the modern political problematic on its religious formulation has not been successfully solved.

In one sense, of course, the objection is correct. If democratic politics is implicitly inconsistent with a given comprehensive conviction, then adherents of that conviction who also affirm democratic politics affirm two inconsistent claims. But the question to which the public view of religious freedom is the answer is not how political order is implicitly consistent with each of a plurality of comprehensive convictions. Clearly, no political order could be so consistent, since differing comprehensive convictions may be inconsistent with each other. In truth, democracy is, to repeat the point already made, inconsistent with all answers to the comprehensive question except the one that appeal to human experience and reason can redeem. Hence, the question to which democratic politics purports to be the answer must be understood as follows: How, if at all, may adherents of a plurality of legitimate religions consistently be democratic citizens, notwithstanding that democracy may be implicitly inconsistent with any given religion? To this question, the public view of religious freedom answers that democracy requires of all religious adherents nothing other than recognition that comprehensive convictions can be validated or assessed by appeal to human experience and reason. This is, of course, the Enlightenment affirmation with which, according to Mead, the rationalist founders made sense of the nation's First Amendment. If agreement with the rationalist founders in this respect is explicitly consistent with every religion, so too is the teaching that politics should be democratic, because the Enlightenment affirmation is, as I will now try to show, a sufficient condition of democratic citizenship.

The affirmation that comprehensive convictions can be assessed by appeal to human experience and reason is, clearly, a necessary condition for commitment to full and free political discourse. Any participant who rejects this condition cannot authentically entertain criticism of her or his claims or assess the claims of others, and, absent the possibility of entertaining and advancing criticism, authentic discussion and debate is impossible. To prescribe religious freedom, then, is to prescribe that all citizens accept the Enlightenment affirmation or what we may also call the way of reason. The state's duty to guarantee the teaching of religious freedom includes teaching not only the negative prescription that the state may not explicitly answer the comprehensive question but also the positive prescription that the political association with its plurality of legitimate religions is constituted by commitment to the way of reason.

But, now, a religious adherent's acceptance of the Enlightenment affirmation is also a sufficient condition of democratic commitment. In her or his religious activity, a citizen asserts some conviction regarding the comprehensive condition of authentic politics. With the recognition that this religion can be assessed by appeal to human experience and reason, this citizen affirms that the state's activities should not imply her or his comprehensive conviction if it cannot be redeemed by the way of reason. A religious adherent's commitment to authentic politics, then, properly expresses both her or his comprehensive conviction and the way of reason, and this inclusive expression *is* commitment to full and free political discourse. Conversely, any religious adherent who rejects democracy denies that her or his religious conviction in its pertinence to the activities of the state can be assessed by appeal to human experience and reason.[5] Given the Enlightenment affirmation, to claim that a given religion is valid is to claim that democratic discourse is not inconsistent with one's religious conviction, because it will be redeemed by the way of reason. Conversely, to recognize that one's religious conviction can be assessed by human experience and reason is to acknowledge that it may be invalidated by full and free political discourse, so that democratic politics is indeed inconsistent with that religion.

But, then, adherents of any religion can consistently be democratic citizens, notwithstanding that democracy may be implicitly

---

5. It is true that some religions deny the significance of politics as such because they identify human authenticity as such as a kind of contemplation or union with an ultimate presence or, perhaps, ultimate absence that requires renunciation or withdrawal from the world. Some may object that at least adherents of these religions cannot consistently accept democratic politics, even if they acknowledge that their own convictions can be assessed by argument, because they deny the authenticity of politics as such. I take the possibility of such religions to mean that a body politic constituted by religious freedom cannot consistently require and the state should not teach that citizens ought to be political participants. As long as there is a world to renounce or withdraw from, however, adherents of acosmic religions acknowledge that there is a community of contemporary individuals that will be ordered in some way or other. Notwithstanding that this world may be understood as illusory or insignificant or provisional, then, those who so believe make some claim about the order of the larger community. Either they disown it altogether or, what is at least equally common, they assert that the political order should not hinder or arrest the activities that their religious convictions require. In either case, the mere assertion that their religious conviction is the valid answer to the comprehensive question implies a full and free political discourse, even if they choose not to be a participant in it. Thus, adherents of acosmic religions can consistently accept the state's explicit insistence that politics should be democratic.

Mutatis mutandis, the same considerations apply to adherents of an anarchistic religion. Even such anarchists assert a comprehensive conviction in terms of which authentic relations among contemporary individuals should be determined. The recognition that this conviction can be assessed by argument allows these religious adherents consistently to accept a full and free political discourse, even if they seek to argue that the political association should be dissolved.

inconsistent with their religion. A democratic constitution and every religious adherent agree in this: Government ought to be informed by the comprehensive truth about reality and human purpose. This agreement permits any religious adherent to be a democratic citizen because every religious conviction claims to be the valid comprehensive conviction and, therefore, claims to be consistent with every other claim that can be redeemed by appeal to human experience and reason. What no religious adherent can consistently accept is a constitutional denial that the comprehensive question has a valid answer, because politics so constituted explicitly denies what every religious adherent asserts, namely, that one's religious conviction can be rationally redeemed. Democracy legitimates an indeterminate plurality of religions because full and free discourse is nothing other than a political expression of the Enlightenment affirmation.

Religious Adherence and Democratic Civility

But if democracy is a political expression of the Enlightenment affirmation, the public view of religious freedom still assumes that adherents of a plurality of legitimate religions can all consistently accept the way of reason. Thus, one might object to the public view by objecting to that assumption. Kent Greenawalt, we may recall, thinks that, for a great many people, "claims about religious truth [or, at least, theistic religious truth] are outside the domain of publicly accessible reasons" (Greenawalt: 75). It is apparent from the earlier discussion in this work that I concur in this judgment. Indeed, I take the belief that religious convictions (or, at least, theistic convictions) are nonrational to be so widespread that the public view of religious freedom cannot be persuasive unless one shows the failure of all attempts to understand religious freedom consistently with this belief. Notwithstanding my arguments that all such attempts are incoherent, moreover, I expect that the public view of religious freedom will continue to seem implausible or impractical to many precisely because of its relation to the Enlightenment affirmation.

But the objection to which we must now attend is more pointed. It does not intend to endorse the theory of religion as nonrational but, rather, depends merely on the fact that others may do so. The fact is that some if not many religions do or, at least, may include the conviction that some particular person, text, or other expression is the infallible or exclusive revelation or interpretation of human life and reality as such. Some religions may claim, moreover, that human life cannot be fully authentic without belief that the valid answer to the comprehensive question is not accessible to reason. If religious freedom requires that the state explicitly endorse the way of reason, this objection contends, religious freedom in truth cannot be consistently accepted by all religious adherents. Because it explicitly denies what some religions assert, the public view of religious freedom denies the legitimacy of at least some religions. In that sense, the objection concludes, the state's duty to guarantee the teaching that politics is constituted as a full and free discourse turns out to be the establishment of a civil religion.

Although this may be, for many, the most persuasive objection, it too, I believe, confuses what the state explicitly asserts or denies with what it implicitly asserts or denies. On my accounting, it is indeed the case that teaching the way of reason is implicitly inconsistent with the claim that human authenticity includes belief in some infallible interpretation or in the superrational character of comprehensive truth. But to imply that these are false religious claims is one thing and explicitly to assert it something else. In truth, to teach that all claims advanced as a part of the political process, including comprehensive convictions, are properly subject to rational assessment is not to teach that any religious conviction is false—and the difference can be marked by saying that religious adherents for whom human activity as such is not fallible or for whom human authenticity as such requires belief in the limits of reason are free to argue for their convictions.

Clarity on this point may be served by comparing to other examples previously discussed the distinction here between the state's explicit assertion and its implications. In the earlier discussions, I argued that particular political prescriptions are distinct from religious convictions because the former are noncomprehensive and the latter are comprehensive claims about human authenticity. If the constitution or statutory legislation proscribes certain forms of racism, for instance, the state only implies religious claims because its explicit claims about human authenticity are noncomprehensive. Even if a given religious community teaches that a belief in racism is an aspect of human authenticity as such, the state has not explicitly denied this religion because in truth the state's explicit moral claim is not a comprehensive one.

In contrast, to teach that comprehensive convictions can be assessed by argument is explicitly to make neither a noncomprehensive nor comprehensive claim about authentic human activity but, rather, simply to affirm that the comprehensive question has a valid answer. Hence, it remains that this teaching only implies religious claims, and the distinction between the two is confirmed by the fact that any implied claim about human authenticity as such is one that can be doubted or contested and can be redeemed only by argument. We can also make the point by insisting that an affirmation by the state does not explicitly deny any answer to the comprehensive question unless it explicitly asserts one, and the claim that answers to this question are validated or assessed by appeal to human experience and reason is not an answer to the question. In truth, to affirm the way of reason is explicitly nothing more than to affirm that the comprehensive question is a sensible one.

To say that a question is sensible is to affirm that it has a valid answer and that there is a criterion in accord with which a valid answer may be distinguished from invalid ones. In the nature of the case, this criterion is distinct from any given answer, because all answers affirm it by virtue of purporting to be valid. The relevant criterion, in other words, is common to all answers and, therefore, belongs to the question itself. Were this not the case, every answer would be its own criterion of validity, and all answers, notwithstanding that they may be mutually exclusive, would be valid. For example, to ask who was elected president of the United States in 1992 is to affirm that the valid answer is determined by the criterion stipulated in the United States Constitution, namely, the candidate who received the majority of electoral votes—and this criterion, because it belongs to the question itself, is common to any claim, whether valid or invalid, that purports to identify the winner.

Moreover, to say that every sensible question includes a criterion in accord with which a valid answer may be identified is to say that answers may be assessed by argument. When there is doubt or disagreement about whether a given answer is valid, considerations may be advanced that serve to determine whether the answer conforms to the relevant criterion. Because the criterion belongs to the question and, in that sense, is distinct from any given answer, to validate any answer is distinct from asserting it. To be sure, there may also be doubt or disagreement about the relevant criterion. Hence, it is always possible to suspend argument about answers to a given question in order first to ask about the criterion proper to the given question. So, for instance, one may doubt that a mere counting of the electoral votes in 1992 is the proper criterion for deciding the winner of that presidential election because one believes that vote fraud occurred in one or more of the fifty states. Accordingly, the criterion for determining the winner must now itself be more precisely determined, namely, by asking about the constitutional and legal prescriptions that prescribe voting procedures in the several states. But the question about the proper criterion for argument is itself a sensible question only because it too has its own proper criterion for argument. Were it not possible to argue about the criterion proper to, say, the comprehensive question, then we could not distinguish valid and invalid understandings of this criterion and, therefore, could not argue about comprehensive convictions themselves.

In sum, a sensible question is a rational question, where this means simply that answers to it can be assessed by argument. On my use of terms, to say that claims and convictions are validated by appeal to human experience and reason is equivalent to saying that every sensible question includes a criterion for argument. The reference to human experience and reason, in other words, does not explicitly intend any particular understanding of the criterion or rational standard proper to any given question, because any formulation of this standard is itself subject to disagreement and, therefore, rational assessment. What is excluded by the way of reason is simply the denial that valid and invalid claims or convictions can be distinguished by argument.

With respect to religious convictions, then, the explicit meaning of religious freedom asserts only that the comprehensive order of reflection is a sensible one, and the rationalist or Enlightenment affirmation that religions can be assessed by appeal to human experience and reason is distinct from any given religious claim just because asking a sensible question is distinct from giving one or another answer to it. To insist that the democratic state should insure the teaching of democracy as a full and free political discourse is insofar nothing more than to reassert that the body politic is constituted by the comprehensive question because it has a valid answer. This teaching can be consistently accepted by all religious adherents, notwithstanding the implications it may have with respect to certain religious claims about the infallibility of some putative revelation or about the limits of reason, because every religious conviction claims to be valid.[6]

---

6. The point here may be reformulated as follows: To affirm the way of reason is not explicitly to deny any religious claim because this affirmation explicitly expresses only the meaning of making or asserting any religious

We may also say that the public view of religious freedom can be consistently accepted by a legitimate plurality of religious communities because adherents of any religion can consistently be self-critical. Because religion is the primary form of culture in terms of which the comprehensive question is explicitly asked and answered, the function of religious activity is so to address this question as to cultivate in the lives of religious adherents comprehensive self-understandings that are authentic. But it is always possible that the understanding of human authenticity identifying any given religion becomes problematic to or is doubted by its adherents. Because the validity of any religion may be questioned, any religious adherent may also ask and answer the comprehensive question critically, and, when this occurs, we may say that religious activity has become self-critical.[7] Becoming self-critical is a strictly formal possibility of religious activity as such, in the sense that it can occur irrespective of the convictions that identify a given religion's answer to the comprehensive question, and it is this formal possibility that makes democracy consistent with a plurality of legitimate religions.

---

claim at all. As we have said, a given religion may include in its answer to the comprehensive question the claim that this answer transcends reason, so that human authenticity as such includes believing this claim. But any religious conviction, whatever claims it may include, claims to be a valid answer to the comprehensive question. Thus, to make or assert any religious claim at all is to affirm that the comprehensive question is a sensible one. If in truth a sensible question is a rational one, then the meaning of making or asserting any religious claim at all is that this claim can be redeemed by argument. It remains that this affirmation may be implicitly inconsistent with the religious claim that a valid comprehensive conviction transcends reason. But this is just to say that any religious claim may be implicitly contradicted by its own claim to be valid. Only in the sense that any religious conviction may be invalid is any religious adherent unable consistently to affirm the way of reason. This teaching, we may say, is not the teaching of a religious claim but, rather, solely the teaching that a valid religious claim is one that answers the comprehensive question validly.

Thus, teaching the way of reason would be an explicit denial of some religious conviction only if the comprehensive question were not rational, in which case the public meaning of religious freedom would explicitly deny all religious convictions. But this is just to say that religious freedom is not a coherent political principle on the theory of religion as nonrational. The objection now under consideration may not intend to endorse that theory, but it would have merit only if that theory were true. To the contrary, then, I have sought to argue that religious freedom is a coherent political principle because the comprehensive question is in truth rational.

7. See the section entitled "Religion and Politics" in chapter 2.

This does not mean that religious activity can be political activity only if the former becomes self-critical. On the contrary, it is perfectly appropriate for religious adherents explicitly to ask and answer the question of the state by making some religious claim and asserting its significance for some political choice or choices. In this sense, any religious association in a body politic constituted by religious freedom is not only permitted but also encouraged publicly to advocate an understanding of the comprehensive purpose in its relevance to the activities of the state. Still, diverse religious associations legitimately participate in the political process only if the claims each association makes about the comprehensive purpose are subject to the critical reflection that is required whenever any claim is doubted and, therefore, whenever the public entertains two or more that conflict. Thus, religious activity properly becomes political in a body politic constituted by religious freedom only with the recognition that such activity may, when required, become self-critical, and this recognition is an expression of the commitment to democratic discourse.

It also follows that individuals or associations that advance distinctively religious claims within the political process are morally bound to affirm full and free political discourse. We may now appropriate Murray's term and endorse his insistence that civility is the constitutive virtue of democratic citizenship—even if, in contrast to Murray, this virtue must now be affirmed without excepting comprehensive convictions because the democratic discourse includes a discussion and debate about human authenticity as such. Democratic civility is a political virtue that each of a plurality of legitimate religious communities is constitutionally bound to teach, at least insofar as it teaches that its religious convictions are politically important.

Indeed, there are practical reasons to hope that the state would not need directly to teach the commitment to democratic discourse, because the teaching of the several religious communities, as well as other voluntary associations, is "good enough" (Mead 1963: 59). This circumstance seems desirable because the state's teaching is less likely to be effective if the teaching of other associations in the lives of citizens, including especially those that represent comprehensive understandings of human authenticity, is contrary to or even silent on civic virtue. Moreover, the affirmation that all political claims are to be assessed by argument is not easily taught in a manner that remains explicitly neutral to all claims in a full and free political discourse or in a manner that readily protects against misunderstanding. In practice, teaching the way of reason may include or may too easily be misunderstood to include the explicit assertion of religious claims that should be only implicit in the activities of the state—for instance, the claim that human activity as such and, therefore, all human expressions are fallible.[8] But that does not gainsay that the state not only may but also must teach democratic civility if nongovernmental institutions are not equal to the task.

The teaching of democratic civility itself becomes especially important if and when there is widespread belief that politics is finally or principally a mere conflict of power because no comprehensive conviction or fundamental principle of political evaluation can be rationally redeemed. Murray was led to insist that "the specifying note of political association is its rational deliberative quality" (Murray: 6) in part because, on his perception, American politics was threatened by the denial of any "universal moral law," so that "soliloquy" had replaced argument. In that perception, Murray concurs with many others in recent decades who have warned that American politics has become widely understood as a process of conflict and compromise among interests or self-interests that cannot itself be rationally evaluated. What is thereby eclipsed is a political commitment to the common good, by virtue of which citizens recognize that interests are properly served by the state only insofar as the proposed activities of the state are consistent with the character of human authenticity as such and, therefore, can be redeemed by argument. In situations where democratic politics is severely compromised by the belief that values or ideals are nonrational, the state is bound to give special attention to the teaching that religious freedom constitutes the body politic by the way of reason alone.

In the sense that democratic civility is the constitutive virtue of democratic citizens, we may also say that democracy is politically prior to religious commitment, and this is just to repeat that democratically taken decisions override one's disagreement with them, even if the disagreement is based on one's comprehensive conviction. Indeed, the state's duty to guarantee the teaching of democratic discourse is in fact nothing other than its duty to unify the political community by insuring that all citizens are taught why they have a moral responsibility to obey the law. Democratic law

---

8. In some previously published formulations, I myself have not been sufficiently attentive to this difference (see, for instance, Gamwell: 208–09).

takes priority because it is democratic, that is, decided through full and free political discourse.

But the priority of democracy on the public view of religious freedom should not be confused with the "priority of right" advanced in the privatist view of Rawls. The latter means that priority is given to some or other freestanding conception of justice, and, as I noted in the previous chapter, we may formulate Rawls's point by saying that some material answer to the question of the state is prior to every answer to the comprehensive question. In contrast, the public view of religious freedom is a strictly formal conception of justice and asserts only the priority of a formal definition of the state to any answer to the comprehensive question—namely, that the state is constituted as a full and free political discourse because all convictions about human authenticity as such are properly assessed by argument.[9]

Moreover, this difference between the priority of a material claim about justice and the priority of a formal definition of the state may be so generalized as to summarize the argument for the public view of religious freedom. On the theory of religion as nonrational, the political community can be unified in principle only by some material conception of justice that claims priority to a plurality of legitimate religions. In addition to Rawls's privatist view, both the partisan view of Murray and the pluralist view of Greenawalt confirm this conclusion. On Murray's account, the natural law is or includes a material answer to the political question that is prior to diverse theistic convictions, and the differences among such convictions are, therefore, irrelevant to politics. On Greenawalt's account, the priority of publicly accessible reasons in any conflict between them and the comprehensive convictions of citizens is the priority of a material answer to the question of the state, and, insofar as this answer is conclusive, the differences among religious convictions are irrelevant to politics. But, I have argued, the claim that some material principle of the state is prior to comprehensive convictions is in fact the denial that any comprehensive conviction is

---

9. We might express the priority affirmed in the public view of religious freedom as "the priority of democracy to philosophy," thereby appropriating a phrase of Richard Rorty's (see Rorty 1988). But Rorty uses this phrase to express his agreement with the "political and not metaphysical" proposal of Rawls (Rawls 1993: 10). It is apparent, then, that the public view of religious freedom may appropriate Rorty's phrase only by giving to it a meaning contradictory to the one he intends.

valid, and, therefore, this claim cannot be consistently accepted by any religious adherent. In contrast to all these proposals, the public view of religious freedom asserts the priority of democratic discourse, that is, a strictly formal definition of the state. It not only can but should be accepted by all religious adherents because any religious adherent claims that her or his comprehensive conviction is valid and, therefore, can be assessed by argument.

The democratic resolution is, we may conclude, both separationist and religionist in the following senses: All religions are separated from the state in the sense that the state may not explicitly endorse any answer to the comprehensive question. At the same time, religion is essential to the body politic in the sense that political decisions should imply the valid comprehensive conviction. Politics is consistent in principle with a plurality of legitimate religions because they are united through democratic discourse, and adherents of all religions can consistently be democratically civil precisely because all religions claim to represent the valid understanding of human authenticity as such.

EPILOGUE: RELIGION AND MODERNITY

I noted at the outset of this work that the constitutional affirmation of religious freedom, at least as this appears in the United States Constitution, is widely understood to be an expression of distinctively modern politics—and this fact gave initial warrant for naming the problem to which religious freedom is the solution "the modern political problematic." Given this understanding, it follows that the proper meaning of religious freedom constrains the manner in which the distinctive character of modernity as such is properly identified. A distinctively modern political principle must be a political expression of the distinctive character of modernity in general, and any definition of modernity that is inconsistent with the principle of religious freedom must be insofar a misunderstanding. If the preceding work has successfully argued that only the constitution of democratic discourse unites a legitimate plurality of religions, then we may conclude that the general character by which modernity is distinguished must be implied by the public view of religious freedom.

This conclusion is significant because a widely affirmed thesis about the modern age is sometimes so understood that religious freedom on the public view could not be a modern political principle. I have in mind the claim that modernity has been marked by the process of secularization. There has been, of course, an extensive debate regarding the proper meaning of "secularization" in relation to the development of modern forms of life, but it is not my intent here to review and attempt to sort out that debate. For present purposes, it will suffice to appropriate the meaning with which Peter Berger, in his widely read sociological analysis of modernity, *The Sacred Canopy*, speaks of "the formation of the modern secularized world" (1967: 128). On his usage, "secularization" refers to "the process by which sectors of society and culture are removed from the domination of religious institutions and symbols" (1967: 107). Given that secularization so removes sectors of society and culture, we may plausibly take Berger to mean by "religion" roughly what I have heretofore meant by "theistic religion." Premodern life, then, was dominated by a "sacred canopy," that is, by the institutions and symbols of a particular theistic religion, and modernity is distinguished by what I have called secularistic understandings of human activity and the larger reality of which it is a part.

The "original 'carrier' of secularization," Berger holds, was "the modern economic process, that is, the dynamic of industrial capitalism" (1967: 109), such that "different strata of modern society have been affected by secularization differentially in terms of their closeness to or distance from" this process (1967: 129). Given the importance of the state to the capitalist economy, "there is a tendency toward the secularization of the political order that goes naturally with the development of modern industrialism" (1967: 130). It is, then, especially pertinent that Berger mentions as an expression of this tendency "the separation of church and state" (1967: 107). On this reading, in other words, the disestablishment of religion is one expression of what Berger calls "an altogether novel situation"; that is, "for the first time in history, the religious [read: theistic religious] legitimations of the world have lost their plausibility not only for a few intellectuals and other marginal individuals but for broad masses of entire societies" (1967: 124).

Berger's analysis is simply one of many in which the increasingly pervasive institutional and cultural control of secularistic understandings is the distinguishing feature of modernity. I will mention only one other instance, namely, the massive research project of Jürgen Habermas, for whom, whatever his differences from Berger, the structure of the modern in distinction from premodern lifeworld is identified in a manner that makes modern social practice, including modern politics, secularistic. Indeed Habermas contrasts the modern worldview with the "religious and metaphysical" worldviews of premodern culture, and it is clear from his description of the latter that, for present purposes, "religious and metaphysical" means what I have called "theistic religious," that is, an understanding in which the norms for human life are derived from an understanding of ultimate reality.

> What is common to religious and metaphysical worldviews is a more or less clearly marked, dichotomous structure that makes it possible to relate the sociocultural world to a world behind it....When it is possible to explain the orders of a stratified class society as homologous to that world-order, worldviews of this kind can take on ideological functions. (Habermas 1987: 189)

It is, then, precisely in transition from such religious and metaphysical worldviews that the "modern understanding of the world" emerges (Habermas 1981: 67). Moreover, Habermas also mentions the separation of church and state as a prominent expression of the transition to modernity (1987: 308).

What Berger and Habermas have in common, so far as I can understand, is an attempt to distinguish modern and premodern in terms of differing *material* understandings or differing convictions or kinds of convictions about the authenticity of human society and culture. Berger betrays this strategy when he speaks of the removal of society and culture "from the domination of religious institutions and symbols," and Habermas does the same when he identifies modernity in contrast to the "religious and metaphysical" worldviews that characterized medieval life. If the argument of the present work has been successful, however, the explicit meaning of religious freedom cannot be the expression of any conviction or kind of conviction regarding human authenticity as such. On the contrary, "the separation of church and state" is explicitly neutral to all comprehensive convictions because it constitutes the body politic as a full and free discourse. On the assumption that religious freedom is a distinctively modern political expression, it follows that the distinctive character of modernity cannot be identified as the increasingly pervasive control of secularistic understandings or, more generally, in terms of any conviction or kind of conviction about the authentic character of human activity and association.[1]

---

1. Given the character of comprehensive convictions as argued in this work, the claim that modernity is secularistic must mean one of the following: (1) The valid answer to the comprehensive question is theistic, and modern life, on the whole, implicitly denies this valid answer. (2) The valid answer to the comprehensive question is secularistic, and modern life, on the whole, implicitly affirms the valid answer. (3) Modern individuals and associations in general understand themselves explicitly in terms of some or other secularistic answer to the comprehensive question; that is, secularism is explicitly asserted. Berger is in fact a theistic religious adherent (see Berger 1979), so that his claim about modernity could mean (1) above. So understood, however, the claim does not distinguish modernity. If modern life on the whole is distinguished by its implicit inauthenticity, then all premodern societies were, on the whole, authentic, and I take it for granted that Berger does not mean so to assert. Habermas's position is secularistic (see Habermas 1981), so that his claim about modernity could mean (2) above. But, so understood, the claim means that all modern societies are, on

In sum, our inquiry into the modern political problematic at least suggests that the distinction between modern and premodern is more properly drawn in terms of formal affirmations about answers to questions about human activity and the world of which it is a part, that is, in terms of affirmations regarding the manner in which material understandings are validated and redeemed. I propose, then, that modern culture is properly distinguished by its formal affirmation that human understandings can be validated or redeemed only by appeal to human experience and reason—and we may call this the modern commitment. In contrast, premodern culture is distinguished by its authoritarian affirmation, namely that human understandings or at least fundamental ones among them can be validated or redeemed by appeal to some inherited expression or tradition or institution. In suggesting this contrast, I do not mean to deny that premodern culture included the affirmation of human experience and reason. Some have argued that this affirmation belongs to Western culture generally because it was "discovered" by philosophic Greece; others hold that it is found both in early and medieval expressions of Judaism and Christianity, in part through the influence of classical Greece. Similarly, the authoritarian affirmation is far from unknown in the modern period, perhaps especially within certain religious communities. The contrast I intend, then, is between dominating commitments, such that, in modern life, the formal commitment to human experience and reason becomes increasingly effective throughout the full range of explicit reflection. On this distinction, we may say that religious freedom is nothing other than a political expression of the modern commitment.

This formal understanding of modernity coheres with the claim that the transition from medieval to modern society and culture includes or is confirmed by the emergence of a plurality of religions

---

the whole, authentic, and it is clear from his critique of modern society that Habermas does not mean so to assert. In truth, then, both Berger and Habermas can only mean (3), namely, that modern individuals and associations in general understand themselves explicitly in terms of some or other secularistic answer to the comprehensive question. Thus, both attempt to distinguish modern and premodern in terms of explicit material convictions regarding the nature of human society and culture. But religious freedom on the only coherent view of it is not an explicitly secularistic understanding of the body politic. Hence, the distinctive character of modernity cannot be the increasingly pervasive control of secularistic understandings if religious freedom is a distinctively modern political principle.

internal to the political community. As the modern commitment becomes increasingly pervasive, the attempt to maintain religious adherence by authoritarian appeal becomes increasingly ineffective. In other words, inherited religions are increasingly opened to explicit question, and the consequence is that religious adherence becomes increasingly a matter of explicit choice.[2]

That politics should legitimate this consequence and, therefore, that the political community should include a plurality of legitimate religions is implied by the modern commitment. It is also worth noting why the emergence of explicit choice with respect to religion may be called *the* modern political problematic. Precisely because this choice concerns the comprehensive grounds for authentic politics, failure to resolve this problematic is, as this work has sought to argue, a failure in principle to resolve all problems of modern politics, because it is the failure coherently to constitute a modern political community. As this work has also sought to argue, then, the public view of religious freedom is a coherent resolution of the modern political problematic because, on this view, religious freedom is nothing other than a political expression of the modern commitment.

Of course, nothing that has been said explicitly argues for or against the validity of any given theistic or secularistic conviction. Precisely because the modern commitment is formal, the burden of this discussion has been to identify modern politics in a manner that is explicitly neutral to an indeterminate plurality of religions. But if there is no argument for a particular religion, our attempt to show how a plurality of religions may be politically unified has also given reason to assert the political importance of religious associations

---

2. In the first chapter of this work, I referred to Berger's later work *The Heretical Imperative: Contemporary Possibilities of Religious Affirmation* in the context of my initial discussion of modern religious plurality. Berger explains that the meaning of "heretical" derives from the Greek verb *hairein*, to choose, and, therefore, the heretical imperative means that modern men and women must explicitly choose their religious convictions (see Berger 1979: 23f.). It might be thought, then, that Berger's thesis about modernity is in fact something like the formal understanding I here advocate, rather than the material understanding I have attributed to him. "It is my position that modernity has plunged religion into a very specific crisis, characterized by secularity, to be sure, but characterized more importantly by pluralism" (Berger 1979: xi). I can only say that I do not think Berger's later work is entirely consistent with the earlier one, and it is the understanding advanced in *The Sacred Canopy* that I here criticize.

generally. Properly understood, modern politics constitutionally affirms religious freedom in order thereby to maximize political decisions that can be redeemed by appeal to human experience and reason. We may say that religious freedom is an expression of modernity's commitment to rational or rationalized politics and, thereby, repeat that religious freedom is incurably an expression of the Enlightenment. It then follows that the political community cannot be rationalized without the political participation of a plurality of religious communities. It is essential to the authenticity of modern politics, in other words, that the political process include critical reflection on the character of human authenticity as such, and this is to repeat that religious freedom constitutes the body politic by the comprehensive question. Absent the participation of religious associations, the democratic process is compromised in its most fundamental respect. It wants for explicit purchase on the abiding purpose of the human adventure.

APPENDIX: ON THE COMPREHENSIVE
ORDER OF REFLECTION

The contemporary philosophical discussion displays widespread suspicion of the Enlightenment and what are taken to be its distinguishing philosophical commitments. Whatever else this suspicion includes, the discussion is marked by understandings of human reflection that bind it to specific traditions, cultural contexts, or communities of discourse in a manner that excludes the kind of universal or transcendental principles characteristically affirmed by Enlightenment thinkers. In contrast, the conclusions I have sought to commend in this work presuppose the possibility of thought about the universal conditions of reality and human purpose. In other words, the affirmation of comprehensive reflection is essential to the public view of religious freedom, and, in this respect, this work is in continuity with the Enlightenment.

To affirm this order of reflection is not to deny that human reflection is also conditioned by its specific historical, cultural, and communal contexts. To say that what we understand includes universal principles does not entail that how we explicitly understand or express those principles is universal. Conversely, to recognize that all human reflection is conditioned by its specific time and place does not entail that only historically specific conditions can be understood. Given the contemporary philosophical discussion, in any event, the purpose of this appendix is to defend more extensively the possibility of comprehensive reflection and to clarify more fully its character.

The preceding work may be taken as a hypothetical argument for comprehensive reflection in the following sense: Only if the comprehensive question is rational is religious freedom a coherent political principle. Of course, one may still deny that religious freedom makes sense. But that denial is, I judge, a considerable price to pay, and, for this reason, I hope that this hypothetical argument alone may give pause to some before they join the current suspicion of the Enlightenment. In the preceding work, however, I have sought to do more than to defend the Enlightenment in the hypothetical sense to which I have just referred. In chapter 2, I sought to show summarily that distinctively human activity is constituted by the comprehensive question, and, in chapter 7, I argued summarily that comprehensive claims may be validated by appeal to the criterion of self-consistency or coherence alone. But these arguments were summary in character, and I seek now to clarify and defend their conclusions more completely.

Human Activity and the Comprehensive Question

On my usage, "human activity" means those moments or states of our lives that are constituted by self-understanding, and a human individual is a series or career of activities, only some of which are distinctively human. I recognize that the terms "human activity" and "self-understanding" are sometimes used such that one has broader application than the other. For instance, some may call all activities of a human individual, even those during dreamless sleep or unconsciousness, human activities. Alternatively, some attribute self-understanding to the activities of creatures or existents that are not called human, for instance, certain nonhuman animals. In contrast, my definition stipulates the same extension for the two terms: Wherever self-understanding occurs, there and only there distinctively human activity occurs. This stipulation helps to simplify the formulation of the present argument, and, I am persuaded, the conclusions I reach would not be substantively altered by a more complicated definition. I also recognize that, on some formulations of theism, the divine reality is constituted by a self-understanding. My identification of self-understanding with distinctively human activity is meant neither to deny theism nor to call God human. Neither is intended because I am convinced by the argument of Schubert M. Ogden that psychic terms, including the term "self-understanding," properly apply to God, if God is, only as symbols and, therefore, not literally (see Ogden 1984). In the literal sense of the term, then, "self-understanding" distinguishes human activity.

Of course, one may deny or refuse to affirm that self-understanding occurs. But one then denies or refuses to affirm the presence of any understanding. This is because understanding necessarily distinguishes. To understand something other than the self is to distinguish the other from the self, and, therefore, to understand the self, at least implicitly. The converse is also true: To understand the self is to distinguish it from at least some others. Self-awareness and awareness of a world of others are inseparable. In one sense, then, it makes no difference whether we say that our distinctive activity is constituted by a self-understanding or constituted simply by understanding. In terms of *what* is understood, however, self-understanding is the inclusive term, because the self includes its relations to others, at least insofar as they are understood. In other words, the self that understands itself is also internally related to at least some others in at least some measure, whereas the others that are understood are not necessarily constituted by relations to the self.

Moreover, to distinguish self and others is always also to understand, at least implicitly, some larger reality of which self and others are parts, because distinction means similarity as well as difference. Complete or absolute difference is not a definite difference at all and, therefore, not an understanding of different things. Thus, to understand something positive about X (for instance, that X is an animal) and to say that Y is absolutely different is to identify Y as merely *not-X* (for instance, not an animal). Since *not-X* is insofar solely negative, it is not the identification of any other thing. Hence, a distinction between self and others implies similarity as well as difference and, in this sense, some larger reality to which both belong. The term "larger reality," in other words, means whatever is implied by the fact of similarity between things that are understood.

Because a human activity understands itself, it is necessarily self-determined in some measure; self-understandings are necessarily chosen. Whatever effects others have on a given activity, these others cannot effect an understanding of their effects, that is, of the self. This is not to deny that each human activity is other-determined by a diversity of causes, and the measure in which a given human activity is other-determined is an empirical question. Still, the completion of an activity that understands itself waits on how it chooses to understand the effects others have on it. So far as I can see, the claim that human activities are in all respects the product of efficient causation or determination by others, so that self-understandings are "epiphenomenal," is self-contradictory.[1]

---

1. There is, we should note, a sophisticated formulation of the claim that self-understandings are epiphenomenal. Some might concede that human activities are self-determined but assert that these activities occur only in the brain and can have no effect on the rest of the human body, so that the behavior of human beings is in all respects other-determined. If this formulation were valid, however, then speech could not express under-

To be sure, we might ask how an activity's self-understanding differs from its understanding of other things. When one understands oneself, what is it that one understands in addition to the others from which one is distinguished? The answer, I believe, can only be one's purpose. If an understanding of others insofar identifies those by which the self is determined, to understand oneself is insofar to identify that by which others will be determined. So far as I can see, in other words, our self-understandings imply a distinction between past and future. We are conditioned by the past, in the sense that others of which we are the effect constitute our past, and we condition the future, in the sense that others of which we will be the cause constitute our future. An activity *is* the condition it imposes on its future. Our self-determination is the decision, within the possibilities that the past presents to us, that completes this condition. The choice of a self-understanding is, then, the choice with understanding of our purpose, and we may also say that a self-understanding is the way in which a human activity chooses to add itself or make a difference to the larger reality of which it is a part.

It is sometimes argued that the notion of self-determination is paradoxical or self-contradictory, because the self that determines must be different than the self that is determined and yet the two must be one. But the apparent paradox disappears, I believe, if we understand the self that is determined as an activity that might have been (in the sense of real, not merely logical, possibility) different than it is. When Robert Frost, facing two roads that diverged, chose the one "less traveled by," he did not simply walk down a particular road; on the contrary, his activity was walking down that particular road when it might have been walking down a more used path. The inclusion of the rejected alternative as something that was rejected is what made the activity the distinct thing that it was—as Frost's poem pertly expresses. This inclusion of the alternative or alternatives that

standing, since speech involves a bodily movement that would be independent of understanding. Hence, communication through speech and action would be impossible, and the attempt by its adherents to communicate this self-understanding would be pragmatically self-contradictory. As I will mention in a moment, I am also persuaded that understanding implies language and communication among human individuals (see also Apel 1975; 1979b), so that the putative affirmation of this sophisticated formulation is also pragmatically self-contradictory.

are not chosen makes the self that is determined and the self that determines the same self.

It is also sometimes argued that the notion of self-understanding or self-reflection is paradoxical or self-contradictory, because the self that reflects must be different than the self on which it reflects and yet the two must be one. But the same notion of something related to itself is, I believe, involved in the concept of determination by others. If X is determined by others, then X is internally related to them, and if X is internally related to others, then X is both its *relations* to others and a *term* constituted by those relations. One might speak of X in the latter sense as a relation to its relations. More precisely, perhaps, X as the term constituted is the manner in which X is related to others. Hence, we may say that understanding is the distinctively human manner of being internally related to others. But then understanding one's own relations to others becomes self-understanding in that the manner of relating to others is self-determined. Understanding is a relation of X to its relations to others because it is also a choice to be X rather than X' or X'', all of which are purposes consistent with being internally related to the others in question. To choose what one is or becomes with understanding is self-understanding.

To claim that distinctively human activity is constituted by self-understanding is not to say that its understanding is in all respects *explicit*. By "explicit understanding" I mean our conscious thoughts. It is, I assume, undeniable that our conscious thoughts are always partial or fragmentary; that is, no human activity explicitly understands all things completely. As a consequence, every human activity includes or is constituted by understandings that are only *implicit*, by which I mean understandings that are excluded from conscious thought but on which explicit understanding is dependent or without which it could not be what it is. For instance, one's conscious thought may attend to things other than the self and could not be what it is without one's implicit self-understanding. Alternatively, one's conscious thought may attend to one's purpose, so that some of one's understandings of other things remain implicit.

In part, the understandings implicit in a particular activity are understandings that were explicit in some previous activity or activities of the individual in question and that are nonconsciously remembered in the present. As I have suggested, we may understand an individual as a series or sequentially ordered career of activities, each of which includes or inherits from its predecessors the identifying character of that individual. Abraham Lincoln, for instance, was the series of activities that began in Hardin County, Kentucky, and ended soon after the assassination in Ford's Theatre and that exemplified throughout its existence the character that distinguished Lincoln from any other individual. In speaking of any given moment of Lincoln's life, we may distinguish between the understandings explicit in the activity of the moment and understandings that were explicit in some previous activities of his life and were nonconsciously remembered in the present. If Lincoln's activity in signing the Emancipation Proclamation was explicitly constituted by whatever conscious thoughts he had at the time, this activity was also constituted by an extensive complex of implicit interpretations of the Union, its order and disorder, that had been conscious thoughts at one time or another in Lincoln's previous activity.

It is apparent that the measure and respects in which explicit understanding is possible for a given activity depend on the measure and respects in which prior learning is implicitly understood. Consciously to understand a Supreme Court decision requires a complexity of prior learning that is nonconsciously remembered. Someone other than Lincoln might have signed the Emancipation Proclamation and done so without approaching the conscious understanding of its significance that, we may assume, characterized Lincoln's activity, because the other individual had not previously learned all that Lincoln did about the Union, its order and disorder. Because conscious thought is dependent on prior learning, moreover, the explicit understanding of any given activity is also dependent on the individual's particular relations to the understanding of others. Lincoln's explicit understanding of the Emancipation Proclamation and of himself as he signed it was dependent on the understandings he had previously learned through associations with a large number of other individuals. Understanding is, we may say, always associational or intersubjective, dependent on communication.

But, now, communication between and among human individuals is also fragmentary, and, for this reason, it is mediated by the particular concepts and symbols with which we express our understandings to others, including especially language. The character of language and its importance in human activity have been central to most recent modes of philosophical thought—and, indeed, "the linguistic turn" is often cited as one of the distinguishing marks of modern philosophy (see, e.g., Habermas 1992: 6). Activity cannot be distinctively human, many have argued, without the use of or participation in language, because conscious thought is linguistically constituted. Whatever differing construals differing philosophers may give to this claim, we have good reason to affirm one of the principal conclusions to which, for many, it leads: Because language is a cultural creation, distinctively human activity is mediated by a particular culture. Given that any explicit understanding depends on prior learning and that prior learning depends on communication, we may say that conscious thoughts are interpretations in terms of cultural concepts and symbols and, therefore, express an individual's participation in a culture or culturally constituted lifeworld.

But the implicit understandings of any given activity cannot be exhausted by the individual's prior learning. Were that the case, self-understanding would be impossible, because an implicit self-understanding is a new understanding. Every particular activity is something new and, therefore, so too is the activity's understanding of itself. To understand the fork in the road and to choose the less-traveled alternative includes an understanding of oneself that cannot be previously and completely received from another or exhausted by prior learning. To be sure, the concepts "less-traveled road" and "more used path" may have been previously learned, but the present self-understanding is that something new now takes the one rather than the other.

Moreover, new self-understandings, implicit or explicit, have new implications. When Lincoln conceived of his signing the Emancipation Proclamation, he implicitly conceived of a certain future for the United States, namely, one in which all future events would be conditioned by the event of the Proclamation, and that implicit understanding of the Union's future was not a possible understanding prior to his conception of the event. This is not to deny that the possibility of Lincoln's new thought with its new implications depended on his prior learning. The point is simply that implicit understandings are not exhausted by what the individual has previously learned but depend also on the self-understanding the activity chooses, for instance, what Lincoln chose to do with his prior learning. Indeed, if all implicit understandings were previously learned, then *that* claim would be implied by all explicit understandings, and each of us would have to learn the truth of that claim before we could have any conscious thoughts at all.

Insofar as explicit understanding is new, it can be culturally creative, that is, can add to or transform the cultural lifeworld in which it participates. New conscious thoughts are creative with cultural concepts and symbols such that new understandings can be communicated to others who also participate in that particular culture.[2] In other words, the dependency between human understanding and culture is a two-way dependency, and a given activity's participation in a cultural lifeworld can also be a contribution to it that depends on the choice of a self-understanding. Thus, if implicit understandings are those excluded from conscious thought and without which conscious thought could not be what it is, they are those so excluded without which self-understanding could not be what it is, whether or not they were previously learned by the individual in question.

But if an activity's implicit understanding is not exhausted by the individual's prior learning, still the implicit understanding constituting a human activity is, like its explicit understanding, always fragmentary. Since implicit understandings are those excluded from conscious thought and without which self-understanding could not be what it is, these implicit understandings could be complete rather than fragmentary only if the self to be understood were constituted by complete relations to all things. I will assume as noncontroversial that the activities of human individuals are always fragmentary, that is, never related to all things completely. Indeed, if there are activities completely related to all things, they are, it seems proper to say, divine rather than human. Accordingly, the understandings implicit in any human activity are also partial. We might formulate this point by saying that explicit understanding represents a fragment of an activity's fragmentary understanding. To be sure, this formulation says that what is understood explicitly is also understood implicitly, but, given the dictum that any proposition implies itself, that consequence need not be troubling.

Because all understanding is fragmentary, moreover, both explicit and implicit interpretations are fallible. If we understood all things completely, then it would not be possible to misunderstand anything. Since our interpretations are partial, we may attribute to some things features that in truth belong or could belong to others. In other words, we misrepresent things by confusing their charac-

---

2. I say "can be" rather than "are" culturally creative in order to express the fact that new conscious thoughts may not ever be communicated to other individuals. Lincoln might have explicitly conceived of the Emancipation Proclamation and never mentioned it to anyone. It remains, however, that his creativity occurred in concepts and symbols that allowed it to be added to the culture.

teristics. For instance, one misunderstands Abraham Lincoln if one believes that he defended slavery in the Lincoln-Douglas debates. One correctly understands that a defense of slavery is a characterization that does or could belong to some human activities, but, failing to understand all things completely, one attributes this characterization to the relevant activities of Lincoln.

Fallibility with respect to self-understanding merits special attention. Given that a human activity chooses its particular purpose with understanding, one can never be simply ignorant of that purpose; because an understanding of one's purpose is an understanding of oneself, we can never be simply ignorant of ourselves. To be sure, our conscious self-understandings may be incorrect, in the sense that one may explicitly understand one's particular purpose to be other than it is. If this occurs, however, one's conscious thought can only be a misrepresentation of the implicit self-understanding by which one's activity is constituted. Given that distinctively human purposes are chosen, the falsity of one's explicit self-understanding implies the choice of another understanding of oneself.

Accordingly, the fallibility of explicit self-understanding includes the possibility of self-deception. Understanding how to exploit other individuals for her or his own maximal advantage, for instance, an individual presently attempts to do so but believes explicitly that she or he pursues what is best for the other individuals. The individual's activity deceives itself or conceals from its explicit attention the implicit self-understanding by which it is constituted. Moreover, self-deception means that one's implicit self-understanding is self-convicting or duplicitous; that is, one chooses a purpose of which one also disapproves or that one also proscribes. Seeking to exploit other individuals, for instance, one may also implicitly believe that one ought not to do so, and it is by virtue of this implicit duplicity that one consciously denies one's true purpose. In order to be what it is, the conscious self-understanding that is false excludes the following implicit self-understanding: to exploit others notwithstanding that I ought not to do so, and, therefore, to deceive myself explicitly.

To say that an explicit misunderstanding of oneself *may be* is not to say that it always or in all respects *is* self-deception. An activity's implicit self-understanding may not be duplicitous or may be authentic, and its explicit misrepresentation may be the result of ignorance or mistake. It simply formulates incorrectly what it implicitly knows about oneself. For instance, an activity may implicitly believe that it ought so to act as to pursue in some specified way the well-being of other individuals and may in fact so act. But it may also explicitly misrepresent this as simply what it wants to do or enjoys doing rather than ought to do—because, say, the individual in question has explicitly learned to associate morality with some rigid or oppressive moralism that she or he rightly rejects. Thus, the activity's implicit purpose is more fully characterized as follows: to pursue in the specified way the well-being of other individuals and to formulate this purpose explicitly as best I can. This is not to deny the importance of an explicit mistake in self-understanding, since the individual in question may subsequently believe it implicitly, such that implicit self-understanding becomes an expression of duplicity. For instance, an individual may subsequently choose not to pursue the well-being of others because, in some situation, she or he does not enjoy it.

Because the fallibility of explicit self-understanding means that one's implicit self-understanding may be explicitly misrepresented, it might seem to follow that one's implicit self-understanding must be infallible. But I have also said that *all* human understanding is fallible, and the sense in which this is the case with implicit self-understanding must be explained. It is certainly true that one's implicit self-understanding is correct, in the sense that one understands the purpose by which one is constituted, because this purpose is chosen, at least implicitly, with understanding. Still, we may say that this self-understanding is fallible in the sense that it may be duplicitous. One may choose an understanding of oneself that one also understands to be invalid; one may choose a purpose that one understands to be morally wrong. To be sure, duplicity is a possibility for all of our activities only if human activity as such is bound by a norm that our self-understandings might contradict. But we are now in a position to see that our choices are always moral choices because every particular self-understanding includes, at least implicitly, a comprehensive self-understanding.

Because the particular implies the general, any understanding of oneself implies an answer to the general question: What are the characteristics common to all self-understandings, actual or possible, or what is the comprehensive character of human activity? We may say that human activity as such is constituted by this comprehensive question, in the sense that it must be asked and answered, at least implicitly, whenever and wherever activities understand themselves. The answer given is always fallible, but invalid comprehensive self-understandings are always duplicitous. The valid answer to this question is implicitly understood by any human activity, so that an invalid answer can only be the simultaneous choice of another comprehensive self-understanding.

Since the choice of a particular self-understanding is the choice with understanding of one's purpose, one's answer to the comprehensive question is an understanding of the comprehensive purpose, the common character or characteristics of all particular purposes. Every distinctively human activity implies and, therefore, exemplifies a valid or invalid understanding of the purpose that identifies human activity as such, and we may say that every particular purpose is authentic or inauthentic. Precisely because duplicity is chosen, it is never simply ignorance. At least implicitly, an invalid or inauthentic self-understanding is a lie.

For this reason, all human activity is moral in character. Our choices are moral because we ought to understand ourselves without duplicity, where "ought" here means that a choice in conformity with the comprehensive purpose is categorically required. Reason requires this choice because understanding is always bound by the norm of validity, and the requirement is categorical in the sense that it cannot be defeated by any other choice the activity in question might make. This does not mean that our particular self-understandings are bound to be complete or, to say the same, that the particular purposes we choose are bound to include a full understanding of our particular past and the relevant future. Human understanding is always fragmentary, and the possible self-understandings present for any given human activity depend on the past that it inherits, including the individual's previous participation in a cultural lifeworld. Given whatever limitations on choice the past presents, however, there remains the choice of how one understands the comprehensive purpose. The valid comprehensive self-understanding, we may say, is the comprehensive condition of human activity.

It follows, if I see the matter clearly, that the character of human activity as such must be understood as a comprehensive variable. In this context, the term "variable" means a general characteristic or set of characteristics that is or may be exemplified in differing particular things in differing measure. However difficult they are to measure, for instance, virtues such as courage or self-control may be understood as variables, meaning that differing human individuals exemplify them in greater or lesser extent. Because the comprehensive purpose is implied by all human activities, it must be exemplified in all human activity; it is the character of human activity as such. Because this purpose is a comprehensive variable, it may be exemplified in greater or lesser measure and, therefore, is also a comprehensive moral norm. In other words, this norm requires human activity so to choose among its possible purposes as to exemplify the comprehensive variable in maximal measure or without duplicity, and duplicity always corrupts this maximization, even while an immoral activity exemplifies the variable in some lesser measure. If John Dewey is correct in saying that pursuit of the all around growth of all human individuals, or the democratic ideal, identifies human activity as such (see Dewey 1957: 186), then moral activity consists in so choosing among one's possible purposes as to maximize pursuit of that ideal. Immoral activity also pursues the all around growth of all but does not maximize that pursuit because immoral activity is compromised by pursuit of something else in contradiction to the democratic ideal.

The comprehensive question, then, may also be formulated: What is the comprehensive condition of human activity—or, again, what makes human activity as such authentic? Because every self-understanding includes an understanding of the larger reality in which self and others are distinguished or of which they are parts, every answer to the comprehensive question includes a comprehensive understanding of the whole of which self and all conceivable or understandable others are parts. In other words, human activity is constituted by some or other understanding, authentic or duplicitous, of reality and human purpose as such. We can also make this point by saying that our distinctively human choices always include, at least implicitly, a comprehensive moral conviction that relates human activity to the metaphysical character of reality.

The Criterion of Comprehensive Reflection

In the preceding work, religion has been defined as the primary form of culture in terms of which the comprehensive question is explicitly asked and answered. If the comprehensive question is asked and answered, authentically or inauthentically, by all human activity, the function of religious activity is so to represent in concepts and symbols the valid answer to this question as to cultivate in human life authentic understandings of the comprehensive purpose. But religious claims, like all claims, are fallible, and any given religion or representation of the comprehensive purpose can become problematic or be called into question. One principal occasion for doubt about its validity is the encounter with others who assert contrary answers to the comprehensive question, and this condition, I have suggested, is both the cause and the consequence of the emergence of religious plurality within modern political communities. The political problematic constituted by that plurality, I have sought to argue, cannot be solved unless valid and invalid religious claims can be critically distinguished by appeal to human experience and reason.

Critical assessment, of course, requires a criterion for argument, and in chapter 7 I sought to show summarily that the criterion for critical reflection on comprehensive convictions is coherence. An answer to the comprehensive question is valid if it is self-consistent or is not self-refuting. The possibility of argument about human activity or reality as such that appeals solely to the criterion of coherence is an aspect of the Enlightenment project of which contemporary philosophical discussion is widely suspicious. Insofar as I am able, then, I will now seek further to defend this possibility.

We may begin this task by repeating that the comprehensive question asks about the character of human authenticity as such. It follows that answers to this question may be expressed in the form "human authenticity as such is X," that is, any such answer substitutes for X the putative character of human authenticity as such. Since the valid comprehensive self-understanding is a comprehensive purpose, all answers to the comprehensive question may also be expressed in the form "human authenticity as such is pursuit of Y." In other words, any such answer substitutes for X "pursuit of Y" and substitutes for Y whatever it is that, on this comprehensive conviction, all human activity ought to pursue—or, as we may also say, whatever this comprehensive conviction asserts as the comprehensive telos. On John Dewey's understanding, for instance, the comprehensive telos is the democratic ideal, so that the valid answer to the comprehensive question may be expressed "human authenticity as such is pursuit of the democratic ideal." Because human authenticity as such is identified by the character of all human activity, an answer to the comprehensive question may also be expressed in the form "human activity as such is X." On this formulation, the claim is that authentic human activity so understands itself as to exemplify without duplicity the character substituted for X, and the character of human activity as such is properly understood as a comprehensive moral variable.

It will be useful to distinguish between comprehensive claims and answers to the comprehensive question, in the sense that every comprehensive claim is not a fully explicit comprehensive conviction. Thus, for instance, "human activity as such is free," "human activity as such chooses with understanding some or other purpose," and "human activity as such is bound by a moral norm" are all comprehensive claims, although none of them is a fully explicit representation of the comprehensive character of human activity. Still, every comprehensive claim purports to identify at least some aspect of this comprehensive character, precisely because it is a comprehensive claim. If, for instance, human activity as such is pursuit of the democratic ideal, then all of the comprehensive claims expressed above are valid comprehensive claims because they represent aspects of this character. Of course, answers to the comprehensive question are also comprehensive claims; the point here is simply that all such claims are not fully explicit statements of the comprehensive purpose.

Because any claim about human activity as such is a claim about the comprehensive self-understanding implicit in all human activity, any such claim is an understanding of an understanding. Since a claim to understand another understanding is often called hermeneutical in character, I will say that answers to the comprehensive question that are expressed in the form "human activity as such is X" are expressed hermeneutically. It is apparent, however, that comprehensive claims are not the only claims that may be expressed hermeneutically. On the contrary, any noncomprehensive claim about human activity, for instance, "this human activity is Anglo-Saxon," also represents an understanding of a possible self-understanding; activities may understand themselves as Anglo-Saxon. There is, we may say, a general class of positive and negative claims about human activity expressed in the form "this human activity is (or is not) X," and we may call this the common form of hermeneutical claims.

To be sure, most of the claims we make about human activity are not, in the first instance, about some particular activity. We say, for instance, "the activities of all those present at the crisis were courageous" or "the activities of all who will be present at the negotiations will be cautious." But any more inclusive claim about human activity may be analyzed into a series of claims in the form "this human activity is X." In the case of claims about past or future human activities, the tense needs to be added. For instance, "the activities of all those present at the crisis were courageous" may be analyzed into a series of claims of the form "it was the case that this human activity is X." Accordingly, even a claim about all past, present, and future human activity may be analyzed into a series of claims in what I have called the common hermeneutical form. Every common hermeneutical claim, then, substitutes for X a characteristic (for instance, the characteristic "Anglo-Saxon") that is asserted or denied of some human activity. Moreover, characteristics of human activity that are comprehensive may also appear in such claims. If human activity as such is free, for instance, then the claim "this human activity is free" is valid for any possible referent of "this human activity" because all human activities must be free. In this sense, I will say that comprehensive claims may also be expressed in the common hermeneutical form.

Now, because every possible human activity implies the comprehensive self-understanding, any positive claim in the general class we have defined implies the character of human activity as such and, therefore, implies every valid comprehensive claim. Moreover, the denial of any claim in the form "this human activity is X" also implies every valid comprehensive claim. On the assumption that human activity as such is free, for instance, "this human activity is free" is implied by "this human activity is Anglo-Saxon" and by "this human activity is not Anglo-Saxon," where "this human activity" refers in each instance to the same activity. We can make this point by saying that the validity of valid comprehensive claims is a necessary condition of the logical possibility of "this human activity is Anglo-Saxon" and, generally, of the logical possibility of any common hermeneutical claim. It now follows that a common hermeneutical claim that identifies a comprehensive characteristic *implies itself*, in the sense that its validity is a necessary condition of its own logical possibility. If human activity as such is free, then "this human activity is free" would not be a logically possible claim unless it were a valid claim. This is simply to repeat, then, that a claim in the form "this human activity is X," where X identifies a comprehensive characteristic, is valid for any possible referent of "this human activity" because all human activities must exemplify that characteristic.

We may also formulate this conclusion by saying that a common hermeneutical claim in which the exemplification of a comprehensive characteristic is asserted is logically necessary. If "this human activity is free" is logically possible and would not be logically possible were it not valid, then its denial is logically impossible or self-contradictory. Hence, "this human activity is free" is logically necessary, because a claim whose denial is logically self-contradictory is logically necessary. Moreover, "this human activity is free" can be logically necessary only if it is valid for any possible referent of "this human activity." Thus, "human activity as such is free" is also logically necessary. In other words, "this human activity is not free," which is logically self-contradictory, is the denial of both "this human activity is free" and "human activity as such is free." It is precisely because the comprehensive order of reflection has this logical character that I could, in chapter 7, defend comprehensive reflection itself by showing that neopragmatism, which may be expressed hermeneutically as "this human activity is not required, explicitly or implicitly, to answer the comprehensive question," and amoralism, which may be expressed hermeneutically as "this human activity is not bound by a moral norm," are logically impossible.

The fact that all valid comprehensive claims expressed hermeneutically are logically necessary means that every such claim implies and is implied by every other such claim; that is, all such claims are mutually implicative. This follows because the logical relations among logically necessary claims about human activity must themselves be logically necessary. Thus, if "human activity as such pursues the democratic ideal" is the valid answer to the comprehensive question, then this claim implies and is implied by the comprehensive claim "human activity as such is free" or "human activity as such chooses with understanding some or other purpose" or "human activity as such is bound by a moral norm."

This relation among valid comprehensive claims clarifies the relation between the formal definition of human activity as such and the valid answer to the comprehensive question. On my formal definition, human activity is the choice of a self-understanding and, therefore, a comprehensive self-understanding. This claim does not explicitly identify the valid comprehensive self-understanding. If I have correctly understood the logic of the comprehensive question, however, the formal definition implies the character of human authenticity as such. Accordingly, we may say that critical reflection on proposed answers to the comprehensive question is nothing other than an attempt to make fully explicit the implications of an explicitly formal definition of human activity as such. To be sure, it is also true that every claim about human activity, whether or not it identifies comprehensive characteristics, implies the character of human authenticity as such. Thus, "this human activity is Anglo-Saxon" implies the valid answer to the comprehensive question, just because this answer is implied by all human activity. Still, it is not the case that any valid comprehensive claim implies that a human activity is Anglo-Saxon, since being Anglo-Saxon is a particular or noncomprehensive characteristic. Among hermeneutical claims, then, it is distinctive of valid comprehensive claims that they are all *mutually* implicative.

Because valid comprehensive claims expressed hermeneutically are *about human activity*, they are not only logically but also pragmatically necessary. If a claim is logically necessary when its validity is a necessary condition of its own logical possibility, a claim is pragmatically necessary when its validity is a necessary condition of the possibility of making the claim. In other words, logical necessity identifies a relation between the propositional content of a claim and the validity of the claim; pragmatic necessity identifies a relation between possible acts of making a claim and the validity of the claim. Pragmatic necessity, we may also say, means that every possible act of making the claim in question requires the validity of the claim.

On the assumption that freedom is a comprehensive characteristic, for instance, the validity of "human activity as such is free" is required by any act of making any claim at all. Hence, the validity of this comprehensive claim is required by every possible act of claiming "human activity as such is free." *Mutatis mutandis*, the same is the case with every valid comprehensive claim. To say this is simply to repeat that every self-understanding implies the valid comprehensive self-understanding. Accordingly, every possible act of denying "human activity as such is X," where X identifies a comprehensive characteristic, is pragmatically self-contradictory, because it requires the validity of the claim that is denied. But if "human activity as such is X," where X identifies a comprehensive characteristic, is pragmatically necessary, then so too is "this human activity is X," where X identifies a comprehensive characteristic. On any possible referent of "this human activity," every possible act of claiming that a human activity exemplifies a comprehensive characteristic requires the validity of the claim, since the act of claiming requires that human activity as such exemplifies all comprehensive characteristics. Hence, every possible act of denying a common hermeneutical claim that identifies a comprehensive characteristic is pragmatically self-contradictory.

With respect to this use of "pragmatically necessary," however, the term "every possible" should be emphasized. The act of claiming "this human activity is Anglo-Saxon" may require the validity of this claim, but only if the claim refers to the activity in which the claim is made and the individual in question is Anglo-Saxon. Similarly, the act of denying this claim may require the validity of the claim that is denied, but only if denial refers to the activity in which it is made and the individual in question is Anglo-Saxon. Moreover, some have used the term "pragmatically necessary" to mean any instance in which the making of a claim requires the validity of the claim that is made (see, e.g., Passmore: 80). On that broader usage, claims about oneself that are not logically necessary may be pragmatically necessary, because some acts of making the claim may require its validity—as for instance, "this human activity is Anglo-Saxon." In contrast, I seek to restrict "pragmatic necessity" to valid comprehensive claims. Hence "this human activity is X" is pragmatically necessary only if *every possible* act of making the claim requires its validity.

If valid comprehensive claims expressed hermeneutically are both logically and pragmatically necessary, the distinction may seem to be pointless. But its significance will become apparent if we consider that claims expressed hermeneutically assume the validity of existential claims. Both the claim that some human activity exemplifies a characteristic and the claim that it does not assume that a human individual exists, in the same manner that "this person is Anglo-Saxon" and "this person is not Anglo-Saxon" both assume that there is a person. If we add this existential assumption to the propositional content of the claim, then "this human activity is (or is not) X" becomes the complex claim "something human exists and this one of her or his activities is (or is not) X." But, now, this complex claim entails the more concise existential claim "something exists that is (or is not) X." So, for instance, "this human activity is Anglo-Saxon," together with its existential assumption, entails the claim "something exists that is Anglo-Saxon." In the sense that comprehensive claims may be expressed in the common hermeneutical form, they too, adding their existential assumptions, entail claims of the form "something exists that is X," and I will say that a comprehensive claim in this form is expressed existentially.

For instance, the claim that human activity as such is bound by a moral norm may be expressed existentially as "something exists that is bound by a moral norm." Assuming that human activity as such is so bound, the expression of the claim in this form remains pragmatically necessary. Every possible act of claiming "something exists that is bound by a moral norm" requires the validity of the claim, and every possible act of denying this claim requires the validity of the claim that is denied. It is a necessary condition of making or denying the claim that the individual doing so exists and her or his activity is bound by a moral norm, and the same is true with respect to any other valid comprehensive claim expressed existentially. Thus, we may also identify valid comprehensive claims as existential claims that are pragmatically necessary or the denials of which are pragmatically self-contradictory. Still "something exists that is bound by a moral norm" is not *logically* necessary; "nothing exists that is bound by a moral norm" is logically possible. This is simply to say that one may deny the existence of all human individuals without logical self-contradiction; a world without humans is conceivable, and, for all we know, the actual world once was and once will be again of this kind.

It might seem, then, that pragmatically necessary existential statements are never logically necessary. But this conclusion is, I now wish to show, illicit because every answer to the comprehensive question includes a metaphysical as well as a moral aspect. Self-understanding, it may be recalled, includes, at least implicitly, an understanding of others and of some larger reality in terms of which self and all conceivable others are distinguished. If an answer to the comprehensive question is a comprehensive moral claim because it identifies human authenticity as such, then the answer includes a claim about the metaphysical character of reality. In other words, human authenticity as such is human activity in relation to ultimate reality, either in the sense that reality as such permits or in the sense that it also authorizes authentic human activity. Or, again, the comprehensive human purpose identifies how human activity as such ought to add itself or make a difference to the larger reality of which it is a part. If, to persist with the example, authentic human activity as such maximally pursues the democratic ideal, then the claim "something exists that pursues the democratic ideal" implies the claim that the metaphysical character of reality is, at the least, consistent with such pursuits.

But another way to make this point is to say that the character of human activity as such includes and is not exhausted by the characteristics of reality as such. A valid understanding of the larger reality in terms of which self and all conceivable others are distinguished is an understanding of oneself as exemplifying the characteristics of reality as such. Let us assume, for instance, that reality as such is temporal, in the sense that every conceivable concrete thing is related to some past and to some future. It follows that temporality is also a characteristic of human activity as such, although the latter also exemplifies other characteristics (for instance, being bound by a moral norm) that are not common to all conceivable concrete things. Hence, "this human activity is temporal" and "this human activity is bound by a moral norm" are both logically and pragmatically necessary, but the first and not the second identifies a characteristic of reality as such. It remains, then, to clarify the criterion in accord with which valid comprehensive claims that identify metaphysical characteristics may be distinguished from those that do not.

If claims about human activity are claims about possible self-understandings and may be expressed in the form "this human activity is (or is not) X," claims about reality are positive and negative claims about conceivable things, that is, objects that may be understood, and may be expressed in the common form "this thing is (or is not) X." If a claim of this form is a valid metaphysical claim, then X identifies a characteristic of reality as such or all possible objects of understanding.

I use the term "thing" here to mean "concrete thing." It is true that the general term "thing" may have a broader meaning, so that "things that may be understood" are of differing logical types. On this broader understanding, an important distinction among things is that between concrete things and abstract things. For instance, "this human activity is Anglo-Saxon" is a claim about a concrete thing; in contrast, "courage is praiseworthy" is a claim about an abstract thing, that is, about a characteristic (i.e., courage) that may be exemplified in many activities and, therefore, many concrete things. In the first instance, then, all claims about reality are not claims in the form "this thing is (or is not) X," where "thing" means a concrete thing. But I hold that the distinction between concrete and abstract things is a logical type distinction because the concrete includes the abstract; that is, all claims about abstract things are claims about characteristics that concrete things may exemplify. Hence, every claim that is, in the first instance, about some abstract thing may be analyzed in terms of a claim or set of claims about concrete things. "Courage is praiseworthy," for instance, entails "each concrete thing that is courageous is, therefore, praiseworthy." I also hold that any claim about any other logical type of things may be analyzed into a claim or set of claims about concrete things, so that, in a summary discussion of metaphysics, it is permissible to say that all claims about reality are claims about concrete things.

This means that any claim of the form "this thing is X" and its denial both imply every valid metaphysical claim, so that the validity of a valid metaphysical claim is a necessary condition of the logical possibility of any claim of the form "this thing is X." It now follows that a valid metaphysical claim implies itself. On the assumption that reality as such is temporal, for instance, the validity of "this thing is temporal" is a necessary condition of its own logical possibility. Hence, a valid metaphysical claim in the common form of claims about reality is logically necessary, and its denial, "this thing is not X," where X identifies a metaphysical characteristic, is logically self-contradictory. But if "this thing is X" is logically necessary on some identification of X, then so too is "reality as such is X" or "all conceivable things are X" on the same identification, because "this thing is X" can be logically necessary only if X identifies a metaphysical characteristic. In other words, "this thing is not X" on some identification of X is also the denial of "reality as such is X" on the same identification.

As with common hermeneutical claims, so also common claims about reality may be restated existentially in the form "something exists that is (or is not) X." In the case of claims about human activity, even valid claims about human activity as such, this restatement includes in its content the existential assumption of any common hermeneutical claim, namely, that some human individual exists. In the case of claims about reality or possible objects of understanding, however, the correlate existential claim, namely that something exists, can no longer be simply an assumption. Since all claims about objects of understanding may be expressed in the form "this thing is (or is not) X," there is no possible claim that does not "assume" that something exists. In other words, "something exists" is presupposed by understanding as such. Hence, "something exists that is X," where X refers to a characteristic of all conceivable things or all possible objects of understanding, is not only pragmatically but also logically necessary. On the assumption that reality as such is temporal, for instance, "something exists that is temporal" is logically necessary, and it is this logical character of valid metaphysical claims that distinguishes metaphysical characteristics from other comprehensive characteristics of human activity.

I recognize that some will reject this understanding of meta-physics on the grounds that "nothing exists" is a logically possible claim, so that all existential claims can be denied without logical self-contradiction. Those who take this position may concede that "this thing is X," where X identifies a metaphysical characteristic, is logically necessary, but they will take this to mean: "If something exists, it is X" is logically necessary. The antecedent in this claim, they will maintain, can be denied without logical self-contradiction, that is, "nothing exists" is logically possible.

But I hold that this account does not make sense, because the assertion that all existential claims are logically contingent contra-dicts the concession that some claims of the form "this thing is X" are logically necessary. On this assertion, the term "thing" cannot refer to every possible object of understanding, because there is a possible object of understanding, namely, the complete absence of existence, that does not exemplify metaphysical characteristics. But if the term "thing" does not refer to every possible object of under-standing, then, so far as I can see, there is no way to identify "thing" such that "this thing is X" could be logically necessary. In showing that "human activity is X" is, on some identifications of X, logically necessary, one may begin with the stipulation that a human activity is constituted by a self-understanding. But how shall we stipulate the meaning of "thing" if we cannot identify it with "object of under-standing?" Some may propose that "thing" means "positive object of understanding." But the meaning of this phrase depends on its distinction from "completely negative object of understanding," and one cannot identify this distinction because "completely negative object of understanding" cannot be distinguished from "putative understanding that has no object at all." Hence the concession that "this thing is X" can be logically necessary implies that "thing" means "object of understanding," and understanding as such presupposes that something exists. So far as I can see, moreover, one is bound to concede that "this thing is X" can be logically necessary because, as I have argued, a self-understanding implies an under-standing of the larger reality in terms of which the self and all other conceivable objects of understanding are distinguished.

If it is now said that "thing" *does* mean "object of under-standing" and that "this thing is something or nothing" is a valid metaphysical claim, the same problem appears. The disjunction "something or nothing" requires that one be able to distinguish "nothing" as an object of understanding from a putative understanding that has no object at all. But it is impossible to distinguish between the claim "nothing exists" and a self-contradictory existential claim, for instance, "something that is a married bachelor exists." In each case, the putative object is completely negative. I conclude that "nothing exists" is a self-contradictory existential claim and represents no understanding at all. It follows that "something exists" is logically necessary, and the same is the case with any valid metaphysical claim expressed in the form "something exists that is X."[3]

Summarily stated, then, valid comprehensive claims are about the characteristics of a human activity or about human activity as such that are both logically and pragmatically necessary. This same class of claims may be identified as existential claims that are pragmatically necessary. Valid comprehensive claims include but are not exhausted by valid metaphysical claims, and the latter are distinguished as existential claims that are also logically necessary.[4]

Because valid metaphysical claims do not exhaust valid comprehensive claims, the former do not imply an answer to the comprehensive question. This is simply to say that the character of reality as such does not imply the character of human activity as such, because the former is more general, and the general does not imply the particular. Hence, an answer to the comprehensive question can be logically necessary only if expressed hermeneutically. If it is valid to say, for instance, that human authenticity as such is pursuit with understanding of the divine telos, then the claim "human activity as

---

3. I have sought to argue more extensively against the logical possibility of "nothing exists" in Gamwell: especially chaps. 2 and 4. This understanding of metaphysics is immensely indebted to the work of Charles Hartshorne (see Hartshorne).

4. In so identifying valid metaphysical claims with logically necessary existential claims, I use "metaphysical" in a strict sense. It is perfectly proper also to use "metaphysical" in a broad sense, so that it refers inclusively to comprehensive claims or claims about human activity as such. So far as I can see, this is the use of the term with which Rawls asserts a theory that is "political and not metaphysical" (1993: 10). It is also, to the best of my understanding, the meaning with which Kant speaks affirmatively of metaphysics. Of course, Kant also denied what I take the comprehensive question to imply, namely, that metaphysics in his sense includes and is not exhausted by metaphysics in the strict sense. In the broad sense, then, valid metaphysical claims are existential claims that are pragmatically necessary and, in the strict sense, those that are also logically necessary. In this work, however, I have confined use of the term "metaphysical" to its strict sense.

such is pursuit of the divine telos" is logically necessary. But the claim "something exists that pursues with understanding the divine telos" can be only pragmatically necessary, even if the metaphysical claim included in this comprehensive conviction—namely, "something exists that is divine"—must be logically necessary. This is simply to repeat that the moral aspect of a comprehensive conviction, which identifies the purpose that all human activities ought to exemplify, is the inclusive aspect.

We are now in a position to return specifically to the assessment of comprehensive convictions and, therefore, to the standard or criterion of a discussion and debate about proposed answers to the comprehensive question. I will assume that such answers are claims of the form "human authenticity as such is X"; that is, each such claim substitutes for X the putative character or variable of human activity as such and means that human authenticity as such exemplifies this variable without duplicity or in maximal measure. It then follows that the valid comprehensive conviction is both logically and pragmatically necessary and its denial is both logically and pragmatically self-contradictory. Accordingly, all invalid answers to the comprehensive question are logically and pragmatically self-contradictory, since every invalid answer implicitly denies the valid comprehensive conviction.[5]

Of course, a claim about human authenticity may be logically and pragmatically self-consistent without being the valid answer to the comprehensive question. For instance, the claim "this human activity pursues the well-being of Anglo-Saxons and is authentic" is both logically and pragmatically possible. In other words, this could be a valid claim about some human activity because, given its particular circumstances, pursuit of the well-being of Anglo-Saxons is a way to exemplify human authenticity as such. But if this pursuit is asserted as a comprehensive conviction, "human authenticity *as such* is pursuit of the well-being of Anglo-Saxons," it is logically and pragmatically self-contradictory. This claim purports to be logically

---

5. One might say that all invalid answers to the comprehensive question are either hopelessly vague or self-contradictory. A putative answer to that question may be neither valid nor self-contradictory because it includes some putative concept or concepts the meaning of which cannot be fixed. But I will assume that a putative answer that is hopelessly vague is not an answer at all, because one cannot say something in concepts that have no fixed meaning.

and pragmatically necessary, but its denial, "this human activity does not pursue the well-being of Anglo-Saxons and is authentic," is both logically and pragmatically possible. Because Anglo-Saxon chauvinism, meaning thereby the assertion that the well-being of Anglo-Saxons identifies the comprehensive purpose, is not logically and pragmatically necessary, it is logically and pragmatically self-contradictory. In other words, the characteristic "Anglo-Saxon" is a specific characteristic of human activity and, therefore, pursuit of Anglo-Saxon well-being cannot possibly be the variable identifying human activity as such. A comprehensive conviction is logically and pragmatically self-contradictory, then, when it asserts as a characteristic of human authenticity as such something that is specific.

In saying this, I affirm the kind of criticism with which neopragmatists typically seek to invalidate comprehensive proposals that have been made, namely, the attempt to show that such proposals escalate some historically specific characteristic into ahistorical status (see, for instance, Rorty 1979). At least, I agree that this is a valid mode of criticism as long as "ahistorical" is taken to mean "historically general" or "historically invariant," in distinction from "nonhistorical" in the sense of "outside of history." Still, this agreement with neopragmatism does not imply, indeed it implicitly precludes, the denial of comprehensive reflection as such.

We should also note, however, that invalid answers to the comprehensive question need not be formulated in terms of characteristics that, like Anglo-Saxon, cannot be identified without reference to some specific time and place. I have previously argued that human activity as such is self-differentiating, in the sense that it implies specific forms of itself. In this sense, for instance, religious activity is a specific form of human activity, because all human activity addresses the comprehensive question implicitly and, therefore implies the possibility of doing so explicitly. Hence, "religious" is not a specific characteristic of human activity in the sense that its identification requires reference to a specific time and place. Still, "religious" is a specific characteristic of human activity. The possibility of such activity is not actualized in all human activity, precisely because religious activity asks and answers the comprehensive question explicitly. Thus, "human authenticity is religious" or "human authenticity is pursuit of religious activity" is an invalid answer to the comprehensive question because it is neither logically nor pragmatically necessary. It too, then, is logically and pragmatically self-contradictory.

We may also say that the valid answer to the comprehensive question is the only logically and pragmatically coherent answer, precisely in the sense that all invalid answers are logically and pragmatically self-contradictory. With respect to human authenticity as such, in other words, a conviction that *could be* valid because it is logically and pragmatically self-consistent *is* valid, and this is just to repeat that the valid comprehensive conviction is logically and pragmatically necessary. Thus, we may use the term "coherence" to identify the proper standard or criterion for assessment in a critical debate of proposed answers to the comprehensive question. The attempt to validate such answers is in principle solely the attempt to identify which claim is coherent, because all invalid answers are incoherent. Moreover, the comprehensive question is the *only* question about human activity that is properly addressed before the bar of coherence alone, because it is the only question that asks about the implications or presuppositions of human activity as such.

It may be apparent that the conclusions in the two sections of this appendix imply each other. Coherence is the criterion of critical reflection on comprehensive convictions precisely because distinctively human activity necessarily asks and answers the comprehensive question, at least implicitly. Conversely, we may conclude that human activity as such is constituted by this question because only the valid comprehensive conviction is coherent. The comprehensive purpose is the inescapable gift to our lives, just as commitment to it is the inescapable demand on us. Coherence is the criterion of the comprehensive order of reflection because human authenticity as such is the life of integrity.

WORKS CITED

Adams, Arlin M., and Emmerich, Charles J.
1990   *A Nation Dedicated to Religious Liberty: The Constitutional Heritage of the Religious Clauses.* Philadelphia: University of Pennsylvania Press.

Apel, Karl-Otto.
1975   "The Problem of Philosophical Fundamental-Grounding in Light of a Transcendental Pragmatic of Language." *Man and World* 8: 239–75.

1979a   "The Common Presuppositions of Hermeneutics and Ethics: Types of Rationality Beyond Science and Technology." *Research in Phenomenology* 9: 35–53.

1979b   "Types of Rationality Today." *Rationality Today.* Ed. Theodor Gereats. Ottawa: University Press, 307–40.

Aquinas, St. Thomas.
1948   *Introduction to Saint Thomas Aquinas.* Ed. Anton C. Pegis. New York: Random House, The Modern Library.

Baier, Kurt.
1989   "Justice and the Aims of Political Philosophy." *Ethics* 99: 771–790.

Bellah, Robert.
1974   "Civil Religion in America." *American Civil Religion.* Ed. Russell E. Richey and Donald G. Jones. New York: Harper and Row.

1975   *The Broken Covenant.* New York: Seabury Press.

Berger, Peter.
1967   *The Sacred Canopy: Elements of a Sociological Theory of Religion.* Garden City, NY: Doubleday, 21–44.

1979   *The Heretical Imperative: Contemporary Possibilities of Religious Affirmation.* Garden City, NY: Anchor Press/ Doubleday.

Bradley, Gerard V.
   1987   *Church–State Relationships in America.* New York: Green-
            wood Press.

Dewey, John.
   1934   *A Common Faith.* New Haven: Yale University Press.

   1954   *The Public and Its Problems.* Chicago: Swallow Press.

   1957   *Reconstruction in Philosophy.* Boston: Beacon Press.

Gamwell, Franklin I.
   1990   *The Divine Good: Modern Moral Theory and the Necessity of
            God.* San Francisco: HarperCollins.

Geertz, Clifford.
   1973   *The Interpretation of Cultures.* New York: Basic Books.

Greenawalt, Kent.
   1988   *Religious Convictions and Political Choice.* New York:
            Oxford University Press.

Habermas, Jürgen.
   1981   *The Theory of Communicative Action, Volume I: Reason and
            the Rationalization of Society.* Boston: Beacon Press.

   1987   *The Theory of Communicative Action, Volume II: Lifeworld
            and System: A Critique of Functionalist Reason.* Boston:
            Beacon Press.

   1992   *Postmetaphysical Thinking: Philosophical Essays.* Cambridge,
            MA: The MIT Press.

Hartshorne, Charles.
   1970   *Creative Synthesis and Philosophic Method.* LaSalle, IL: Open
            Court.

Hick, John.
   1989   *An Interpretation of Religion: Human Responses to the Trans-
            cendent.* New Haven: Yale University Press.

Kant, Immanuel.
   1949   *Fundamental Principles of the Metaphysic of Morals.*
            Indianapolis: Bobbs-Merrill.

Levy, Leonard W.
   1986   *The Establishment Clause: Religion and the First Amend-
            ment.* New York: Macmillan.

McElroy, Robert W.
  1989   *The Search for an American Public Theology.* New York: Paulist Press.

Mead, Sidney E.
  1963   *The Lively Experiment: The Shaping of Christianity in America.* New York: Harper and Row.

  1975   *The Nation with the Soul of a Church.* New York: Harper and Row.

Murray, John Courtney, S. J.
  1960   *We Hold These Truths: Catholic Reflections on the American Proposition.* Kansas City, MO: Shead and Ward.

Niebuhr, Reinhold.
  1942   "Religion and Action." *Science and Man.* Ed. Ruth Nanda Anshen. New York: Harcourt, Brace and Company, 44–64.

  1944   *The Children of Light and the Children of Darkness: A Vindication of Democracy and a Critique of Its Traditional Defense.* New York: Charles Scribner's Sons.

  1949   *Faith and History: A Comparison of Christian and Modern Views of History.* New York: Charles Scribner's Sons.

Ogden, Schubert M.
  1984   "The Experience of God: Critical Reflections on Hartshorne's Theory of Analogy." *Existence and Actuality: Conversations with Charles Hartshorne.* Ed. John B. Cobb, Jr., and Franklin I. Gamwell. Chicago: The University of Chicago Press.

  1992   *Is There Only One True Religion or Are There Many?* Dallas: Southern Methodist University Press.

Passmore, John.
  1961   *Philosophical Reasoning.* New York: Basic Books. (Basic books ed., 1969).

Popper, Karl R.
  1966   *The Open Society and Its Enemies.* 2 vol. Princeton, NJ: Princeton University Press.

Rawls, John.
  1971   *A Theory of Justice.* Cambridge, MA: The Belknap Press.

  1980   "Kantian Constructivism in Moral Theory." *The Journal of Philosophy,* 77: 515–73.

1985   "Justice as Fairness: Political not Metaphysical." *Philosophy and Public Affairs*, 14: 223–51.

1987   "The Idea of an Overlapping Consensus." *Oxford Journal of Legal Studies*, 7: 1–25.

1988   "The Priority of Right and Ideas of the Good." *Philosophy and Public Affairs*, 17: 251–76.

1993   *Political Liberalism*. New York: Columbia University Press.

Rorty, Richard.
1979   "Transcendental Arguments, Self-Reference, and Pragmatism." *Transcendental Arguments and Science*. Ed. Peter Bieri, Rolf Horstman, and Lorenz Kreuger. Dortrecht, Holland: D. Reidel, 77–103.

1982   *Consequences of Pragmatism*. Minneapolis: University of Minnesota Press.

1988   "The Priority of Democracy to Philosophy." *The Virginia Statute for Religious Freedom: Its Evolution and Consequences in American History*. Ed. Merrill D. Peterson, and Robert C. Vaughn. New York: Cambridge University Press, 257–88.

Skinner, Quentin.
1978   *The Foundations of Modern Political Thought*, 2 vols. Cambridge: Cambridge University Press.

Stout, Jeffrey.
1981   *The Flight from Authority: Religion, Morality and the Quest for Autonomy*. Notre Dame, IN: University of Notre Dame Press.

Tillich, Paul.
1951   *Systematic Theology*, vol. 1. Chicago: The University of Chicago Press.

Toulmin, Stephen.
1990   *Cosmopolis: The Hidden Agenda of Modernity*. New York: The Free Press.

Whitehead, Alfred North.
1938   *Modes of Thought*. New York: The Free Press.

1961   *Adventures of Ideas*. New York: The Free Press.

INDEX